D0205638

Books in the **Contemporary World Issues** series address vital issues in today's society such as genetic engineering, pollution, and biodiversity. Written by professional writers, scholars, and nonacademic experts, these books are authoritative, clearly written, up-to-date, and objective. They provide a good starting point for research by high school and college students, scholars, and general readers as well as by legislators, business-people, activists, and others.

Each book, carefully organized and easy to use, contains an overview of the subject, a detailed chronology, biographical sketches, facts and data and/or documents and other primary source material, a forum of authoritative perspective essays, annotated lists of print and nonprint resources, and an index.

Readers of books in the Contemporary World Issues series will find the information they need in order to have a better understanding of the social, political, environmental, and economic issues facing the world today.

CONTEMPORARY WORLD ISSUES

Science, Technology, and Medicine

LGBT Youth Issues Today

A REFERENCE HANDBOOK

David E. Newton

ABC-CLIO

Santa Barbara, California • Denver, Colorado • Oxford, England

Copyright 2014 by ABC-CLIO, LLC

All rights reserved. No part of this publication may be reproduced, stored in a retrieval system, or transmitted, in any form or by any means, electronic, mechanical, photocopying, recording, or otherwise, except for the inclusion of brief quotations in a review, without prior permission in writing from the publisher.

Library of Congress Cataloging-in-Publication Data

Newton, David E.
   LGBT youth issues today : a reference handbook / David E. Newton Ph.D.
      pages cm. — (Contemporary world issues)
   Includes bibliographical references and index.
   ISBN 978–1–61069–315–8 (hardback : alk. paper) — ISBN 978–1–61069–316–5 (ebook) 1. Gay youth—Handbooks, manuals, etc. 2. Gay and lesbian studies—Handbooks, manuals, etc. I. Title.
HQ76.27.Y68N498   2014
306.76'60835—dc23   2013041522

ISBN: 978–1–61069–315–8
EISBN: 978–1–61069–316–5

18 17 16 15 14   1 2 3 4 5

This book is also available on the World Wide Web as an eBook.
Visit www.abc-clio.com for details.

ABC-CLIO, LLC
130 Cremona Drive, P.O. Box 1911
Santa Barbara, California 93116-1911

This book is printed on acid-free paper ∞

Manufactured in the United States of America

This book is dedicated to Phil Bockman,
after all these many years,
a reconnection,
with appreciation for a patient
and understanding ear and kind heart.

Nicholas' brief life was not a very happy one. He was constantly teased and harassed at school for not being "masculine enough." His classmates just assumed that he was a "fag." One day, they threw him into the school pool, while fully clothed. Both the perpetrators of the prank and Nicholas' teacher thought the event was a "big joke." When one of his teachers tried to come to his defense, he was advised not to say anything about the problem; his teaching contract was not renewed. The day after the swimming pool event, Nicholas killed himself by jumping from a bridge in town. (Dorais and Lajeunesse 2004, 3)

Alex Morse came out as a gay man while still a sophomore in high school. He organized his school's first gay-straight alliance club and was instrumental in planning a faculty training session on lesbian, gay, bisexual, transgender, and questioning (LGBTQ) issues at his school. He was able to attend Brown University at least partly because of a scholarship awarded [to] promising LGBT students by the Point Foundation. In 2011, he was elected mayor of the city of Holyoke, Massachusetts, the youngest openly gay mayor of a U.S. city. (Alex Morse 2013)

These two stories could not be more different as descriptions of what it is like to be a young lesbian, gay man, bisexual, or transgendered person in the United States today. As Alex Morse's story illustrates, many LGBT youth today are able to achieve as much as any one of their non-LGBT counterparts. For these individuals, the American dream is well within reach. For many other LGBT youth, however, that dream is a distant fantasy, the journey there more a nightmare than a dream. They face an array of problems similar to those of their heterosexual peers but much, much greater in their severity and eventual consequences. LGBT youth are statistically more likely to be verbally and physically harassed in school and in their communities, more likely to be thrown out of their families because of their sexual orientation or gender presentation, more likely to end up homeless on the streets, more likely to consider and/or attempt suicide, and more likely to experience a host of long-term effects such as depression, anxiety, problems in completing their education and gaining employment, and inability to develop loving relationships with others.

Same-sex relationships have been the subject of hatred, opprobrium, and abuse since the beginning of time. Young gay men, lesbians, bisexuals, and transgendered people have not been immune from these widespread and general negative feelings. They have been in the unusual and unfortunate situation of having to defend themselves not only against the homophobia of society in general, but also against the lack of attention and disregard from members of their own same-sex-loving community. For much of history, gay and lesbian adults have been reluctant to make common cause with their younger counterparts at least in part because of fears that they would be accused of "recruitment" or "child molestation."

Over the past few decades, a new era appears to have been dawning for LGBT youth. At last, allies from both within the gay and lesbian community as well as from the general public have been struggling to become better informed about the unique problems facing LGBT youth in their everyday lives and to develop systems and programs for dealing with those problems. Perhaps the signal step forward in this battle was the foundation in 2010 of the It Gets Better project by Dan Savage and Terry Miller. That project lays out the simple, if somewhat revolutionary, concept that being gay, lesbian, bisexual, or transgender during childhood and adolescence may be difficult, but one needs to persevere because life does get better. Such is the case because LGBT individuals have learned how to stand up for themselves, how to become more supportive of each other, and how to battle for their rights in society. In addition, they have discovered how to be happy and productive members of American society.

The purpose of this book is to review what is known about the role of LGBT youth in history and the way societal attitudes have shifted over the past century on this issue. The book also lays out some of the most critical issues and problems facing LGBT youth today, including bullying in schools and the general community, homelessness, and suicidal ideation and suicide attempts. Much of the book consists of materials that can be used for those who wish to learn more about the topic, including chapters on a chronology of important events in history, a glossary of important terms, a profile of important individuals and organizations associated with the problems and successes of LGBT youth, and an annotated bibliography of print and electronic resources. Of special interest is the chapter on perspectives, in which 10 individuals write of their own specific experiences with LGBT issues and the ways in which those experiences shaped their own lives and that of the community in general.

References

Dorais, Michel, and Simon Louis Lajeunesse. *Dead Boys Can't Dance: Sexual Orientation, Masculinity, and Suicide.* Montreal: McGill-Queen's University Press, 2004.

Morse, Alex. Point Foundation. http://www.pointfoundation. org/sslpage.aspx?pid=543. Accessed on May 3, 2013.

LGBT Youth
Issues Today

From the U.S. Supreme Court case *Nabozny v. Podlesny, Davis, Blauert* (92 F.3d 446 [1996]):

> Jamie Nabozny was a student in the Ashland Public School District ... in Ashland, Wisconsin throughout his middle school and high school years. During that time, Nabozny was continually harassed and physically abused by fellow students because he is homosexual. ...
>
> Around the time that Nabozny entered the seventh grade, Nabozny realized that he was gay. Many of Nabozny's fellow classmates soon realized it too. Nabozny decided not to "closet" his sexuality, and considerable harassment from his fellow students ensued. Nabozny's classmates regularly referred to him as "faggot," and subjected him to various forms of physical abuse, including striking and spitting on him. ...
>
> Following the holiday season [in 1988], student harassment of Nabozny worsened ... in a science classroom, [a fellow student] grabbed Nabozny and pushed him to the floor. [The fellow student and a friend] held Nabozny down and performed a mock rape on Nabozny, exclaiming

Demonstrators carry signs calling for protection of homosexuals from discrimination as they march in a picket line in front of Independence Hall in Philadelphia in 1967. (AP Photo) that Nabozny should enjoy it. The boys carried out the mock rape as twenty other students looked on and laughed. Nabozny escaped and fled to Podlesny's office. Podlesny's alleged response is somewhat astonishing; she said that "boys will be boys" and told Nabozny that if he was "going to be so openly gay," he should "expect" such behavior from his fellow students.

For lesbian, gay, bisexual, and transgendered (LGBT) students, stories such as this one may not seem particularly unusual. Harassment and bullying are a normal part of the everyday school experience of many LGBT students. This story is different only because Jamie Nabozny decided to file suit against the Ashland School District, alleging that it had failed to provide equal protection for him under the law, as required by the Fourteenth Amendment of the U.S. Constitution (for more details about this case, see Chapter 5). One cannot help but ask, however, why a young man who is openly gay can be subjected to such humiliating, degrading, and physically painful harassment as Nabozny was for virtually all of his five years in Ashland secondary schools. Simply put, why did Ashland students hate Nabozny so completely that they subjected him to such experiences?

There is no simple answer to that question. Indeed, scholars have been engaged for decades in the study of homophobia, the irrational fear and hatred of homosexuality. Their findings can hardly be summarized in one brief chapter in this book. It can be instructive, however, to ask how various societies and cultures have viewed same-sex relationships over the long stretch of human civilization. How would the people of ancient Sumeria some 6,000 years ago, or the citizens of classical Greece during its ascendancy in the third and fourth centuries BCE, or the residents of largely Roman Catholic Europe in the tenth century CE, or the English population of the Victorian Period, or the early settlers of the new United States in the 1600s have viewed Jamie Nabozny's experience? Would they have supported his attackers? Called them to account for their actions? Not understood what the controversy about homosexuality was all about? One way to understand the issue of same-sex relationships among the young in the twenty-first century in the United States is to take a look back at the way such relationships have been viewed by other cultures.

Homosexuality in History

Within the long and complex history of same-sex relationships in human societies, one fact stands out very clearly: opposite-sex relationships lie at the very heart of human civilization. The goal of the human species, like that of any other plant or animal species, is to perpetuate itself; to ensure that a new generation will be available to replace the existing generation. Same-sex relationships clearly cannot contribute to achieving that goal. Two men or two women cannot produce a new child on their own. Given that fact, one might ask how any society can permit, let alone approve of, same-sex relationships. The decision by two men or two women to reject societal norms and abandon the opportunity of childbearing certainly appears to be a threat to the general community.

And there have been any number of human societies throughout history that have taken this position. As one of the oldest prohibitions against same-sex behavior, the Roman Catholic church has long taught that such behavior is sinful simply because it cannot result in procreation (Ministry to Persons with a Homosexual Inclination 2013). Even in the twenty-first century, a number of countries, tribes, and groups continue to hold to that belief. For example, same-sex relationships are prohibited in many nations around the world today. In many cases, those prohibitions are accompanied by severe penalties: same-sex behavior is punishable by death in five nations—Iran, Mauritania, Saudi Arabia, Sudan, and Yemen—and parts of Nigeria and Somalia. Such behavior is also punished by severe prison terms ranging from a few months up to a few years (as much as 14 years in Gambia, Kenya, Malawi, Seychelles, and Zambia and 25 years in Trinidad and Tobago) and even life in a few nations (Guyana, Sierra Leone, Tanzania, and Uganda) (Itaborahy 2012).

The argument that same-sex couples cannot procreate is still popular among some groups in the United States today. For example, groups opposed to same-sex marriage in the United States often base their position on the fact that same-sex couples are unable to procreate. In a news release explaining its support for California's Proposition 8, which sought to amend the state constitution to prohibit same-sex marriages, the Church of Jesus Christ of Latter Day Saints (the Mormon church) pointed out that

> The sacred nature of marriage is closely linked to the power of procreation. Only a man and a woman together have the natural biological capacity to conceive children. This power of procreation—to create life and bring God's spirit children into the world—is sacred and precious. Misuse of this power undermines the institution of the family and thereby weakens the social fabric (Divine Institution of Marriage 2013).

Given the long and deep association between human sexual relationships and procreation, it is somewhat surprising that many societies at many times in history have, in fact, taken a quite different view about same-sex relationships, sometimes simply ignoring them, other times, accepting the fact that they exist without necessarily approving or disapproving of them, and at still other times, providing them with recognition equal to that accorded to opposite-sex relationships. In some instances, same-sex relationships have even been honored or given special sacred significance. It is beyond the scope of this book to provide even a brief review of the hugely diverse ways in which various societies have thought about same-sex relationships. We can, however, provide a hint of that diversity with a few examples from human history. (One of the best resources for a much more detailed look at the variety of ways in which human societies have dealt with same-sex feelings and behaviors is David Greenberg's book *The Construction of Homosexuality* [1988].)

One place to begin this review is with a very early society that appears to have had a generally favorable view of same-sex relationships, that of the Sumerian civilization that arose in at least the fourth millennium BCE. The greatest of all Sumerian texts is the *Epic of Gilmagesh*, which dates to at least 2750 BCE. The story concerns the powerful king of that name, a man more god-like than human, with enormous strength and ferocity. At one point in his life, the gods decide to try to "rein in" Gilmagesh by sending him a male companion, Enkidu, to serve as a moderating force in his life. The two soon develop an intense personal relationship, whose precise nature has been the subject of debate for centuries. The language with which the relationship is described in the epic poem certainly seems explicit in many places. Even before Enkidu appears in Gilmagesh's life, the king dreams about his future companion. He imagines that Enkidu falls from the sky in the form of a stone, is aroused, and turns into a living human only when Gilmagesh takes him in his arms and caresses him. When asked to explain the dream, the king's mother tells her son that the stone/man who has fallen from the sky

> stands for a dear friend, a mighty hero
> You will take him in your arms, embrace and caress him
> the way a man caresses his wife. (Mitchell 2004, 42)

For a number of critics, passages such as this one make clear the fact that the relationship between Gilgamesh and Enkidu is similar in many ways to that between two men or two women in today's world. Other observers have gone even farther, suggesting that the prominent role played by Enkidu in the Gilgamesh story reflects societal values of the time and that same-sex relationships in Sumeria must have been accepted and even valued. As one writer has said:

> Since it is inconceivable that the central figure in a legend or epic would not reflect the values and sentiments of its intended audience, it follows that homosexual relationships between masculine men were known and even admired among the Sumerian city-states where the Gilgamesh legend originated, and among the later Akkadian and Babylonian civilizations which wrote down the legend. (Neill 2009, 88–89)

The story of Gilgamesh and Enkidu is mentioned here primarily as an example of any number of same-sex relationships that have been described, often in admirable terms, throughout the ages. In classical Greece, one of the most famous of those relationships was between Achilles and Patroclus. This relationship is described in detail in the great Greek classic the *Iliad*, which was written about 1100 BCE. According to the story, the two men had been friends since childhood, a friendship that may well have been sexual for all or part of their lives. As with the story of Gilgamesh and Enkidu, it is virtually impossible for modern analysts to decide how physically extensive this relationship was, but the language used to describe it certainly seems suggestive at some points. In the *Iliad*, for example, Homer writes that Achilles, upon hearing of the death of Patroclus, weeps that

> I could suffer nothing worse than this, not even if I learned my father's died ... or if I heard my dear son had died ... Up to now, the heart in my chest hoped that I alone would perish here in Troy ... You'd return to Phthia, taking my child in your swift black ship away from Scyros. (Homer 2013)

As is so often the case with tales of close relationships between two men (or two women), some critics suggest that the intensity of feelings between the two individuals is nothing more than a close connection between two "good buddies," such as the ones that exist between any two individuals of the same sex who really like each other a great deal but have no sexual feelings for each other. While such may certainly be the case, another view is that the relationship might well have a physical component also. For example, in the case of Achilles and Patroclus, one historian has written that

> It is senseless to assume that Achilles would lie in the arms of a dead man whom, living, he had kept at the discrete distance appropriate to one who is no more than a "companion." (Clarke 1978, 393)

References to same-sex behaviors and relationships are common in ancient Chinese, Japanese, Hindu, and other non-Western societies. In China, four anecdotes seem to set the theme for societal attitudes about same-sex relationships: the "shared peach" (the story of Mizi Xia), the story of Lord Lang Yang and the fish, the tale of Pan Zhang and Wang Zhongxian, and the tale of the cut sleeve (the story of the Emperor Ai). In the first of these tales, dating to about 500 BCE, a handsome court official, Mizi Xia, is strolling in an orchard with the Duke Ling. After biting into a peach, Mizi gives to the rest to the Duke, who notes: "How sincere is your love for me! You forget your own appetite and think only of giving me good things to eat." He later forgives Mizi when the court official steals the Duke's carriage to visit his ailing mother, an act that would normally have resulted in the amputation of his feet (from Sima Qian, quoted in Crompton 2003, 214).

The second story is set in the third century BCE and tells of an episode involving the king of Wei, King Anxi, and his male companion, Lord Long Wang. While the two are fishing, the handsome Lord Long suddenly begins to cry. When asked by the king the reason for his tears, he answers that he had just thrown the fish back into the water, hoping to catch a larger fish. But then he realized that the king might feel the same way about him and "throw him back" if he found another man that he loved more. To reassure Lord Long, the king issues a proclamation prohibiting anyone from mentioning any other handsome man in his presence, upon pain of death for that person and all of his family (Hinsch 1992, 32–33; Long Yang Club 2013).

The third story tells of the student Wang Zhongxian, who comes to study with a famous scholar, Pan Zhang. The two "fell in love at first sight" and not only worked together, but also began to sleep together "like man and wife." They continued their relationship throughout their lives, and when they died, they were buried together on Lofu Mountain. Soon thereafter, a tree began to grow on their gravesite with branches that intertwined each other. Residents called the tree the Shared Pillow Tree in honor of the two men (Crompton 2003, 216-216; also see Hinsch 1992, 24–25; Song 2004, Chapter 5).

The final story deals with the last adult emperor of the Han Dynasty, Emperor Ai, who ruled from 6 BCE to 1 CE, and his male lover, Dong Xian. Dong had come to the palace as a common man who eventually captivated the emperor and rose rapidly in the imperial government. The story is told that on one occasion, the emperor was called to an important meeting after Dong had fallen asleep on his arm. Rather than waken Dong, the emperor ordered his sleeve to be cut off. Ever since that time and to the present day, same-sex lovers have been referred to as "those of the cut sleeve." According to tradition, other male homosexuals in the Chinese court also took to wearing short-sleeve shirts to boast of their own sexual proclivities (Crompton 2003, 214–215; Hay 2013; Hinsch 1992, 53).

A striking feature of the discussion of same-sex relationships in history thus far must be the apparently complete absence of female-female relationships. In some respects, this lacuna can hardly be surprising. With rare exceptions, the history of the human race until only very recently has been largely that of males. Throughout history in virtually all cultures, women have been assigned to a subsidiary role, with the result that their lives and their accomplishments have been relegated to footnotes in the historical record. Crudely put, we know little about same-sex relationships among women at least partly because women were not thought worthy of comment, either favorably or unfavorably.

Some notable exceptions exist throughout history, however, usually anecdotal reports of particular female couples who quite obviously had strong personal feelings (and, perhaps, sexual relations) with each other. Perhaps the most frequently mentioned of these relationships in ancient China was that of Nenuphar and Pivoine, described in a famous Chinese novel called *The Dream of the Red Chamber*. The two girls had played opposite each other as lovers in a production by the acting troupe of which they were members. At one point, apparently, the two had become so comfortable with their roles that they also became lovers in real life. When Pivoine died, Nenuphar was heartbroken and expressed her sorrow by burning "spirit money" in her friend's memory. Asked by an observer what it was that Nenuphar was memorializing, a friend explained that the two girls were "more than friends." The story ends with the following moral: "The cock-bird who mourns his mate is found to be a hen and a true heart is able to sympathize with a strange kind of love" (quoted in Crompton 2003, 236; also see Lesbianism 2013).

Probably the most famous reference to same-sex relationships among women in history centers on the life of the Greek poet Sappho (ca. 630–612 BCE–ca. 570 BCE). She was described by her contemporaries as "among the greatest of poets" or sometimes simply "the Poetess" (in comparison with "the Poet," Homer) ("Sappho" 2013). Although we know virtually nothing with certainty about her personal life, there is no question that many of her love poems were written explicitly to or about women, and historians generally agree that her romantic relationships were largely, if not exclusively, with other women. In fact, the modern term for same-sex relation-ships among women, *lesbianism*, is derived from the island on which Sappho was born and where she spent most of her life. (A somewhat older term for lesbianism, *sapphic love*, also derives from her name.)

The following segment of one of Sappho's poems provides a hint of the passion that other women aroused in her. Observing a beautiful women sitting next to a man, she writes:

To me it seems that man has the fortune of the gods,
whoever sits beside you, and close,
who listens to you sweetly speaking
and laughing temptingly;
my heart flutters in my breast,
whenever I look quickly, for a moment—
I say nothing, my tongue broken,
a delicate fire runs under my skin,
my eyes see nothing, my ears roar,
cold sweat rushes down me,
trembling seizes me,
I am greener than grass,
to myself I seem needing but little to die. ("Isle of Lesbos"
    2013; one of six translations of this fragment)

Same-Sex Behavior in Adolescence

Of special interest for this book is the question of what we know about same-sex activities during adolescence. Evidence from a number of fields of study seems to suggest that such activities have been a normal and natural part of adolescence in many cultures throughout human history. Anthropological studies have found, for example, that ritualized same-sex behav-ior is common in many so-called primitive societies, such as those of the South Pacific. Adults sometimes believe that a boy is unable to develop fully and normally into a man until and unless he has been exposed to a variety of same-sex experiences. Within the Sambia tribe of New Guinea, for example, adults believe that a young boy "must be initiated and orally inseminated, otherwise the girl betrothed to him will outgrow him and run away to another man" (Kimmel 2006). Interestingly enough, members of the tribe do not think of these ritualistic practices as being "homosexual." Rather, they are seen to be part of the normal process of becoming heterosexual adults. Similar ritualistic practices have been reported for a wide variety of primitive cultures. Sometimes they are viewed as true same-sex experiences and at other times, as preparation for adult heterosexuality, as with the Sambias (for an extensive review of such studies, see Herdt [1984]).

Same-sex relationships can develop among adolescents even in the most homophobic of societies. Muslim countries are perhaps the best example of this truism. Although most Islamic scholars condemn same-sex behaviors and the most severe penalties against same-sex acts exist in Muslim nations, such behaviors are common among adolescents of those nations. The reason for this pattern is relatively clear. Any type of opposite-sex behavior is absolutely prohibited outside of marriage, and certainly before a male reaches adulthood. Such behaviors are even more reprehensible than are same-sex acts, so essentially the only sexual outlet for a young Muslim boy is another male. As the young male reaches adulthood and is able to marry, the motivation for same-sex experiences disappears, and he is able to enter into an approved form of sexual expression, an opposite-sex relationship (for an extensive review of this point, see Schmitt and Sofer [1992]).

In many societies—especially Western societies—same-sex activities among adolescents have often been viewed as a normal feature of the growing up process. Adults have viewed boy-on-boy or girl-on-girl sexual activity during adolescence as a "phase" through which individuals grow as they experiment with a variety of sexual expressions. This hypothesis was a common feature of psychoanalytical and psychiatric theory during the first two-thirds of the twentieth century in many cultures, including in the United States. Many mental health experts during the mid-twentieth century counseled parents not to be concerned if their children engaged in same-sex behaviors. They should, however, be very concerned if those practices continued in adulthood. The psychiatric and psycho-analytical professions taught that same-sex feelings and behaviors in adulthood were not normal or natural; rather, they represented perversions that required consultation and treatment by professional mental health experts (see, for example, Bieber and colleagues [1962]).

This viewpoint was reversed by the American Psychiatric Association in 1973 when the organization removed homosexuality from its list of mental disorders, an action taken also by the American Psychological Association in 1975 and the World Health Organization in 1990. (The American Psychoanalytic Association has never formally taken a position on homosexuality per se, although it has issued position statements supporting gay-related issues since the early 1990s [Goode 1998].)

Man-Boy Love

If there is any constant in the long story of same-sex relationships in cultures around the world throughout human history, it is the theme of age differences. Regardless of the symbolic importance of the relationship between Gilgamesh and Enkidu, the coupling of two adult males is very much the exception rather than the rule in same-sex relationships. Far more common are associations between an older man and a younger man, usually an adolescent. The pattern in ancient Greece is instructive.

The practice of an older man's choosing a younger man as his lover appears to have had its beginning in about the seventh century BCE. The practice became known as *paiderastia* (παισεραστία), from which the modern term *pederasty* eventually developed. The original term comes from two Greek words meaning "lover of children," although, over time, it became more specifically associated with the concept of love between an adult male and a younger boy.

The term *pederasty* is not to be confused with a similar term, *pedophilia*, although the two words are sometimes used synonymously. The term *pedophilia*, literally, "the love of children," is generally reserved for adults who have a sexual interest in prepubescent children. The condition is today, and has throughout history, been almost universally condemned and regarded in many times and locations as a mental disorder and/or criminal act. More commonly today, pedophilia is described as *child molestation* [see De Coninck-Smith (2013)].

The origin of man-boy relationships is clouded in the mists of history, but most authorities believe that the practice was originally based in a number of classic Greek tales of the lives of the gods. The most common example is that of the relationship between Zeus, the father of all gods and goddesses, and a young boy named Ganymede. The story is told that Zeus (who was married to the goddess Hera at the time) saw Ganymede tending sheep on the slopes of Mount Ida and became infatuated with him. He sent an eagle to transport Ganymede to Mount Olympus, home of the gods, where he became Zeus's cupbearer and, ultimately, his intimate companion (Calimach 2013).

By about 630 BCE, pederasty had become so thoroughly imbedded in Greek culture that writers of the time ascribed boy lovers to all of the major Greek gods, including Apollo, Dionysus, Hercules, Hermes, Orpheus, Pan, and Poseidon. The sole exception appears to have been Ares, the god of war, who remained unmarried (although not chaste) throughout his life (Percy 1996, 54).

The customary format of pederasty among Greek males had become fully entrenched by that time. The pattern was for an older man (who was almost inevitably married) to choose a younger male to be his companion. The companionship was expected to include a sexual relationship as well as an emotional bond. The boy involved in the relationship was usually in his early teens, probably soon after puberty, an age that his female companions were being joined in a traditional heterosexual marriage. One big difference between the male couple and the heterosexual couple was that the girl generally had nothing to say about her husband, who was commonly much older than she, while the boy traditionally was able to choose among interested and eligible suitors.

After a certain number of years had passed, the older male–younger boy relationship was dissolved. At that point, the older man might select another young boy to take the place of his abandoned lover. The boy, who had by that time probably become a man, was then likely to select a female to whom he became married in a traditional heterosexual marriage. After a period of years, he also would likely select a younger man to become his companion, repeating the cycle that had begun with his own apprenticeship. (Greek pederasty has been the subject of a number of major books. See, for example, Hubbard [2003], Lear and Cantarella [2008], Percy [1996], and Skinner [2005].)

So-called man-boy relationships in Greek culture were probably much more ambiguous and complex than described here and as generally understood in the nonspecialized literature. An authority on the topic, John E. Boswell, has noted that the terms commonly used to describe the members of a same-sex couple, ἐραστής ("lover") and ἐρώμενος ("beloved"), did not necessarily refer to the older and the younger partners, respectively, but sometimes to the more attractive and the less attractive members of the couple, respectively. He notes as an example that Alcibiades, widely known for his beauty, was the "beloved" in same-sex relationships throughout his life. Similarly, same-sex couples did not inevitably consist of an older man and a young boy. Two well-known couples, for example, consisted of the 72-year-old Euripides and the 40-year-old Agathon, and the 65-year-old Parmenides and the 40-year-old Zenon (Boswell 1980, 28).

The intriguing point about the role of pederasty in Greek society of the time was that the tradition appears to have been far more than a quaint social custom that may have permitted adult males to satisfy their own peculiar sexual interests. Instead, it appears to have been considered an essential feature of the culture's philosophical, political, social, military, and artistic life. In the *Symposium*, for example, Plato points out that man-boy relationships are a positive political value for a society because such relationships are more amenable to democracies than they are to tyrannies. He and other writers provide specific examples of tyrants who have been overthrown largely through the efforts of same-sex couples who shared strong common political views. One example frequently mentioned both by Plato and his contemporaries is that of Harmodius and Aristogeiton, an adult same-sex couple who became known as "the Tyrannicides" because of their role in overthrowing the tyrant Hipparchus and converting Athens to a democracy (Plato 2013; Thucydides 2013).

Greece was by no means the only region where man-boy relationships flourished over a significant period of time with at least some level of approval and, perhaps at least as often, with admiration and respect. One source for the popularity of pederastic practices around the world is the Sibylline Oracles, a collection of observations attributed to the Greeks Sibyls, women who issued revelations while in a state of frenzy. Only fragments of these Oracles remain, dating from the second century BCE to the seventh century CE. Their summary of the observance of man-boy relationships is instructive:

> they [the Jews] are mindful of holy wedlock;
> and they do not engage in impious intercourse with male
>   children,
> as do Phoenicians, Egyptians, and Romans,
> spacious Greece and many nations of others,
> Persians and Galatians and all Asia, transgressing

the holy law of immortal God, which they transgressed.
(Gathercole 2013, 147; Troxel 2013; for the original text, see Sibylline Chronicles 2013, line 750)

The inference from this passage is that man-boy relationships were present in just about every culture of which the writer was aware.

The same can be said for parts of the world other than the Middle East and Greece. In Japan prior to its exposure to Western ideas, for example, same-sex relationships between older men and young boys were common, particularly in two settings: religious institutions and the military. In monasteries, for example, it was considered both common and acceptable for senior members of the institution, such as monks and abbots, to take younger lovers both for sexual purposes and as teachers and guides. As in Greece, such relationships were expected to conclude as the younger man reached adulthood, after which he himself might repeat the cycle of man-boy lover (Childs 1980; Leupp 1995; Pflugfelder 1999). Interestingly enough, some writers at the time justified man-boy relationships based on the fact that no women are mentioned in chronicles of the earliest ages of Japanese society, so the gods must have procreated by homosexual means.

Pederasty was also widespread within the samurai, the Japanese military class. Again, adult males accepted younger men and boys as their partners and lovers, with the responsibility of teaching them about proper procedures in preparation for warfare. As the younger partner grew to adulthood, the relationship was dissolved, usually to be replaced by new lovers for both members of the partnership. In some cases, the two members of the partnership even signed a formal agreement specifying that they would be loyal to each other, perhaps even unto death (Leupp 1995, 54).

A list of famous—or at least well-known—men who have been in long-term relationships with boys or younger men is probably long. An abbreviated list of this type has been prepared by the North American Man/Boy Love Association

(NAMBLA, about whom more will be said later). It includes names such as Alexander the Great (356–323 BCE), the Roman Emperor Hadrian (76–138 CE), Leonardo da Vinci (1452–1519), Michelangelo (1476–1564), Christopher Marlowe (1564–1593), Horatio Alger (1834–1899), Oscar Wilde (1854–1900), Friedrich Alfred Krupp (1854–1902), and Andre Gide (1869–1951) ("15 Famous Men Who Had Boy Lovers" 2013).

The character of man-boy relationships in Japan (and other cultures) described here differed significantly from that in Greece. In the latter case, pederasty was a relatively common practice seen among many males in the community of free men. In the former case, man-boy relationships were largely limited to all-male institutions, such as the military and the priesthood. And it is the Japanese model that persisted through the centuries until well into at least the eighteenth century.

Variations of man-boy relationships appear to have been common in other civilizations also. Such relationships are the topic of extended discussions at various points in history throughout the Muslim world. In all times and places, Muslims were required to tread carefully when considering same-sex relationships among males. Although strictly forbidden by the Qur'an, such relationships were apparently widespread. One observer from the twelfth century wrote, for example, "He who claims that he experiences no desire when looking at beautiful boys or youths is a liar, and if we could believe him he would be an animal, and not a human being" (Monroe 1997, 117). In a recent analysis of Arabic poetry from 1500 to 1800, Harvard professor of Islamic intellectual history Khaled El-Rouayheb suggests that large portions of the Muslim poetic canon during the period were written in praise of young boys— not girls, as has been traditionally thought. He claims that this poetry is a reflection of Islamic "passionate but chaste" love between men and boys (El-Rouayheb 2005, 3).

With the fall of Rome and the spread of Christianity throughout Europe, all types of sexual behavior, except those associated directly with procreation, were outlawed as sinful by the church. Any form of contact between man and boy was prohibited, as was every form of homosexuality, adultery, masturbation, and premarital sex. Condemnation of man-boy relationships has continued throughout most parts of the world to the present day, with only rare exceptions. Indeed, such relationships are now frequently conflated with pedophilia and are regarded not only as sinful and evil, but also as exploitative of and harmful to the younger member of the partnership. Physical contact (and often less intimate contact) between adult males and underage boys is now a crime almost everywhere.

One of the few exceptions to this trend has been the North American Man/Boy Love Association (NAMBLA). NAMBLA was founded in December 1978, largely in response to a raid by Boston police on a private home in the suburb of Revere. Twenty-four men were arrested and accused of operating a "sex ring" involving underage boys. Although those charges were eventually dropped, members of the Boston gay community were sufficiently outraged to meet and form a new group to bring together men who believed in their right to have relationships with underage boys. That group was NAMBLA ("Brief History of the Modern Childlove Movement" 2013).

The fundamental position espoused by NAMBLA is that in the modern world, man-boy relationships are not well understood and, more important, are often mischaracterized. Such relationships are not, they say, generally exploitative; rather, they are mutually supportive for both the men and the boys involved in a relationship. They are, according to the NAMBLA website,

> based on mutual respect and affection, and strongly desired by both partners. Such relationships do not harm anyone, and often entail many benefits for both man and boy. Boy-lovers and boys alike respond to the needs of those they love—needs for affection, understanding, and freedom. (What Is Man/Boy Love? 2013)

One of the organization's publications, *Boys Speak Out on Man/Boy Love* (2013), includes testimonials from boys who have been engaged in man-boy relationships, explaining how those relationships have been helpful, comforting, supportive, and even life-saving in their own lives.

Since its founding, NAMBLA has been the focus of vigorous debate both within the gay and lesbian community itself and among the general public. The nature and significance of that debate will be discussed later in this chapter.

The Making of a Gay Community

Apologists for same-sex relationships sometimes attempt to justify the legitimacy of such relationships by pointing to famous men and women of history who were gay men or lesbians, a list that might include names such as Alexander the Great, Socrates, Sappho, Hadrian, Richard the Lionhearted, Saladin, Sir Francis Bacon, Frederick the Great, Lord Byron, Walt Whitman, Oscar Wilde, Marcel Proust, Gertrude Stein, Alice B. Toklas, Federico Garcia Lorca, Cole Porter, Virginia Woolf, Pope Julius III, Tennessee Williams, James Baldwin, Michelangelo, Leonardo Da Vinci, Christopher Marlowe, and Herman Melville ("Famous GLB People in History" 2013).

The problem with such lists is that prior to the eighteenth century, it probably would have been impossible to call someone *gay* or *lesbian*, terms that define an individual primarily in terms of his or her sexual interests. Virtually all of the individuals in the preceding list who lived prior to the Industrial Revolution lived fairly traditional heterosexual lives: they were married and had children; they belonged to political clubs that had nothing to do with their sexual orientation; they attended churches that despised their sexual proclivities; they were similar to other members of their families, their neighbors, and other members of their community . . . except for the fact that they had emotional attachments to members of the same sex and acted on those feelings in more or less secret ways.

This seeming ambiguity of sexual activity and experience has led to almost endless debates as to whether a particular individual was really "gay" or "lesbian." In the case of Alexander the Great, for example, some writers insist there is no doubt that his good friend Hephaestion was the real love of his life, while other historians point out that Alexander was married and the father of at least two children, one legitimate and one illegitimate, as well as the lover of a number of other women (Alexander the Great 2013; Children of Alexander III the Great 2013; Upbin 2011).

So how does the Industrial Revolution mark a turning point in the nature of same-sex relationships and the rise of the modern gay and lesbian movement? Prior to the Industrial Revolution, virtually all societies worldwide were essentially agrarian cultures that were focused on the family and the local community. Most people were born, grew up, lived, and died surrounded by close relatives and near neighbors. They tended to follow their parents' lifestyle as a farmer, a butcher, a shop owner, a tradesman, or a housewife. One's life was devoted to earning a living and raising a family. For the ordinary man or woman, finding expressions for any same-sex feelings that one might have would of necessity have been fairly low on a list of personal priorities, and one that could be realized only in furtive, out-of-the-way experiences. Two men or two women could hardly move in together and build a life with each other as heterosexual couples in the community were not only able to do, but were expected to do. Probably the only major exception to this type of lifestyle was a religious community, where individuals could at least escape the expectations of a heterosexual family lifestyle and experience a same-sex community, whether or not actual sexual experiences were ever a realistic option in such communities. It is hardly surprising, then, that some religious communities (in spite of their teachings) may have acknowledged the validity of same-sex relationships and even, upon occasion, have instituted religious rituals for recognizing such relationships (see, for example, Boswell [1994]).

The rise of industrialism made possible, for the first time in history, an alternative to that lifestyle. Industrialization required the construction of factories, where strong men and women, boys and girls, could be brought together to work. Individuals now found it necessary and advantageous to leave their families as soon as possible, move to urban areas, set up their own households, and develop new friendships based on their jobs rather than their own families. For the first time, it became relatively easy for men and women who were sexually attracted to their own sex to find like-minded individuals and pursue same-sex relationships. As a consequence, true same-sex communities became a possibility, probably for the first time in modern society. As John D'Emilio, a pioneer in the analysis of this movement has written,

> Gradually finding methods of meeting one another, these men and women staked out urban spaces and patronized institutions that fostered a group life. . . . a subculture of gay men and lesbians was evolving in American cities that would help to create a collective consciousness among its participants and strengthen their sense of identification with a group. (D'Emilio 1998, 12–13)

This sense of community resulted in the creation of bars and clubs catering almost entirely to gay men and lesbians, newspapers and magazines aimed at the community, specialized literary societies and other social institutions, and other mechanisms for bringing together like-minded gay men and lesbians for all types of interaction.

Nor was the United States the only nation where such changes were taking place. Indeed, any country in which industrialization and capitalism had taken root was experiencing a similar evolution. Perhaps the leading nation in the growth of a self-identified gay and lesbian subculture was Germany. The rise of the gay and lesbian movement in Germany was due at least in part to the introduction of strong new anti-same-sex legislation in the German parliament that resulted in the adoption of Paragraph 175, which outlawed virtually all same-sex activity. One response to the adoption of this legislation was the formation of a committee to work for the rights of gay men and lesbians, the Wissenschaftlich-humanitäres Komitee (Scientific-Humanitarian Committee), founded in 1897 by physician Magnus Hirschfeld, publisher Max Spohr, lawyer Eduard Oberg, and writer Franz Joseph von Bülow. The committee sought the repeal of Paragraph 175 and the adoption of new legislation protecting the rights of lesbians and gay men. The organization was the first of its kind in history. By 1922, there were 25 chapters of the organization in Germany, Austria, and the Netherlands (Beachy 2010). Hirschfeld later went on to found the Institut für Sexualwissenschaft (Institute for Sex Research) in 1919 and the Weltliga für Sexualreform (World League for Sexual Reform) in 1921, although none of his efforts survived the rise of the Nazi Party in Germany in the early 1930s. (For more detail on the early German gay rights movement, see Lauritsen and Thorstad [1995].)

Gay Liberation and Gay Rights

Efforts to achieve political rights for lesbians and gay men in the United States, like those in Germany, did not surface until the early 1950s with the establishment of the Mattachine Society for gay men and the Daughters of Bilitis for lesbians in 1950 and 1955, respectively. (For details of the history of the gay and lesbian movement in the United States prior to the late 1960s, see especially D'Emilio [1998] and Pre–Gay Era Bibliography [2013].) For many historians, however, the defining moment in the development of a gay and lesbian consciousness in the United States occurred on the evening of June 27–28, 1969, when a group of New York City police officers staged a raid on a popular Greenwich Village bar the Stonewall Inn. Such raids were not uncommon in New York City, or almost any other community in the United States where homosexuals gathered for social interaction. In such raids, patrons of the bar typically cowered at the back of the room or ran away as fast as they could to prevent having their names, addresses, and—sometimes—photos printed in the next day's newspapers.

The Stonewall raid was different, however, in that bar patrons, many of whom were drag queens, chose to fight back against the police. (A drag queen is a man who dresses up as a woman primarily for the purpose of entertaining others.) Instead of leaving quietly, stepping into waiting police paddy wagons, or running away as fast as possible, bar patrons and a gathering crowd from the surrounding area chose to fight back. They threw beer cans, bricks, and other objects at police officers, locked them inside the bar, and set the bar on fire. (No one was seriously injured in the resulting melee.) (Possibly the best description of the Stonewall riots is Teal [1971]. Also see Carter [2004] and Garcia [2013].) A number of factors were involved in the decision by Stonewall patrons and others in the neighborhood to fight back, not the least of which was a general reaction to persons in authority that had evolved out of the long period of despair over the war in Vietnam. As one participant in the riot later said,

> We all had a collective feeling like we'd had enough of this kind of s***. . . . There was something in the air, freedom a long time overdue, and we're going to fight for it. It took different forms, but the bottom line was, we weren't going to go away. And we didn't. (quoted in Carter 2004, 160)

In another unusual turn of events, the riots did not simply die out in the early morning hours of July 28. Instead, skirmishes between police and homosexuals and their supporters continued over the next two days. More important, the riots set into motion actions that were to mark the real beginning of a gay and lesbian protest movement, both in New York and in cities across the country. For example, activists began to explore more organized ways of responding to the harassment and persecution of homosexuals by New York police in particular, but also by persons and organizations in authority throughout society. At first, these activists attempted to work through existing organizations such as the Mattachine Society. But they were discouraged by the relatively moderate view of the Mattachine about gay-related issues. These activists eventually decided to form a new organization of their own, which they called the Gay Liberation Front (GLF). GLF survived only two years but during that time became a powerful force on behalf of gay liberation in the city (Gay Liberation Front 2013a; Gay Liberation Front 2013b). Upon its demise, it was replaced by organizations with similar objectives, including the Gay Activists Alliance, Radicalesbians, Radicalqueens, Lesbian Feminist Liberation, Third World Gay Revolution, Street Transvestite Action Revolutionaries, The Effeminists, Red Butterfly, and Gay Flames.

What were the goals of these new groups? Although various groups had somewhat different objectives, one theme was constant throughout all of them: lesbians and gay men had decided to take the offensive against negative images that U.S. (and, to a large extent, world) society had constructed of them. They no longer accepted the premise that same-sex acts were sinful, pathological, criminal, or harmful to other individuals. They took as their theme a slogan first proposed by long-term activist Franklin Kemeny: "Gay is good." Among the activities promoted by various gay liberation groups were the publication of New York City's first newspaper for gay men and lesbians, sit-ins at various social and political events to make their concerns known, sponsorship of city legislation to protect the rights of lesbians and gay men in the city, and the first gay pride parade in the United States on June 28, 1970. (An interesting insight into the activities of an early gay liberation front group can be found at Gay Liberation Front–DC [2013], with special attention to "first fact sheet" addendum. Perhaps the best overview of the aims of the gay liberation front movement was the Gay Liberation Front Manifesto, published by the British organization of that name; see Gay Liberation Front: *Manifesto* [2013].)

Proponents of gay rights in the last quarter of the twentieth century faced an uphill battle. Public opinion was strongly arrayed against any sort of positive attitude toward same-sex activities, relationships, and rights. Most public opinion polls found that Americans thought that same-sex acts were "always wrong" or "wrong most of the time"; that gay men and lesbians should not have equal rights with regard to housing, employment, and access to public accommodations; and that lesbians and gay men should be banned from a number of occupations, such as teaching and medicine (Yang n.d.). In one survey conducted in 1974, for example, researchers found that three-quarters of white Americans disapproved of same-sex relationships, and 83.8 percent said they thought that such relationships were "obscene and vulgar" (Levitt and Klassen 1976).

The proportion of respondents to polls who held such attitudes remained relatively constant over the next two decades but then began to fall rather rapidly. According to the long-term NORC poll conducted by the University of Chicago, the fraction of those queried who thought that same-sex relationships were "always wrong" hovered around 70 percent between 1973 and 1991. That fraction began to drop, however, reaching 62.2 percent in 1993, 54.3 percent in 1998, and 43.5 percent in 2010 (Smith 2013, 2). The prestigious Gallup organization found similar patterns over the same time period. When asked in 1977 if same-sex relationships should be legal, respondents were evenly divided on the question, with 43 percent answering "yes" and 43 percent answering "no" to the question. Rates of those who favored legalizing same-sex relationships gradually increased over time, however, and reached a high of 64 percent in 2012. At the same time, the fraction opposing legalizing same-sex relationships dropped to 33 percent (Gay and Lesbian Rights 2013). On another topic, Gallup asked respondents whether gay men and lesbians should have equal rights in terms of job opportunities. In 1978, a majority of respondents (56 percent) responded "yes" to the question, with 33 percent opposing equal rights for lesbians and gay men. By 2010, those numbers had changed to 89 percent and 8 percent, respectively (Gay and Lesbian Rights 2013).

Perhaps at least partly in response to increased acceptance of gay and lesbian lifestyles, the political emphasis of the gay and lesbian movement itself has evolved over the past half century. Today, one hears relatively little about gay liberation, the right of a gay man or lesbian to be himself or herself and live his or her own life without fear of oppression or harassment. For most gay men and lesbians in the United States and other developed nations of the world, that goal has been achieved. Instead, the emphasis in the gay movement has turned to civil rights: the right to employment, housing, equal access to public accommodations, as well as the right to marry and adopt children. In one sense, the gay movement has evolved from wanting the right to be free and independent of societal expectations to wanting to become equal members of the overall society.

But What about LGBT Youth?

For readers of this book, a crucial question at this point might well be why there has been—with the exception of man-boy relationships—so little mention of same-sex relationships among boys and girls. What do we know about the occurrence of such relationships, say, between two teenage boys or two teenage girls and about societal attitudes about and restrictions of same-sex feelings and acts?

One fact that does seem to be clear is that a significant number of boys and girls do recognize in themselves an erotic attraction to members of the same sex at a relatively young age. Studies have shown that gay men and lesbians recall experiencing same-sex feelings in high school, middle school, elementary school, or even earlier. In one study of 1,752 college students, for example, 17 percent of gay men and 11 percent of lesbian knew of their sexual orientation as early as elementary school, and 20 percent of men and 6 percent of women had made that recognition by high school (Lesbian, Gay, Bisexual, and Transgendered Youth Issues 2001, 1). In one comprehensive study of the development of sexual orientation, two researchers came to the conclusion that

> the development of sexual attraction may commence in middle childhood and achieve individual subjective recognition sometime around the age of 10. As these studies [referring to earlier studies by these authors] have shown, first same-sex attraction for males and females typically occurs at the mean age of 9.6 for boys and between the ages of 10 and 10.5 for girls. (Herdt and McClintock 2000, 597; a number of online blogs also provide interesting insight on this question)

Another matter of interest with regard to younger LGBT is the phenomenon of childhood gender nonconformity. The term *childhood gender nonconformity* (CGN) refers to instances in which a young boy or girl behaves in ways that are not considered typical of the person's biological sex. For example, a young boy might want to dress in girl's clothing and play with dolls rather than take part in sporting activities. A girl might act like a "tomboy," preferring boy's activities and clothing to those usually associated with girls. A great deal of research has been done on CGN, and there is now a strong consensus among researchers that a strong correlation exists between the phenomenon and adult sexual orientation. That is, CGN boys have a strong likelihood of growing up to become gay men and CGN girls, to become lesbians. In fact, one researcher has observed that

> It is difficult to identify an example of a pattern of childhood behaviors that is as predictive of an essential adulthood behavioral phenomenon as is early cross-gender

behaviors with later homosexual orientation. (Green 2008, 17)

This observation suggests that one's adult sexual orientation may often be predictable on the basis of a child's early behavior. To the extent that this is true, same-sex orientation may become an issue (and often a problem) at a relatively early age. It would seem likely that any adult same-sex organization would be concerned about providing support, assistance, and guidance to young LGBT. But generally speaking, that has not been the case.

(It is necessary to point out that the association between CGN and adult sexual orientation is much more complex than indicated here. For example, one's *gender* orientation [whether one sees oneself as a male or female] may not necessarily have anything to do with one's *sexual* orientation [the choice one makes for a sexual partner]. For more on this point, see Special Issue on Childhood Gender Nonconformity and Development of Adult Homosexuality [2008].)

Homosexuality and Child Molestation

Opposition to same-sex behavior has traditionally been based on a number of arguments: such behavior is not "normal" or "natural"; religious teachings condemn such practices; people who practice same-sex behavior are mentally disordered; or same-sex acts are a type of criminal behavior. An additional argument of particular interest to LGBT youth and their friends is that homosexuals prey upon young children, usually for their own sexual satisfaction or for the purpose of recruiting new members for the homosexual community.

This argument is relatively new in the long history of human society. Its origins can be traced to the rise of the modern gay movement in Western societies in the 1960s and 1970s. Perhaps the best-known effort to link homosexuality and child molestation during the period was the Save Our Children campaign organized by former popular singer and born-again Christian activist Anita Bryant in 1977. That campaign was organized in response to the adoption of an ordinance by Dade County, Florida, prohibiting discrimination against gays and lesbians in housing, employment, and public accommodation. Bryant's fundamental argument was that the ordinance violated her constitutional right to teach her children Christian values. The main thrust of her campaign, however, was an effort to portray gay men (lesbians were hardly mentioned) as child molesters who were out to recruit new members for their community. Her most memorable quotation during the campaign was, "As a mother, I know that homosexuals cannot biologically reproduce children; therefore, they must recruit our children" ("HBO Eyes Biopic about Anti-Gay Activist Bryant" 2013). (For an excellent discussion of the Save Our Children movement, see Palmer [2013]).

Bryant's Save Our Children campaign successfully overturned the Dade County antidiscrimination ordinance by a margin of 70 percent to 30 percent in the largest turnout of voters in the county's history to that date. Similar campaigns based largely on the dangers posed by homosexual men as child molesters overturned similar ordinances in Eugene, Oregon; St. Paul, Minnesota; and Wichita, Kansas. The Dade County success also emboldened antihomosexual activists in California to put forward an initiative petition that would have banned homosexual men and women from teaching positions in state schools and, more broadly, would have prohibited the mention of same-sex issues in any state school. That initiative, Proposition 6 (widely known as the Briggs Initiative, after sponsoring legislator John Briggs), was ultimately defeated in the November 1978 general election (Harbeck 1997, 39–60).

Bryant's argument and that of the Save Our Children campaign was hardly an anomaly in the United States in the late 1970s. Indeed, warnings of the dangers posed by gay men to young boys could be found almost everywhere. (As usual, any threat that lesbians may have posed to young girls was never mentioned.) A popular health science textbook for high schools of the time, for example, showed a shadowy figure hiding by a tree near a school yard with the caption "A male homosexual may wait patiently around a high school day after day, until he thinks he can safely approach and befriend a student" (Friend 1993, 215; also see Newton 1979; Newton 1992).

Groups opposed to granting equal rights to gay men and lesbians also used the threat of child molesters as a theme in their own campaigns. In 1982, for example, the far right religious organization Christian Voice Moral Government Fund based its fund-raising efforts on the theme that

> Thousands of innocent American children may soon be molested by sex deviates—if Congress votes for a proposed "civil rights" law now being considered—including precious Christian children in your Sunday school. (Kirchick 2013)

(Possibly the foremost spokesperson for the position that gay men are child molesters is Paul Cameron, who wrote extensively on the topic for more than two decades. See, for example, Cameron [1993]. For a more recent discussion of the topic, see Baldwin [2002], who argues that "homosexual behavior threatens the foundation of Western civilization—the nuclear family. An unmistakable manifestation of the attack on the family unit is the homosexual community's efforts to target children both for their own sexual pleasure and to enlarge the homosexual movement" [267].)

It should be noted that the purported connection between homosexuality and child molestation is not generally supported by the vast majority of experts in the field. In an extended review of the topic, one researcher has concluded that

> The empirical research does not show that gay or bisexual men are any more likely than heterosexual men to molest children. This is not to argue that homosexual and

bisexual men never molest children. But there is no scientific basis for asserting that they are more likely than heterosexual men to do so. (Herek 2013; also see Schlatter and Steinback 2013)

The problems created by the panic over child molestation following the Save Our Children campaign were perhaps most clearly expressed in the response of gay liberation organizations to the existence and activities of NAMBLA. At first, those organizations were opened to the fundamental concerns of NAMBLA, especially the way age of consent laws were used as a tool against same-sex activities. (For example, a 20-year-old man can be prosecuted for child molestation if he is engaged in same-sex activities with an 18-year-old male if the age of consent in a state is 19 years.) As reactionary politics swept the nation in the early 1980s, however, most gay activists began to see their relationship with NAMBLA as a significant handicap in moving forward with their other objectives. They began to distance themselves from the organization and to disavow its philosophy and activities.

In the first gay march on Washington, DC, in October 1979, a number of participants objected to the presence of NAMBLA members in the parade. A year later, the Lesbian Caucus of the New York City Gay Pride Parade threatened to withdraw from the event if NAMBLA was also allowed to participate (Thorstad 1991). By the middle of the 1980s, essentially all mainstream gay and lesbian organizations had abandoned NAMBLA and rejected everything for which the organization stood, a trend from which they have never reversed direction. For example, in 1994, the board of directors of one of the most influential gay and lesbian groups in the United States, GLAAD (Gay and Lesbian Defenders against Defamation), issued a policy statement saying that NAMBLA's goals "constitute a form of child abuse and are repugnant to GLAAD" (GLAAD/USA Position Statement Regarding NAMBLA 2013). In the same year, the National

Gay and Lesbian Task Force (NGLTF) issued a similar statement, saying that NGLTF

> condemns all abuse of minors, both sexual and any other kind, perpetrated by adults. Accordingly, NGLTF condemns the organizational goals of NAMBLA and any other such organization. ("Brief History of the Modern Childlove Movement" 2013)

Thus, although NAMBLA remains in existence in the second decade of the twenty-first century, it has been disavowed by all mainstream gay and lesbian organizations, and the topic of man-boy love is absent from the websites of all major mainstream organizations.

The point of this discussion is not to argue one side or another in the homosexuality and child molestation debate; rather, it is to try to explain the situation that the gay rights movement in the last decades of the twentieth century faced in dealing with young lesbians, gay men, bisexuals, and transgenders. Any effort to work aggressively for specifically youth-oriented concerns faced the risk of validating the homosexuality–child molestation link posed by opponents of gay and lesbian rights.

The Growth of LGBT Organizations

Still, prior to the Save Our Children movement in Florida, an estimated 35 school- and community-based groups designed specifically for gay and lesbian youth had been established, primarily in large urban areas like New York City and San Francisco. One of the best known and longest-lasting of these groups was Gay Youth (GY), which began as a subsidiary of GLF but became independent in February 1970. Membership in GY was limited to males and females under the age of 21 (later 22) and for much of its existence was run largely without adult supervision. GY later changed its name to Gay & Lesbian

Youth of New York (GLYNY); Bisexual, Gay and Lesbian Youth of New York (BiGLYNY); and finally Bisexual, Gay, Lesbian and Transgender Youth of New York (BiGLTYNY). The activities of BiGLTYNY have since been absorbed by the Lesbian, Gay, Bisexual & Transgender Community Center of New York (Gay and Lesbian Youth of New York Records 2013) (for an in-depth description of three New York City groups, see Cohen [2007]).

The late 1970s and early 1980s were, therefore, a difficult time for groups working for the advancement of gay and lesbian civil rights. That challenge was made even more difficult in the early 1980s with the advent of the HIV/AIDS crisis. For most of that decade, gay men and lesbians largely set aside their efforts to achieve equality in the American political system to concentrate on dealing with the horrendous medical problem with which the federal government and most nongay organizations were not interested in dealing. (President Ronald Reagan, for example, refused to acknowledge the AIDS crisis during the first seven years of his presidency and did not say the word *AIDS* in public until 1987, seven years after the disease first appeared in the United States ["Nancy Reagan and the AIDS Crisis" 2013].)

Non-AIDS activism did not become totally moribund, however. Indeed, the formation of a wide variety of social and political organizations continued throughout the 1980s. And such efforts accelerated as progress eventually began to be made in bringing the HIV/AIDS epidemic under some measure of control in the 1990s. As an example, the Indiana Youth Group (IYG) was founded in 1978 by a small group of lesbians and gay men who were then working on the Gay and Lesbian Switchboard in Indianapolis, Indiana. These men and women were motivated by the problems they regularly heard about from young lesbians, gay men, bisexuals, and transgenders calling to the switchboard for help. The organization was eventually able to purchase its own building in 1992 and became a member of the local United Way Community Fund which provided a dependable source of funding for the first time in its history. Perhaps its signal accomplishment in recent years was gaining approval from the Indiana Bureau of Motor Vehicles for a specialty license plate carrying the IYG name, the first such program in the United States (Indiana Youth Group 2013).

Stories like those of IYG are probably far more common than many people might imagine. Support groups for lesbian, gay, bisexual, and transgender youth have been springing up throughout the United States for well over three decades, often in cities and towns that one might not imagine. In 1991, for example, Tonda Taylor—a native of Charlotte, North Carolina—decided to found an organization for gay, lesbian, bisexual, and transgender youth, which she called Time Out Youth (TOY). TOY and Taylor organized the first local conference on homosexuality the same year and a year later sponsored the city's first LGBT prom. As with most LGBT youth organizations, TOY offers a safe space for young people to gather, activities focused on their specific interests, resources on which they can call for additional information and guidance, and support for parents and friends of LGBT youth. (The TOY website is at http://www.timeoutyouth.org/index.html.)

The last two decades of the twentieth century also saw the appearance of school-centered groups to bring LGBT students together with their nongay peers interested in discussing topics of common interest. The first of these so-called gay-straight alliances (GSA) was formed in 1988 by teacher Kevin Jennings at Concord Academy, a private secondary school in Concord, Massachusetts. The first GSA in a public school was formed three years later at South Newton High School in Newton, Massachusetts, by teacher Robert Parlin. These two groups later grew into two national organizations, the Gay, Lesbian and Straight Education Network (GLSEN) and GSANetwork.

GLSEN evolved out of a series of organizations that began in 1990 when Jennings organized a group of about 70 volunteer teachers in the Boston area who were concerned about the special problems of LGBT students, such as harassment, bullying, depression and other emotional problems, and lack of support within the traditional educational community. Jennings named the organization the Gay and Lesbian Independent School Teachers Network (GLISTN), reflecting the dominant sexual orientation of its members as well as its center in independent schools. Within a year, the organization had changed its name to simply the Gay and Lesbian School Teachers Network (GLSTN) as an indication of its rapid and growing appeal to teachers in a wider range of school settings. GLSTN gained recognition from official circles almost immediately when Massachusetts governor William Weld invited the group to advise his newly created Commission on Gay and Lesbian Youth, which was organized to deal with many of the same issues about which GLISTN had originally been formed.

In 1994, GLSTN became a truly national organization when it opened an office in New York City and hired Jennings as executive director. The organization changed its name once again, this time to the Gay, Lesbian and Straight Teachers Network (GLSTN) to take note of the increasing role of heterosexual allies in the campaign to provide support for LGBT youth. One final name change occurred in 1997 when GLSTN took on its current name of Gay, Lesbian and Straight Educators Network (GLSEN) in an effort to expand its outreach to adults and youth in all types of educational environment. GLSEN currently maintains its national headquarters in New York City with a public policy office in Washington, DC. It also oversees 39 local chapters in 22 states that coordinate and advise local chapters in their regions. As of late 2013, more than 4,000 individual gay-straight alliances had registered with GLSEN.

GSA Network had its origins in a 1998–1999 school year effort to bring together 40 separate gay-straight alliances in high schools in the San Francisco Bay area. The goal of that effort was to provide a mechanism by which such groups could contact and otherwise interact with each other and to find ways of drawing on the resources of local communities in attaining their individual and collective objectives. By 2001, the organization had spread throughout the state of California, and three years later it had become a national organization. Today it acts as a coordinating and advisory body for more than 900 gay-straight alliances in 35 states.

In recent years, there has been a trend toward the development of new organizations that deal with specific issues in the lives of LGBT youth. One example is Faces for Change, a group formed in January 2013 after 15-year-old Jadin Bell, a student at La Grande High School in La Grande, Oregon, hanged himself. In his suicide note, Bell said that he could no longer tolerate the bullying he experienced on a daily basis for being openly gay at school. Friends of the Bell family, Bud Hill, Heather Martin, and Jayne Baremore, decided to form a new organization designed to educate students about the importance of accepting everyone just for who they are. The organization had no immediate plans to expand beyond the local area; rather, it planned to focus on what it could do in La Grande to create a more caring and understanding community. (The Faces for Change website is at http://www.facesforchange.com/.)

A Word about Words

A number of terms have appeared in this chapter without having been specifically defined. Yet knowing the meaning of those terms is essential in any discussion of LGBT youth issues. So let us review those terms.

Perhaps most fundamental of all are the terms *sex* and *gender*. These two terms are used so widely in discussions of LGBT issues that they are sometimes made to sound equivalent or even identical. For people who study sexual issues closely, that is not the case. Generally speaking, the term *sex* is used to describe those biological characteristics that make males different from females. Those characteristics in humans include the so-called primary sexual traits (those used in the process of reproduction), including sex organs such as the penis and testes in males and the vagina and ovaries in the female; as well as secondary sexual characteristics, such as facial hair, a deep voice, broad shoulders, and relatively larger muscle mass and strength in males, compared to growth of breasts, wider hips, and generally smaller hands and feet than in males for females. Primary sexual characteristics are present at birth but tend to develop during puberty, while secondary sexual characteristics are largely absent until the onset of puberty ("Human Development" 2013).

By contrast, the term *gender* for humans is more properly used to describe a person's public presentation as a man or woman, a boy or girl. The World Health Organization defines gender as "the socially constructed roles, behaviours, activities, and attributes that a given society considers appropriate for men and women" ("What Do We Mean by 'Sex' and 'Gender'?" 2013). Thus, it is possible for a person who is biologically a male to present himself publicly as a feminine person by choosing the clothing and lifestyle that his society usually associates with a female. In such cases, members of that society may react by stigmatizing that male as a "sissy," "cream puff," "momma's boy," "namby-pamby," "wuss," or some other derogatory term. Similarly, a biological female who presents herself with masculine characteristics may be labeled by her peers as a "tomboy," "butch," or "amazon."

To emphasize the difference between *sex* and *gender*, the terms most properly used for the former are *female* and *male*, and for the latter *feminine* and *masculine*.

At one time, the most common words used to describe a person's sexual orientation were *homosexual* and *heterosexual*. Surprisingly, perhaps, both words are relatively recent terms with which to talk about one's sexuality. They were first used in 1869 by the Austrian-born writer Károly Mária Kertbeny (1824–1882) in a pamphlet opposing strong new Prussian laws against same-sex relationships. Kertbeny suggested the words *homosexual* and *heterosexual* to describe two classes of individuals who are sexually attracted primarily to people of the same sex or people of the opposite sex, respectively. He thought that these scientifically neutral terms would allow a more rational, less impassioned debate over the new laws than more traditional value-laden terms such as *pederast* and *sodomite* (Burroway 2013). By extension, many discussions today (including some comments in this book) refer to *homosexuality* as if it were some all-encompassing condition by which a person can be defined.

It is for just this reason that many people prefer not to use the words *homosexual* and *heterosexual* when talking about someone. The practice appears to suggest that a person can be defined by his or her choice of sexual attraction. That presumption is almost certainly not true. One would not expect to call a person a Christian or a Michigander or a philanthropist and know everything of importance simply based on one of those general designations. People who write and think about sexuality, then, often prefer to use the words *homosexual* and *heterosexual* as adjectives that describe certain types of sexual acts. That makes it easier to talk about someone whose primary sexual encounters are with someone of the same sex or someone who is married but has occasional sexual contacts with someone of the same sex or someone who is celibate but may have intense thoughts about same-sex encounters (on this point, see Swartz [2013, 5]).

That having been said, it is true that the practice of categorizing people on the basis of their sexual interests is still very common today, as evidenced by a book on lesbian, gay, bisexual, and transgendered youth (as if that is all we need to know about those individuals!). Of those terms, *lesbian* and *gay* refer, at one level, to females who are erotically attracted to other females and males who are erotically attracted to other males, respectively. But the terms also have more complex and subtle meanings. Many gay men and lesbians use these terms to describe themselves not only because they *are* attracted to someone of the same sex, but at least as importantly, because they have acknowledged that aspect of their personality. They refer to that process of acknowledgment as "coming out."

Coming out is one of the most crucial events in the life of a lesbian or a gay man, and it usually occurs in phases. The first stage of coming out is admitting to oneself that one is "different" from one's peers. A 10-year-old boy may realize, for example, that he is not really interested in talking about girls with his male friends and that he is more interested sexually in those friends than they are in him. A second stage of coming out is self-acceptance, a time when one not only acknowledges being different, but also accepts the fact that being different is not an evil, unhealthy, sinful, or otherwise negative condition. Rather, it is simply a condition that makes one different from most other people. Yet another level of coming out is revealing one's sexual orientation to one's family, neighbors, friends, co-workers, and even the general public. One reaches the point where it is just as easy to talk about one's girlfriend (if one is a female) as it is to talk about one's boyfriend. Coming out, then, is really a range of experiences, from the intensely personal to the very public.

One of the serious problems in using the terms *the homosexual* or *the heterosexual* is that many individuals simply do not belong in one category or the other: they find sexual gratification from both sexes. Such individuals are called *bisexual.* Abundant scientific evidence points to the fact that many humans find themselves attracted to both sexes to one degree or another: perhaps 10 percent same sex and 90 percent opposite sex; or 50 percent toward each sex; or some other fraction. A number of social and psychological factors are probably involved in getting people to "choose" which category they belong in, gay or lesbian, and many just refuse to make that choice and call themselves bisexual.

The fourth category in the LGBT acronym, the *T* category, consists of transsexual or transgendered individuals. Some disagreement exists about the precise meaning of these two terms. To some individuals and organizations, they may refer to almost the same phenomenon, a situation in which an individual feels that she or he belongs to a gender that is different from the biological sex with which she or he was born. That is, an adolescent boy almost certainly knows that he is a male because of his primary and secondary sexual characteristics. The fact that he has a penis, however, may not match his feelings that he wants to dress in girl's clothing, take part in traditional female activities, and, therefore, is really a female or at least wants to behave as a female at least part of the time.

Other individuals disagree. They point out that a significant range of feelings is subsumed in the terms *transsexual* and *transgender*. Some individuals may be perfectly happy dressing and acting like someone of the opposite sex for part of the time while continuing to maintain a traditional gender role in most other aspects of their lives. Research shows that transsexuality or transgenderism is probably most common among married heterosexual males who enjoy dressing in women's clothing upon occasion and appearing in public in an attempt to "pass," at least temporarily, as a women. Transsexual/transgender males who fit this description are perfectly happy to remain biological males and would never consider having hormone therapy, surgery, or other procedures that would change the biological sex with which they were born. This pattern of behavior might logically be called *transgenderism* because the married heterosexual male wants to change the public presentation of his gender, not the biological features that determine his sex and make him a male. (Interestingly enough, this form of transsexuality or transgenderism is much less common among heterosexual women, for whom dressing in men's clothing and displaying traditional male behavior is not only acceptable, but actually quite common.)

In this view, the term *transsexuality* should perhaps be reserved for individuals who want to change not only the public presentation of their sexuality (their gender), but also their actual biological sex. That is, males want to lose their male sex organs and the hormonal balance that determines their secondary sexual characteristics, and females want to lose their female sex organs and their characteristic female sex hormone production.

Yet this set of terms, as logical as it might seem, is not necessarily the way that transsexuals and transgenders actually talk about themselves. Much of the literature on transsexualism, for example, focuses on the way that individuals present themselves in public (which is normally defined as a person's gender), while people who think of themselves tend to deal with issues of how far they are willing to go to accept changes in their physical bodies that will provide them with a different (opposite) biological sex from the one with which they were born. Generally speaking, groups that include *T* individuals tend to focus on those men and women, girls and boys, who hope for and expect hormonal and surgical procedures as the ultimate means of achieving the sex-gender congruence they currently do not experience in their lives.

Transgendered individuals have historically experienced among the most severe rejection of any gender nonconforming group. For many years, even gay and lesbian groups were unwilling to adopt transgenderism as an issue with which they should be concerned. They felt that transgendered individuals were too marginal to be included in many gay and lesbian groups and activities, and that the presence of such individuals was likely to distract from the core efforts of their groups (gay and lesbian groups often had similar views toward bisexuals, who—they sometimes thought—were simply gay men or lesbians who "couldn't make up their minds") (Alexander and Yescavage 2004). These prejudicial views have largely disappeared today, and most groups concerned with gay and lesbian issues include bisexual and transgender issues with equal emphasis (even if they don't include *B* and *T* in their names; see, for example, "Transgender Issues" [2013]).

Many LGBT organizations now use a somewhat more detailed acronym: LGBTQ or LGBTQQ. To what do these additional *Q*'s refer? The first *Q* stands for *queer*, a term that has long had a derogatory meaning for gay men and, to a lesser extent, lesbians. According to the Merriam-Webster dictionary, the word was first used in 1508 and has traditionally meant worthless, counterfeit, questionable, eccentric, unconventional, suspicious, or "differing in some odd way from what is usual or normal" (Merriam-Webster 2013). The word itself is thought to have been derived from the German *quer*, meaning "cross-wise" or "at right angles" (Shannon 2011, 176).

During the late nineteenth and early twentieth centuries, the word became associated especially with unconventional sexual practices. It was frequently used to describe male homosexuals who took the passive role in anal intercourse. (Interestingly, the man who took the active role was regarded as heterosexual or "straight," even if he was in a long-term committed relationship with "the queer" [Robertson 2002, 103].) By the late nineteenth century, the word *queer* had become an intensely offensive term for homosexuals, just as had become the case for terms such as *nigger, wop, dago, chink, jap,* and *wetback*.

By the beginning of the twentieth century, however, gay men and lesbians had begun to adopt a practice previously undertaken by black women and men, who had adopted a previously pejorative term (*nigger*) for self-description. Thus, black men (in particular) began to call each other nigger as a term of bonding and pride, although no nonblack would ever be allowed to follow the same practice. Similarly, gay men and lesbians began talking about themselves as queers, throwing back into the face of nongays and nonlesbians a once-offensive label now used as an expression of pride. Indeed, some observers suggest that the term can be used as a political expression to describe anyone with empathy for the goals of the gay movement, including

> the straight ally who marches during pride, the republican
> *[sic]* lesbian, the person who highly values queer theory
> concepts and would rather not identify with any particular
> label, the gender fluid bisexual, the gender fluid

heterosexual, the questioning GLBT person, and the person who just doesn't feel like they quite fit in to societal norms and wants to bond with a community over that. ("A Definition of 'Queer' " 2013)

The addition of the letter *Q* for *queer* in LGBTQ youth, then, emphasizes the inclusion of a person in a group that recognizes not only lesbians, gay men, bisexuals, and transgenders, but also individuals who have a broader and often more aggressive understanding of the meaning and objectives of the gay movement (Snyder 2013).

And the second *Q*, as in LGBTQQ? This *Q* stands for *questioning*, a reminder that many individuals, especially young people, are still uncertain about their own sexuality. Adolescence is a time of growth and rapid change, and it often raises issues about which an individual is uncertain: what type of career to pursue, whether to continue one's education, whether to continue living at home or move away, and what gender one is most attracted to. Over the past few decades, then, LGBT groups have acknowledged that many young people just do not know if they are gay, lesbian, bisexual, transgendered, or some other condition of sexual orientation. These groups have welcomed those individuals into their own debates, discussions, activities, and organizations (Monroe 2013).

And the question of naming can become even more complex. In an effort to be hospitable to boys and girls, young women and young men of all sexual persuasions and conditions, some groups have taken on even longer names and acronyms. For example, acronyms such as LGBTQQISA and LGBTQIA can now be found in books and articles, in campus LGBT organizations, and in political manifestoes. These terms mean, respectively, lesbian, gay, bisexual, transgender, queer, questioning, intersex, same-gender loving, and ally; and lesbian, gay, bisexual, questioning or queer, intersex, and ally or asexual (Schulman 2013; "What Is LGBTQIA?" 2013).

References

"15 Famous Men Who Had Boy Lovers." NAMBLA.org. http://www.nambla.org/famousmen.html. Accessed on February 27, 2013.

Alexander, Jonathan, and Karen Yescavage. *Bisexuality and Transgenderism: InterSEXions of the Others.* New York: Harrington Park; Northam, UK: Roundhouse, 2004.

"Alexander the Great." GayHeroes.com. http://www.gayheroes.com/alex.htm. Accessed on March 2, 2013.

Baldwin, Steve. 2002. "Child Molestation and the Homosexual Movement." *Regent University Law Review.* 14: 267–282. Available online at http://mail.famguardian.org/Subjects/SexualImmorality/Pedophilia/14_2baldwin.pdf. Accessed on March 4, 2013.

Beachy, Robert. 2010. "The German Invention of Homosexuality." *Journal of Modern History.* 82(4): 801–838.

Bieber, Irving et al. *Homosexuality: A Psychoanalytic Study.* New York: Basic Books, 1962.

Book III [Sibylline Chronicles]. http://www.sacred-texts.com/cla/sib/sib05.htm. Accessed on October 26, 2013.

Boswell, John. *Christianity, Social Tolerance, and Homosexuality.* Chicago: University of Chicago Press, 1980.

Boswell, John. *Same-Sex Unions in Premodern Europe.* New York: Villard, 1994.

Boys Speak Out on Man/Boy Love. NAMBLA. http://www.nambla.org/boys.html. Accessed on February 28, 2013.

"Brief History of the Modern Childlove Movement." http://www.freerepublic.com/focus/f-news/1794584/posts. Accessed on February 28, 2013.

Burroway, Jim. "Today In History: The Love That Dares Not Speak Its Name Gets a Name." Box Turtle Bulletin. http://www.boxturtlebulletin.com/2008/05/06/1942. Accessed on February 23, 2013.

Calimach, Andrew. "The Zeus and Ganymede Myth: Analysis and Resources." http://www.gay-art-history.org/gay-history/gay-literature/gay-history/zeus-ganymede-analysis/zeus-ganymede-analysis.html. Accessed on February 27, 2013.

Cameron, Paul. *Child Molestation and Homosexuality.* Washington, DC: Family Research Institute, 1993.

Carter, David. *Stonewall: The Riots That Sparked the Gay Revolution,* 2nd ed. New York: St. Martin's, 2004.

"Children of Alexander III the Great." Pothos.org. http://www.pothos.org/content/index.php?page=children-2. Accessed on March 2, 2013.

Childs, Margaret H. 1980. "Chigo Monogatari. Love Stories or Buddhist Sermons?" *Monumenta Nipponica.* 35(2): 127–151.

Clarke, W. M. 1978. "Achilles and Patroclus in Love." *Hermes.* 106(3): 381–396.

Cohen, Stephan. *The Gay Liberation Youth Movement in New York: "An Army of Lovers Cannot Fail."* New York: Routledge, 2007.

Crompton, Louis. *Homosexuality and Civilization.* Cambridge, MA: Belknap Press of the Harvard University Press, 2003.

De Coninck-Smith, Ning. "Pedophilia." *Encyclopedia of Children and Childhood in History and Society.* http://www.faqs.org/childhood/Pa-Re/Pedophilia.html. Accessed on February 28, 2013.

"A Definition of 'Queer.'" PFLAG. http://community.pflag.org/page.aspx?pid=952. Accessed on March 7, 2013.

D'Emilio, John. *Sexual Politics, Sexual Communities: The Making of a Homosexual Minority in the United States, 1940–1970,* 2nd ed. Chicago: University of Chicago Press, 1998.

"The Divine Institution of Marriage." The Church of Jesus Christ of Latter-Day Saints. http://www.mormonnewsroom.org/article/the-divine-institution-of-marriage. Accessed on February 24, 2013.

El-Rouayheb, Khaled. 2005. "The Love of Boys in Arabic Poetry of the Early Ottoman Period, 1500–1800." *Middle Eastern Literatures.* 8(1): 3–22.

"Famous GLB People in History." http://www.lambda.org/famous.htm. Accessed on March 2, 2013.

Friend, Richard A. "Choices, Not Closets: Heterosexism and Homophobia in Schools." In Lois Weis and Michelle Fine, eds. *Beyond Silenced Voices: Class, Race, and Gender in United States Schools.* Albany: State University of New York Press, 1993, 209–236.

Garcia, Michelle. "From Our Archives: The 1969 Advocate Article on the Stonewall Riots." *Advocate.* http://www.advocate.com/society/activism/2012/06/29/our-archives-1969-advocate-article-stonewall-riots. Accessed on March 3, 2013.

Gathercole, Simon James. "After the New Perspective: Works, Justification and Boasting in Early Judaism and Romans 1–5." Doctoral Thesis, University of Durham, March 2001. http://etheses.dur.ac.uk/1654/1/1654.pdf. Accessed on February 28, 2013.

"Gay and Lesbian Rights." Gallup. http://www.gallup.com/poll/1651/gay-lesbian-rights.aspx. Accessed on March 3, 2013.

"Gay and Lesbian Youth of New York Records." Lesbian, Gay, Bisexual & Transgender Community Center of New York. http://www.gaycenter.org/community/archive/collection/008. Accessed on March 5, 2013.

"Gay Liberation Front." http://www.outhistory.org/wiki/Gay_Liberation_Front. 2013a. Accessed on March 3, 2013.

"Gay Liberation Front." Pagan Press. http://paganpressbooks.com/jpl/GLF.HTM. 2013b. Accessed on March 3, 2013.

"Gay Liberation Front: *Manifesto.*" http://www.fordham.edu/halsall/pwh/glf-london.asp. Accessed on March 3, 2013.

"Gay Liberation Front–DC, The." http://www.rainbowhistory .org/html/glf.htm. Accessed on March 3, 2013.

"GLAAD/USA Position Statement Regarding NAMBLA." http://www.qrd.org/qrd/orgs/GLAAD/general.information/ 1994/position.on.nambla-02.22.94. Accessed on March 7, 2013.

Goode, Erica. 1998. "On Gay Issue, Psychoanalysis Treats Itself." *New York Times.* December 12, 1998. http://www .nytimes.com/1998/12/12/arts/on-gay-issue-psychoanalysis -treats-itself.html?pagewanted=all&src=pm. Accessed on February 26, 2013.

Green, Richard. 2008. "Childhood Cross-Gender Behavior and Adult Homosexuality: Why the Link?" *Journal of Gay and Lesbian Mental Health.* 12(1/2): 17–28.

Greenberg, David F. *The Construction of Homosexuality.* Chicago: University of Chicago Press, 1988.

Harbeck, Karen Marie. *Gay and Lesbian Educators: Personal Freedoms, Public Constraints.* Malden, MA: Amethyst, 1997.

Hay, Bob. "Comrades of the Cut Sleeve; Homosexuality in China." http://bobhay.org/_downloads/_homo/11%20 Comrades%20of%20%20the%20Cut%20Sleeve.pdf. Accessed on February 25, 2013.

"HBO Eyes Biopic about Anti-Gay Activist Bryant." Reuters. http://www.reuters.com/article/2010/02/02/us-bryant -idUSTRE6110QZ20100202?type=entertainmentNews. Accessed on March 4, 2013.

Herdt, Gilbert H., ed. *Ritualized Homosexuality in Melanesia.* Berkeley: University of California Press, 1984.

Herdt, Gilbert, and Martha McClintock. 2000. "The Magical Age of 10." *Archives of Sexual Behavior.* 29(6): 587–606.

Herek, Gregory M. "Facts about Homosexuality and Child Molestation." http://psychology.ucdavis.edu/rainbow/html/ facts_molestation.html. Accessed on March 4, 2013.

Hinsch, Bret. *Passions of the Cut Sleeve: The Male Homosexual Tradition in China.* Berkeley: University of California Press, 1992.

Homer. *The Iliad.* Translated by Ian Johnston. http://www .mlahanas.de/Greeks/Texts/Iliad/iliad19.htm. Accessed on February 23, 2013.

Hubbard, Thomas K. *Homosexuality in Greece and Rome: A Sourcebook of Basic Documents.* Berkeley: University of California Press, 2003.

"Human Development." Encyclopædia Britannica. http:// www.britannica.com/EBchecked/topic/275624/human -development/63848/Development-of-the-reproductive -organs-and-secondary-sex-characteristics. Accessed on April 15, 2013.

Indiana Youth Group. http://www.indianayouthgroup.org/ about-us. Accessed on March 6, 2013.

"Isle of Lesbos." http://www.sappho.com/poetry/sappho2 .html. Accessed on February 26, 2013.

Itaborahy, Lucas Paoli. *State-Sponsored Homophobia: A World Survey of Laws Prohibiting Same Sex Activity between Consenting Adults.* May 2012. http://old.ilga.org/ Statehomophobia/ILGA_State_Sponsored_Homophobia _2012.pdf. Accessed on February 24, 2013.

Johnson, Matthew D. "NAMBLA." In Claude J. Summers, ed. *An Encyclopedia of Gay, Lesbian, Bisexual, Transgender, and Queer Culture.* http://www.glbtq.com/social-sciences/ nambla.html. Accessed on March 7, 2013.

Kimmel, Michael. 2006. "Ritualized Homosexuality in a Nacirema Subculture." *Sexualities.* 9(1): 95–105.

Kirchick, James. "The Stranger." *New Republic.* http://www .newrepublic.com/article/politics/the-stranger. Accessed on March 4, 2013.

Lauritsen, John, and David Thorstad. *The Early Homosexual Rights Movement, 1864–1935*, rev. ed. Ojai, CA: Times Change Press, 1995.

Lear, Andrew, and Eva Cantarella. *Images of Ancient Greek Pederasty: Boys Were Their Gods*. London; New York: Routledge, 2008.

"Lesbian, Gay, Bisexual, and Transgendered Youth Issues." 2001. *SEICUS Report* Supplement. 29(4): 1–5.

"Lesbianism." Cultural China. http://history.cultural -china.com/en/171H11947H14606.html. Accessed on February 26, 2013.

Leupp, Gary P. *Male Colors: The Construction of Homosexuality in Tokugawa Japan*. Berkeley: University of California Press, 1995.

Levitt, Eugene E., and Albert D. Klassen Jr. 1976. "Public Attitudes toward Homosexuality: Part of the 1970 National Survey by the Institute for Sex Research Journal of Homosexuality." *Journal of Homosexuality*. 1(1): 29–43.

Long Yang Club (of Philadelphia). http://philadelphia.long yangclub.org/LYStory.html. Accessed on February 25, 2013.

Merriam-Webster. http://www.merriam-webster.com/ dictionary/queer. Accessed on March 7, 2013.

"Ministry to Persons with a Homosexual Inclination: Guidelines for Pastoral Care." United States Conference of Catholic Bishops. November 14, 2006. http://old.usccb.org/ doctrine/Ministry.pdf. Accessed on October 26, 2013.

Mitchell, Stephen. *Gilgamesh: A New English Version*. New York: Free Press, 2004.

Monroe, Irene. "Questioning Sexuality through the Q's." *A Globe of Witnesses* (The Witness Magazine). http://www .thewitness.org/agw/monroe092904.html. Accessed on March 7, 2013.

Monroe, James T. "The Striptease That Was Blamed on Abu Bakr's Naughty Son: Was Father Being Shamed, or Was the Poet Having Fun?" In J. W. Wright and Everett K. Rowson, eds. *Homoeroticism in Classical Arabic Literature.* New York: Columbia University Press, 1997, 94–139.

Murray, Stephen O., Will Roscoe, et al. *Islamic Homosexualities: Culture, History, and Literature.* New York: New York University Press, 1997.

"Nancy Reagan and the AIDS Crisis." PBS Newshour. http://www.pbs.org/newshour/nancy-reagan/2011/01/ other-headline-9.html. Accessed on March 6, 2013.

Neill, James. *The Origins and Role of Same-Sex Relations in Human Societies.* Jefferson, NC: McFarland & Co., 2009.

Newton, David E. "Homosexuality and Child Sexual Abuse." In William O'Donohue and James H. Geer, eds. *The Sexual Abuse of Children: Theory and Research*, vol. 1. Hillsdale, NJ: Lawrence Erlbaum Associates, 1992, 329–358.

Newton, David E. 1979. "Representations of Homosexuality in Health Science Textbooks," *Journal of Homosexuality.* 4(3): 247–254.

Palmer, David. "Normal Politics: Negotiating Sexuality and Child Endangerment in 1977 America." Master's Thesis, University of North Carolina at Chapel Hill, 1977. http:// books.google.com/books?id=b-RuxHLUJN4C&pg=PA16 &dq=%22save+our+children%22+anita+bryant&hl=en&sa =X&ei=dRU1UcDJIY7OyAGc9oDgAw&ved=0CEMQ6 AEwBA#v=onepage&q=%22save%20our%20children %22%20anita%20bryant&f=false, Chapter 2. Accessed on March 4, 2013.

Percy, William Armstrong, III. *Pederasty and Pedagogy in Archaic Greece.* Urbana: University of Illinois Press, 1996.

Plato. *The Symposium.* http://classics.mit.edu/Plato/ symposium.html. http://classics.mit.edu/Plato/symposium .html. Accessed on February 27, 2013.

Pflugfelder, Gregory M. *Cartographies of Desire: Male-Male Sexuality in Japanese Discourse, 1600–1950*. Berkeley: University of California Press, 1999.

"Pre-Gay Era Bibliography." OutHistory.org. http:// 209.200.244.13/wiki/Pre-Gay_Era_Bibliography. Accessed on March 3, 2013.

Robertson, Stephen. 2002. "A Tale of Two Sexual Revolutions." *Australasian Journal of American Studies*. 21(1): 98–110.

"Sappho." Poetry Foundation. http://www.poetryfoundation. org/bio/sappho. Accessed on February 26, 2013.

Schlatter, Evelyn, and Robert Steinback. "10 Anti-Gay Myths Debunked." Southern Poverty Law Center. http://www .splcenter.org/get-informed/intelligence-report/browse-all -issues/2010/winter/10-myths. Accessed on March 4, 2013.

Schmitt, Arno, and Jehoeda Sofer. *Sexuality and Eroticism among Males in Moslem Societies*. New York: Haworth, 1992.

Schulman, Michael. "Generation LGBTQIA." *New York Times*. January 9, 2013. http://www.nytimes.com/2013/01/ 10/fashion/generation-lgbtqia.html. Accessed on October 26, 2013.

Shannon, Laurie. "King Lear: Lear's Queer Cosmos." In Madhavi Menon, ed. *Shakesqueer: A Queer Companion to the Complete Works of Shakespeare*. Durham, NC: Duke University Press, 2011, 171–178.

[Sima Qian]. Ssu-Ch'ien. *Records of the Grand Historian of China [Shih chi]*. Translated by Burton Watson, 2 vols. New York: Renditions, Columbia University Press, 1993.

Skinner, Marilyn B. *Sexuality in Greek and Roman Culture*. Malden, MA: Blackwell, 2005.

Smith, Tom W. "Public Attitudes toward Homosexuality." NORC/University of Chicago. http://www.norc.org/PDFs/ 2011%20GSS%20Reports/GSS_Public%20Attitudes%

20Toward%20Homosexuality_Sept2011.pdf. Accessed on March 3, 2013.

Snyder, Molly. "What Does the 'Q' in LGBTQ Really Mean?" OnMilwaukee.com. http://onmilwaukee.com/buzz/articles/queerarticle.html. Accessed on March 7, 2013.

Song, Geng. *The Fragile Scholar: Power and Masculinity in Chinese Culture*. Hong Kong: Hong Kong University Press, 2004.

Special Issue on Childhood Gender Nonconformity and Development of Adult Homosexuality. 2008. *Journal of Gay and Lesbian Mental Health*. 12(1/2): whole.

Swartz, Aaron. 2013. "Why I Am Not Gay." *The Gay & Lesbian Review*. 20(2): 5.

Teal, Donn. *The Gay Militants*. New York: Stein and Day, 1971.

Thorstad, David. 1991. "Man/Boy Love and the American Gay Movement." *Journal of Homosexuality*. 20(1/2): 251–274.

"Thucydides: On Aristogeiton and Harmodius: From The History of the Peloponnesian War, 6th Book." Translated by Richard Crawley.http://www.fordham.edu/halsall/pwh/thuc6.asp. Accessed on February 27, 2013.

"Transgender Issues." National Gay and Lesbian Task Force. http://www.thetaskforce.org/issues/transgender. Accessed on March 6, 2013.

Troxel, Ronald L. "Sibylline Oracles." http://hebrew.wisc.edu/~rltroxel/JHL/Sibyllines.htm. Accessed on February 28, 2013.

Upbin, Bruce. 2011. "Alexander the Great: Gay or Straight?" *Forbes*. http://www.forbes.com/sites/booked/2011/02/10/alexander-the-great-gay-or-straight/. Accessed on March 2, 2013.

"What Do We Mean by 'Sex' and 'Gender'?" World Health Organization. http://www.who.int/gender/whatisgender/en/. Accessed on April 15, 2013.

"What Is LGBTQIA?" University of Missouri–Kansas City. http://www.umkc.edu/HOUSING/lgbtqia.asp. Accessed on March 7, 2013.

"What Is Man/Boy Love?" http://www.nambla.org/whatis .html. Accessed on February 28, 2013.

Yang, Alan. *From Wrongs to Rights, 1973–1999*. Washington DC: Policy Institution of the National Gay Task Force, n.d. Available online at http://www.thetaskforce.org/downloads/ reports/reports/1999FromWrongsToRights.pdf. Accessed on March 3, 2013.

When Scott Morrison (a biological female at the time) began getting ready for high school each morning, he laid out two sets of clothing, a "boy outfit" and a "girl outfit." Then he decided which of the two outfits to wear to school that day. After a while, Scott noticed that he was always choosing the "boy outfit." He decided that it was time for him to stop identifying as a female and to begin identifying exclusively as a male. Today he is undergoing hormone therapy as the first step in transitioning from a female to a male. (Dungca 2013, A4)

Adolescence is a difficult time in any person's life. In fact, among psychologists and psychiatrists, adolescence is sometimes characterized as a period of *Sturm und Drang* (storm and stress), a phrase first coined for the period by American psychologist and educator G. Stanley Hall in 1904 (Arnett 1999). Almost every teenager understands the meaning of this expression. Adolescence is a period when one's hormonal system begins to undergo a significant change, basically for the purpose of preparing males and females to be able to reproduce.

Gizmo Lopez, left, who identifies herself as bisexual and homeless, sits with her boyfriend Tiny Jenkins and all their possessions inside a fast food restaurant, waiting to ride the subways for a night's sleep in New York in 2012. Almost half of the city's homeless youth are part of the LGBT population. (AP Photo/Bebeto Matthews)

But these hormonal changes go far beyond adapting a person's body to sexual activity; they engender new feelings and emotions that one has scarcely, if ever, experienced as a child. Adolescence is also a period during which children begin to feel independence, and they often resent the need to depend on parents and the family to make decisions about their own lives. An adolescent is, therefore, constantly torn between wanting to strike out on his or her own and needing the support and security of a family. According to one classic study of this period, adolescents experience an average of two conflicts with their parents every three days, or an average of 20 conflicts per month (Montemayor and Hanson 1985, 27). Although this study is now more than two decades old, more recent studies tend to confirm this frequency of conflict between adolescents and parents (see, for example, Laursen, Little, and Card 2012, 68).

Given this fact about adolescence, it is nonetheless true that some categories of teenagers tend to experience different types of issues during these years, as well as different levels of intensity with which those issues occur. In the area of human sexuality, for example, most white middle-class American teenagers (as well as some other categories of adolescents) gain an early understanding of societal expectations from a host of social clues, such as television programs; social media; magazines, both general interest and those aimed specifically at teenagers; parental pressure and other family influences; and peer expectations. Twelve-year-old boys and girls in the United States probably have a fairly good idea as to the kind of clothes they are expected to wear, the language they should use in talking with peers and adults, the way to make contact with members of the opposite sex for friendships and intimate relationships, the type of short- and long-term relationships they are expected to develop, the type of family they are expected to create, and on and on.

But what about teenagers who do not fall into that vast social category known as "average" or (very incorrectly) "normal" adolescents, for example, those who are sometimes referred to as LGBTQ youth? Where do they learn how to grow up in such a way as to be true to their own natures, how to meet and develop relationships with other LGBT youth, and how to deal with a host of those special problems that are generally unknown and unknowable to nongay, nonlesbian, nonbisexual, nontransgendered youth? In many cases, the answer to that question may be "nowhere." In fact, until fairly recently, LGBT youth had very few role models or sources of information to which they could turn in their efforts to learn how to grow up as a lesbian, gay, bisexual, or transgendered person. Even today, with the availability of gay-straight clubs in schools; the visibility of successful lesbians, gay men, bisexuals, and transgendered people in politics, the arts, entertainment, sports, and other aspects of life; the presence of LGBT people in television, radio, motion pictures, and other popular media; and other aids to understanding themselves and their roles in society, LGBT youth continue to experience a number of problems largely unknown to their non-LGBT counterparts. Those problems fall into six major categories:

- Coming out to oneself
- Coming out to one's family
- Coming out to one's friends and peers
- Handling rejection, harassment, bullying, and other negative responses to one's sexual personality at school and at work
- Dealing with problems of homelessness
- Understanding issues of self-worth and suicidal ideation

This chapter will deal with the problems and issues related to each of these categories, along with a review of some solutions that have been proposed and introduced for them.

Coming Out to Oneself

Probably the first issue with which most LGBT youth have to deal is the question of being sexually "different." In some cases, this "difference" may actually be a biological or physiological issue, a situation in which a person has sexual anatomy and physiology that varies from that expected by parents, peers, medical workers, or the child himself or herself. One example of this situation is a condition known as *intersexuality*. The Intersex Society of North America defines intersexuality as "a variety of conditions in which a person is born with a reproductive or sexual anatomy that doesn't seem to fit the typical definitions of female or male" (What Is Intersex? 2013). For example, a person might be born with genitalia that are not easily identifiable as typically female or male; a girl with an unusually large clitoris, for example, or a boy with an unusually small penis.

At one time, such individuals were called *hermaphrodites*, but that term is no longer considered appropriate for intersex individuals. Hermaphrodites are defined as plants or animals that have both male and female sex organs, a definition that virtually never applies to intersex individuals.

The issues raised by intersexuality, especially among younger children prior to or just at the age of puberty, became a topic of considerable interest in the third quarter of the twentieth century when a number of researchers began to ask what the best treatment might be for individuals of ambiguous sex. One of the first and most widely discussed books on the topics was *Man & Woman, Boy & Girl: The Differentiation and Dimorphism of Gender Identity from Conception to Maturity*, by American psychologists and sexologists John Money and Anke A. Ehrhardt. In this book, Money and Ehrhardt discussed the sex reassignment of a young boy who experienced genital mutilation during circumcision and who the researchers decided should have surgery to reassign him as a girl. The eventual results of that surgery became a topic of extensive discussion in the medical and psychological community, and debate continues on the best way of dealing with males and females who have ambiguous sex (Walker 2013).

As serious as the problems of intersexuality may be, it should probably be admitted that the sexual issues with which most LGBT adolescents have to deal are not based on the problem of having ambiguous genitalia or reproductive systems, or other biological or physiological problems. Another group of individuals, however—those who see themselves as transgender—may feel a disconnect between their biological sex and their *affirmed gender*, the gender with which one feels most comfortable. This condition is probably most commonly described as "being a man in a woman's body," or vice versa. Although this condition has been recognized for more than 150 years as one that deserves attention, it has been only in the past few decades that such individuals have begun to feel comfortable "coming out" and talking about the issues with which they have to deal.

Those issues are often profound, especially as some boys and girls begin to recognize very early in their lives that they are "the wrong gender" (or "the wrong sex"). That realization may or may not be followed by the additional realization that they want to undergo sex reassignment procedures that involve the use of hormone therapy and surgery to gain the type of body that is congruent with the sexuality experienced in their brains.

Until fairly recently, sex reassignment procedures were used only with adults who were old enough to realize the consequences of their actions and could give the kind of consent needed for such procedures to be used. Increasingly today, boys and girls in their preteens or early in puberty are beginning to make those same decisions, with which parents, other adults, the medical profession, and health caregivers may or may not agree.

An indication of this trend is the increasing attention being given to so-called gender nonconforming children (GNC), boys and girls who see themselves as belonging to the gender opposite that of their biological sex. Some gender nonconforming children are even more gender fluid, in that they may see themselves as both male and female and take on the gender role of each sex at one or another time in their lives. One of the interesting features of GNC is that they often are very comfortable with their condition and do not quite understand the concerns that parents, teachers, and other adults express about their lack of commitment to one gender or the other or to the challenge of aligning their biological sex with the "appropriate" gender. Adults, especially parents, often do not experience this level of comfort about their nonconforming children and wonder what actions they should take, if any, to deal with this "problem" (see, for example, Padawer [2012]).

At one time, some medical authorities recommended sexual reassignment procedures, with the goal of providing a boy or girl with the sexual characteristics of the gender with which she or he felt most comfortable. That approach fell out of favor, however, as many experts felt that childhood was too early for a person to make a decision of this magnitude. They believed that in many cases, gender ambiguity was a "stage" through which some children went and that by puberty, they would sort out the gender that matched their biological sex.

But that has turned out not to be the case in many instances. Today, a significant number of boys and girls have come to the conclusion that they truly have the wrong biological and physiological structures, and they want to have whatever procedures are necessary to eliminate that dissonance. The surgical procedures required to make the ultimate changes necessary in sex reassignment are generally not available until a person has reached the age of 18. But transgender children can begin the process of sex reassignment at a much earlier age. They may start taking so-called *puberty blockers*, which suppress the body's production of sex hormones, such as estrogen and testosterone. The primary effect of puberty blockers is to inhibit the development of secondary sex characteristics, which are (or would be) responsible for so much of the body dysphoria (dislike of the body) that transgender children feel (Spack 2013). After puberty has begun, physicians may also prescribe a hormone regimen that makes use of the hormone required to produce male (testosterone) or female (estrogen) primary and sexual characteristics. One advantage of using puberty blockers—beyond the emotional boost they provide a child—is that their use can be discontinued without producing long-term harmful effects to a child's body.

Relatively few statistics are available on the number of GNC and transgender children, the number who go on to have gender or sex reassignment surgery, and the age of children who make tentative or definite decisions on these matter. Such is hardly surprising given the social stigma and emotional trauma associated with such decisions. Available research does suggest that children may begin having such feelings and making at least temporary decisions at very young ages. According to Jenn Burleton, founder and executive director of TransActive, a counseling, case management, and medical referral service in Portland, Oregon, some parents report children as young as 18 months expressing body dysphoria, reacting strongly when they are praised for being a "good boy" or "good girl," when they prefer the opposite sexual characteristic. Burleton notes that expressing gender dysphoria this early is unusual, however, and that the average age at which children "know their gender" is about four, with most having apparently made "final judgments" about this issue by the age of seven (Mirk 2013).

In any case, it is no longer unusual to find stories of children under the age of puberty who have expressed gender dysphoria long enough and intensely enough that they have convinced their parents, friends, medical workers, and other adults that sex reassignment is an option that all need to consider very seriously. Margaret Talbot's touching article about a young girl who began the transition to male sex at the age of 14 (identified in the article only as "Skylar") and who had the first stages of surgery at the age of 16 provides a revealing overview of the issues faced by transgender children and the solutions they find for dealing with those issues (Talbot 2013).

Nor is Skylar any longer particularly unusual. Specialists who work with GNC and transgender children now report parents coming to them with questions about boys and girls as young as five or six years who are faced with problems of everyday living as a result of their gender dysphoria (see, for example, Payne and Fantz [2013]; Trans Parent Journeys [2013]).

Gay, Lesbian, and Bisexual Children and Teenagers

Gay, lesbian, and bisexual children and adolescents face many of the same issues as do intersex individuals and transgenders. At some point in their lives, they begin to realize that they are attracted primarily to someone of the same sex or, in the case of bisexuals, to individuals of the same and opposite sex equally or to some other degree. Many (probably most) lesbians, gays, and bisexuals believe that their sexual orientation was determined before they were born, that is, that they were "born that way." So childhood and adolescence are a period of *recognizing* one's sexual orientation rather than *becoming* gay, lesbian, or bisexual.

(A warning: The question as to what "causes" homosexuality is one of the most contentious issues in all of human sexuality, with a variety of very controversial explanations having been offered. See, for example, "What Causes Homosexuality/ Bisexuality?" [2013]. Perhaps the single most interesting aspect of this question is that the comparable query—what causes heterosexuality—is virtually never asked, suggesting that inquiring about the causes of homosexuality may imply something abnormal about that type of sexual behavior. See Bettcher [2013]; Gross and Woods [1999, 185].)

In retrospective studies, most lesbians, gay men, and bisexuals seem to have recognized at a relatively early point in their lives that they were somehow "different" from their peers in that they were sexually attracted to others of the same, rather than or in addition to the opposite, sex. In one of the most widely cited of all studies on the question, nearly half (48 percent) of a sample of 1,752 self-identified gay, lesbian, and bisexual college students had recognized their sexual orientation while they were still in high school. Of that number, 20 percent had attained that realization while they were still in middle school, and 11 percent while they were in elementary school (Elliott and Johnson 1997, 163–164). Those data would appear to confirm comments made by LGB people themselves on the web and on social media outlets in the early 2010s (see, for example, "At What Age Were You Sure That You Were Gay/Lesbian/Bisexual and It Wasn't a Phase?" [2013]; "To the Gay/Lesbian/Bi Society?" [2013]; "What Age Did You Come Out?" [2013]). Perhaps the most comprehensive review of literature on the age of coming out for LGB individuals found that the age of "first sexual awareness" of same-sex attraction reported in a number of studies was 10 (Board on the Health of Select Populations, 2011, 143–145).

A striking feature of this question is that the age at which LGB individuals acknowledge their sexual orientation appears to have been decreasing substantially over the past few decades. Among the most recent evidence of this trend was the result of 2010 poll conducted by the British LGB organization Stonewall. In its poll of 1,536 gay, lesbian, and bisexual individuals, Stonewall found that the average age at which people are coming out is now 15, compared to an average coming out age of 37 for people over 60. The organization credited a number of factors, including a generally more favorable view of same-sex relationships, for the willingness of individuals to come out at an increasingly younger age ("Average Coming Out Age Has Fallen by over 20 Years," 2013). A similar finding was reported for LGB individuals in Israel in 2011. According to that study, the average age of coming out for Israeli LGB youth is now 16 years, compared to 25 years as recently as 1991 (Shilo and Savaya 2011, 321). Similar trends have also been reported in the United States (see, for example, Denizet-Lewis 2009).

What about the Q in LGBTQ?

Many lesbians, gay men, bisexuals, and transgenders claim to know at an early age about their sexual orientation. When asked when or how they came out, these boys and girls, men and women often say that they just "always knew" or "never had any doubt" about their sexual orientation (e.g., see nearly 800 comments on this issue at "When Did You Realize You Were Gay?" [2013]). But many other children and young adults are less certain about their sexual orientation. They represent the "Q," questioning, part of the LGBTQ acronym. How do such individuals deal with their uncertainty about their sexual orientation?

In situations like this, professionals who deal in human relationships often suggest that a person talk with trusted adults in positions of authority: parents, other trusted family members, physicians, school counselors, teachers, sport coaches, or members of the clergy. A modest amount of research and a considerable body of anecdotal evidence suggests, however, that these sources are rarely the individuals to whom LGBTQ youth turn for advice and support in their struggle to understand their sexual orientation. In one of the most comprehensive studies on the resources to whom LGBTQ adolescents turn, for example, clergy (often the first resource to whom people turn for support and guidance) were the least trusted of all adults to whom LGBTQ youth turned. Coaches and members of the medical community were the next least trusted of traditional helping professions. Even teachers and members of an extended family were significantly less trusted by LGBTQ youth than were close friends and classmates ("Growing Up LGBT in America" [2012, 11]; see later in this chapter for more detail; also see "Fact Sheet: Lesbian, Gay, Bisexual and Transgender Youth Issues," [2013]; "LGBT: Who Do You Trust the Most?" [2013]).

So to whom can a young person turn with questions about and support for one's own sexual orientation? It is always possible, of course, that the answer to that question is a parent, a sibling, a "special" teacher, an understanding member of the clergy, or one's tennis coach. But it is far more likely to be an individual or an organization that has a special interest in working LGBTQ teenagers who need their support and guidance. A number of national organizations fall into that category, such as Advocates for Youth, Bisexual Resource Center, Campus Pride, Family Acceptance Project, Human Rights Campaign, It Gets Better Project, Matthew Shepard Foundation, National Gay and Lesbian Task Force, Parents and Friends of Lesbians and Gays (PFLAG), Safe Schools Coalition, Stop Bullying Now, Trans Youth Family Allies, and the Trevor Project (most of which are described in Chapter 4 of this book). Most communities in the United States today also have local organizations and/or services that have personnel trained especially to deal with LGBTQ issues and questions. The best way to locate such agencies is an Internet search for LGBTQ services for a specific city, town, county, or state. One of the most complete resource guides is provided by Lambda Legal on its website at http://www.lamb dalegal.org/sites/default/files/publications/downloads/fs_resources -for-lgbtq-youth-by-state_1.pdf. That resource lists a host of agencies throughout the United States, such as GLBT Advocacy & Youth Services, Inc., in Huntsville, Alabama; NWA Center for Equality, in Fayetteville, Arkansas; J.U.S.T. for Youth, in Wilmington, Delaware; the Boise GLBT Center, in Boise, Idaho; Ozone House, in Ann Arbor, Michigan; Western Montana Community Center, in Missoula; U21 in Albuquerque, New Mexico; Gay Lesbian Bi Youth Group, in Tulsa, Oklahoma; and the Sexual Minority Youth Assistance League, in Washington, DC.

The Trevor Project has an interactive search function for use in locating local agencies and organizations at http://www .thetrevorproject.org/youth/local-resources. The search function can be used to find specific types of services (such as bisexuality or bullying) and for specific locations (such as a city or state). For most young people, local chapters of the Gay, Lesbian and Straight Education Network (GLSEN) or a local gay-straight alliance club may be the best single resource. The GSA Network reports that as of late 2013, there were more than 900 GSA clubs throughout the United States. The

scale, with the vast majority of them falling somewhere between 0 and 6.

Still, many young people (and adults) today feel as if they must make a choice about their sexual orientation, and they ask which choice, gay/lesbian or nongay/nonlesbian, fits them best. In trying to help young people make that decision, a number of individuals and organizations have provided recommendations as to how one can know one's sexual orientation. They suggest that a person ask herself or himself questions such as:

- When you dream or fantasize, do you think about someone of the same sex or the opposite sex?
- Have you ever had intense emotional and/or sexual feelings for someone of the same sex?
- Are you fairly certain about the way you feel and the strength of your emotions?
- Do you become sexually excited when you see photographs of someone of the same sex?
- Are you comfortable when your friends talk about their own experiences with someone of the opposite sex?
- Do you worry about how you present yourself to peers and friends, that is, seeming to be "too gay"?
- Do you make special efforts to avoid looking, talking, or acting like a lesbian or gay man? (See, for example, "How Do I Know if I'm Gay?" [2013]; "How Do I Know if I'm Gay or Lesbian?" [2013]; "I Think I Might Be Gay. Now What Do I Do?" [2013]; Penzel 2013)

In addition to suggesting question such as these, many individuals and organizations who attempt to aid questioning youth make the greater point that understanding one's sexual orientation often takes a long period of time, and there is no reason one should rush to find an answer that might not come for years. Instead, it is probably better to be open-minded about the subject, learn more about all types of human sexuality, and wait to see how one's feelings develop and evolve. More important than anything else, they often say, one needs to work on developing and improving one's own self-esteem, learning to be proud and happy of whatever type of person one turns out to be.

Coming Out to Family

Recognizing one's own sexual orientation is only the first step in the long process of coming out. The next step is sharing that information with someone else, someone, one hopes, who will be understanding and supportive. What should that "someone" be? One's mother and/or father; a trusted aunt, uncle, or cousin; one's best friend; a high school teacher or counselor; a trusted member of the clergy? Given the diversity of attitudes about same-sex relationships in society, it is almost impossible to answer that question. In close-knit families where trust and love have always been an essential component, the answer might be one's parents. In a household where there has been misunderstanding, mistrust, abuse, or neglect, talking to a parent may not necessarily be the best idea. Every young adult has to decide to whom to talk based on her or his own experience with family, peers, and other adults. A number of Internet websites share the experiences of specific LGBT youth in this regard, and they are truly as diverse as one might expect (see, for example, "The First Person You Told" [2013]; Friedrichs [2013]; "Gay, but Scared to Come Out to My Parents" [2013]; "When I Came Out" [2013]).

What kind of response can LGB youth expect if and when they come out to their parents, siblings, and other members of their families? It is almost impossible to answer that question, since families are so different from each other in the way they interact with each other. Numerous studies have been done on this question, however, and a trend is reasonably clear:

A large fraction of family members tend not to be supportive of their children's announcement that they are gay, lesbian, or bisexual. And that disapproval is often expressed in terms of verbal, emotional, and/or physical abuse, sometimes in the most extreme forms.

Some examples of the more extreme reactions that families have produced include the following:

- In a 2011 stand-up "comedy" act in Nashville, "comedian" Tracy Morgan announced that if his son told him he was gay, he would "pull out a knife and stab that little nigger to death" ("Tracy Morgan Goes on Anti-Gay Tirade at Nashville Show" 2013).

- A New York man severely beat his gay son, threw him out of the house, and threatened to kill him and bury him in the backyard if he came back (Siciliano 2013).

- A minister in the Church of the Nazarene in rural Delaware attacked his son when he learned he was gay, attempted to strangle him, and threw him out of the house (Morgan 2013).

- In October 2012, political commentator Ann Coulter tweeted to her followers that "Last Thursday was 'coming out' day. This Monday is national 'disown your son' day" ("Ann Coulter's National 'Disown Your Son' Day Tweet Slammed by LGBT Rights Advocates" 2013).

(Two of the four examples cited here were reputedly meant as "jokes" by those who made the comments, which in and of itself is a commentary on the way in which some people view violence against LGBT children and adolescents by their parents and family members.)

Such examples are hardly the exception to the way in which most families treat children and adolescents who have come out to them. A number of studies have showed that as many as half of all LGBT youth who come out to their families are forced out of their homes or choose to leave because of harassment, abuse, and rejection ("Today's Gay Youth: The Ugly, Frightening Statistics" 2013). A recent study of homeless LGBT youth found that nearly half of those teenagers (46 percent) were homeless because they had been rejected by their families and, in some cases, thrown out of their homes. Nearly as many of the homeless LGBT youth (43 percent) had been forced out of their homes because of their sexual orientation, and about a third (32 percent) had experienced physical, emotional, or sexual abuse for that reason (Durso 2012, 4).

The short- and long-term harmful effects of parental rejection on LGBT individuals have now been clearly documented. In one extensive study, researchers at San Francisco State University found that LGBT youth who experienced severe family rejection as children or teenagers experienced suicidal ideation at 8.4 times the rate of non-LGBT youth, were 5.9 times more likely to suffer depression, were 3.4 times more likely to use illegal substances, and were 3.4 times more like to engage in unprotected sex (Ryan et al. 2009). Ironically, many of the parents involved in this study had no idea that their actions would produce such harmful results; they believed that they were simply practicing "tough love" to get their children to abandon a sexual orientation with which they (the parents) were so uncomfortable. Providing these new data on the actual effects of parental actions turned out to be one of the most useful tools in helping parents, children, and adolescents deal more humanely and more effectively with issues raised by boys and girls, young men and women, coming out to their families. (For more on suicidal ideation in this regard, also see Kitts [2005].)

So is there some type of strategy that a person can follow in coming out to one's family? Again, the answer probably is that no one road map works for every LGBT youth who has decided to tell his or her family about his or her sexual orientation. Every person has to decide the best time and best approach to use in coming out. Nonetheless, many people who have thought about this question have tried to come up with ideas as to how best to come out to one's family. Some of those suggestions include the following:

- Perhaps it is obvious, but one should be sure about one's sexual orientation, or at the very least willing to talk about the possibilities, before bringing up the issue with parents. For many (although certainly not all) parents, learning that a son is gay or a daughter is a lesbian can be one of the most stressful pieces of information they ever hear. Better to be reasonably sure that that information is accurate before making a crisis out of its disclosure.

- Try to be sure that your information will not produce a reaction that may pose a risk, physical, emotional, sexual, or otherwise. As noted earlier in this chapter, a significant number of parents may be so upset by news of a child's same-sex attractions that they may actually physically attack the child and throw her or him out of the house.

- Think of some of the questions or concerns that parents may have about the announcement and try to have some responses ready.

- Be as direct and forthcoming as possible. Providing hints rather than simply making a statement may actually make the news more difficult for parents.

- Give parents time ... time ... time. Some parents know that their children are gay, lesbian, bisexual, or transgender even before the child knows. But for other parents, the news is a shock, and it may take them time to incorporate the news, adjust to a "new reality," and figure out how to deal with a new perception of their child.

- Understand that one's news will almost certainly affect a wider range of individuals than parents and children, including siblings, aunts and uncles, cousins, and even more distant relatives. Christmas get-togethers, for example, are almost certainly never going to be the same again.

Recognize that parents need to rethink not only their own opinions and attitudes about same-sex relationships, but they may have to ask the most important people in their lives to do the same.

- Choose the right time, place, and method for coming out. An email sent to parents during a family reunion is probably not the best possible way to make this kind of announcement.

- Try to have a support system of some kind in case it is needed after you talk with your parents. If they are not able, or refuse, to provide the support you need after this traumatic moment, it is useful to have another person or group of people who can and will do so.

- Make sure that sharing information about your sexual orientation is the primary purpose of this conversation. Young adults may feel the need to announce this information in a moment of anger or frustration resulting from some other family crisis, which is not the most positive situation in which to raise such an important matter.

- As one source says in summary, "Remember: Coming out is a process. It takes time—don't rush the process" (Lesley V. et al. 2013).

(These suggestions are summarized from a number of sources, including *Be Yourself: Questions and Answers for Gay, Lesbian, Bisexual, and Transgender Youth* [1999, 2002]; "Coming Out Issues for Latinas and Latinos" [2013]; "Coming Out to Your Parents" [2013]; Lesley V. et al. [2013]; Neece [2013]; Savin-Williams [2001]; Signorile [1994].)

Coming Out as an Issue for Family

Of course, the problem of coming out is not one that a child or teenager alone has to deal with. Family members may also be confronted with new challenges, new problems, new issues, and new opportunities. It is certainly true that many adults know or suspect that their own child is gay, lesbian, bisexual, or transgender. But for others, the news of a child's sexual orientation can be a shock or surprise that can potentially be one of the most profound events in a parent's life. How can and should parents (and other close relatives) respond to this new information?

At one time in the not-too-distant past, there were relatively few good answers to that question. Same-sex attraction was still regarded as an embarrassment, a sin, a moral turpitude about which the less said, the better. Young men and women knew enough to keep their sexual orientation private information, even from their own family, and many families were happy to keep things that way.

But times have changed dramatically over the past few decades. Today, as is the case with LGBT youth themselves, a large number of individuals, agencies, and organizations are concerned with helping LGBT youth talk with their parents about their sexual orientation and with helping parents respond in a supportive and loving way. Again, a search of the Internet provides a host of resources for parents and families members as they respond to, assist, and support their gay, lesbian, bisexual, and transgender children.

One of the first recommendations that experts make is for parents to take a deep breath and not respond with the first thoughts that spring to mind. Especially if the idea of a child's being LGBT is a new one, a parent needs to take a step back and allow herself or himself a chance to think about the new information rather than responding "off the cuff." In any case, the single most important thing a parent can do is remind the child or young adult that he or she is still a loved member of the family, and no matter how the parent feels at the moment, that love remains. It might be unreasonable to expect a parent to process such unexpected news without experiencing some level of fear, concern, anguish, or worry, but those are emotions that can be analyzed and dealt with at a later moment.

The recommendation to parents that they try simply to stay calm when confronted with a child's information about her or his sexual orientation is based on the reality that for at least some parents, this revelation may challenge some of their most basic and important beliefs. Most religious organizations tend to hold fairly strong anti-same-sex views and to learn that one's own child is gay, lesbian, or bisexual can shake one's theological, philosophical, and ethical views. Parents should attempt to hold off on trying to reconcile this kind of conflict until a later moment when they can think about the issues involved in a somewhat less emotional and more detached manner.

Another immediate response by some parents is that professional help is needed to change a child or adolescent's sexual orientation. At one time, it was not at all unusual for parents to send their children to psychiatrists or psychologists, medical doctors, or other specialists in a search for a "cure" for their same-sex feelings. That day is now long past, although the concept of "curing" homosexual feelings has not completely disappeared. Indeed, there is a moderately robust movement in the United States (and other parts of the world) today for a procedure sometimes known as *reparative* or *conversion therapy*. That procedure is based on the assumption that same-sex attraction is a learned behavior, not a genetic or inborn trait and, furthermore, that it is a mental aberration that can be cured by exposure to the proper types of treatment (see, for example, Nicolosi [1991]; Nicolosi [2013]).

The vast majority of medical, psychological, counseling, educational, and related professional organizations have now expressed the view that reparative therapy is based on a false assumption (namely, that same-sex attraction is abnormal and unhealthy) and that it is essentially ineffective in changing a person's sexual orientation. Policy statements to this effect have been issued by a host of organizations, including the American Academy of Pediatrics, American Association for Marriage and Family Therapy, American Counseling Association, American Medical Association, American Psychiatric Association, American Psychoanalytic Association, American Psychological Association, American School Counselor Association, National Association of Social Workers, and Pan American Health Organization (PAHO): Regional Office of the World Health Organization ("The Lies and Dangers of Reparative Therapy" 2013).

Most of the position statements from these organizations and from private health workers point out that reparative therapy tends to be not only ineffective, but also positively harmful. In its position statement on reparative therapy, for example, the International Society of Psychiatric-Mental Health Nurses noted that "harmful sequelae of reparative therapy reported in the literature include anxiety, depression, avoidance of intimacy, sexual dysfunction, PTSD, loss of self-confidence and self-efficacy, shame/guilt, self-destructive behavior, and suicidality" ("Position Statement on Reparative Therapy" 2013). In fact, the California state legislature passed a law in 2012 banning reparative therapy for minors that was signed on September 30, 2012, by Governor Jerry Brown. A few months later, the state of New Jersey adopted a similar law, signed by Governor Chris Christie on August 19, 2013 (Elias 2013).

Many experts in the field suggest that parents also try to develop empathy for their child at the moment of revelation. Certainly they will already understand how traumatic this news can be for themselves, but it may help if they can also realize how difficult it is for a child to talk with his or her parents about this subject, how much the child potentially has to lose from the conversation. At the same time, as the parent may feel confused and uncertain about what it means when a child says that he or she is gay, lesbian, or bisexual, it may help for the parent to understand that the child may be as confused, uncertain, and even uninformed as to what the implications are of acknowledging this sexual orientation.

Finally, parents should be as honest about their feelings as their child is about her or his feelings about being gay, lesbian, or bisexual. In some cases, a parent may feel so overwhelmed that he or she just does not know what to say, how to react, or how to provide support for his or her child. In such an instance, it may be helpful for the parent to seek help from professionals with experience in this area. Most communities today have public health facilities or private agencies or individuals with knowledge about and skills related to working with LGBT youth and their parents in dealing with coming out issues. Some good sources of information and referrals for parents of LGBT youth are the Get Help Resource Center of the It Gets Better Project (http://www.itgetsbetter.org/pages/ get-help/); Trevor Lifeline of the Trevor Project (866-488-7386); GLBT National Help Center (888-THE-GLNH [888-843-4564]); referral web page of Parents, Families, and Friends of Lesbians and Gays (http://community.pflag.org/ sslpage.aspx?pid=803); Ten Tips for Parents of a Gay, Lesbian, Bisexual, or Transgender Child of Advocates for Youth (http://www.advocatesforyouth.org/parents/173-parents); True Colors' Reading Materials for Heterosexual Parents of LGBT Children (http://www.ourtruecolors.org/Resources/Reading/ straight-parents.html); Advice for Parents when Your Child Comes Out, by Youth Pride, Inc. (http://www.youthprideri .org/Resources/ComingOutAdviceStoriesArt/AdviceforParents WhenYourChildComesOut/tabid/225/Default.aspx); and the referral page provided by CenterLink, a coalition of local LGBT community centers (http://www.lgbtcenters.org/Centers/ find-a-center.aspx). A good resource for referrals to local specialists with expertise in LGBT issues is provided by the Psychology Today Therapy Directory at http://www.psychology today.com/blog/gay-and-lesbian-well-being/201008/parents-gay -children-and-courtesy-stigma, "Find a Therapist."

Coming Out to One's Friends and Peers

One would like to believe that the very first place a LGBT child or adolescent would go for understanding and support when coming out is one's family. In many cases, that assumption is a correct one, and many families readily acknowledge that their love for their child is more important than anything else about their relationship; they reach out—either immediately or after a period of reflection—to offer their daughter or son support, understanding, assistance, and, most important, love. (Of the many print and electronic resources that tell stories of support for LGBT children, one of the best is "Fortunate Families: Catholic Families with Lesbian Daughters and Gay Sons," at http://www.fortunatefamilies.com/stories/our-stories/.)

Yet as the previous section has demonstrated, complete understanding and acceptance by parents do not always follow a child or adolescent's coming out statement. In many cases, LGBT children and youth tell friends and peers first, before they announce their sexual orientation to members of their own family. An extensive study conducted by the Human Rights Campaign (HRC) in 2012, for example, found that 91 percent of respondents were out to their closest friends, 64 percent to their classmates, and 61 percent to other individuals at their schools, compared to just 56 percent to their immediate families ("Growing Up LGBT in America" 2012, 11). Although the report does not discuss the significance or meaning of this finding, it might be taken to reflect the expectation that LGBT children and youth have of greater understanding and support from their peers than from their own families. Trust in other traditional counselors and advisors is even lower, with respondents reporting that they are out to their sports coaches in only 11 percent of all cases; to their doctors, in 16 percent of cases; and to their religious leaders, in only 5 percent of all instances, the lowest of all categories ("Growing Up LGBT in America" 2012, 11).

The implication that friends and schools may be more supportive than parents and families is only just barely confirmed by the HRC report. When asked the biggest problems they face in their daily lives, LGBT children and youth name nonacceptance by their families as their number one concern (26 percent of respondents), followed closely by problems at school, such as harassment and bullying (21 percent). By comparison, these two matters of concern are not listed by any measurable number of non-LGBT youth ("Growing Up LGBT in America" 2012, 7). Some of the specific issues with which LGBT youth have to deal in schools, according to the HRC report, are verbal harassment (twice as common among LGBT as among non-LGBT youth), physical harassment and abuse (reported by 17 percent of LGBT youth compared to 10 percent of non-LGBT youth), and exclusion and isolation by their peers (48 percent for LGBT youth compared to 26 for non-LGBT youth).

Some of the suggestions for coming out to one's friends are not so different from those for coming out to parents and families. For example, it is important to choose the right time and place to bring up the subject, to be prepared for either a positive or negative first response, and to think about possible questions one might have to answer and what those answers will be. But friends are also different from parents and families, and other issues may arise. For example, a young man or women is likely to know his or her friends reasonably well, and he or she may have a fairly good idea that news about one's sexual orientation may not be taken all that well. In fact, some young people who have come out to their "very best friends" have found that they are completely rejected out of hand. A long-term friendship can come to an immediate end as soon as the friend learns that his or her buddy and pal is gay or lesbian. In such a case, it may be best simply not to come out at all . . . at least at this time under the present circumstances.

A coming out announcement also should be prepared very carefully so that the person to whom it is delivered does not feel threatened by the message. One's sexual orientation *is*, of course, a very personal and emotional topic. But it is often best to approach the coming out process in an objective way, allowing a person to think about its implications without becoming stressed, frightened, angry, or upset.

When a coming out announcement produces a negative response from a friend, it is often a good idea not to take that response too personally. One of the remarkable facts about public attitudes regarding same-sex relationships is how much those attitudes are influenced by whether a person actually knows a gay, lesbian, bisexual, or transgendered person. A number of scientific studies have found that individuals who actually know a gay or lesbian person are more likely to be accepting of same-sex relationships and more supportive of LGBT issues. For example, a study reported by the Gallup organization in 2010 found that 88 percent of individuals who know a gay man or lesbian are comfortable being around LGBT people, while only 64 percent of individuals who say they do not know a gay or lesbian admit to being comfortable. Even more dramatically, 67 percent of those who know a gay or lesbian say that same-sex relationships should be legal, while only 40 percent who do not know a gay or lesbian person take that view (Morales 2013). The effect of knowing or not knowing a gay man or lesbian is perhaps most significant in the recent increase in approval of same-sex marriage seen in the United States. A 2012 ABC News/Washington Post poll found that people who know someone who is gay or lesbian are about 20 percent more likely to support same-sex marriage (59 percent to 39 percent) than those who say they do not know a lesbian or gay man (Ergun 2013).

The point of these statistics for the coming out process is that a person's friends may never have met someone who is out as gay, lesbian, or bisexual and may not ever have had to think about or deal with their feelings on the subject. Given time, a person's views about same-sex relationships may evolve into a more understanding and more accepting position.

Finally, a young lesbian, gay, or bisexual person may want to emphasize to a friend that her or his coming out announcement does not have to affect the personal relationship they have had up to this time. A person's sexual orientation is only one facet of his or her personality and for the most part, the person he or she has been in the past is no different from the person making the announcement today. (For experiences of LGBT youth coming out to friends, see Bembrey [2013]; "Coming Out

Stories" [2013]; Egregiously Homosexual et al. [2013]; "When I Came Out" [2013]. For advice from professionals on coming out to friends, see, for example, "Coming Out" [2013]; Seba [2011].)

School Issues

The level of homophobia in American schools has been studied extensively, and research suggests that a large majority of American adolescents hold strongly negative views about same-sex relationships. Probably the most comprehensive and most current research on this issue—as well as on a wide variety of issues dealing with gay issues in American schools—is the annual National School Climate Survey conducted by the Gay, Lesbian & Straight Education Network (GLSEN). In its 2011 report, GLSEN noted that nearly two-thirds (61.3 percent) of all students surveyed for the study reported hearing a gay-related term used in a pejorative way "frequently," 23.6 percent heard such a term "often," and 10.7 percent heard such a term "sometimes." The comments most often mentioned were terms, such as *faggot*, *dyke*, and *homo*, and phrases such as *that's so gay* and *no homo* (Kosciw et al. 2012, Figure 1.1, 14). The GLSEN survey does not specifically define the terms *frequently*, *often*, and *sometimes*, although a similar study by Egale Canada Human Rights Trust does provide that perspective. In the organization's 2011 report, *Every Class in Every School: The First National Climate Survey on Homophobia, Biphobia, and Transphobia in Canadian Schools; Final Report*, Egale states that 70.4 percent of the general school population surveyed reported hearing the phrase *That's so gay* "frequently" in the sense of "at least once a day," and 21.5 percent heard the phrase "sometimes" ("weekly") (Taylor et al. 2011, Figure 1, 48).

Interestingly enough, these comments were being made not only by students, but also by administrators, teachers, and other school personnel. In the 2011 GLSEN report, just over half (56.9 percent) of the general school population reported hearing negative comments about gay, lesbian, bisexual, or transgender students with at least some frequency (Kosciw et al. 2012, Figure 1.6, 17). The Egale survey reported somewhat similar trends, with almost 10 percent of LGBTQ students having noticed homophobic comments from teachers on a daily or weekly basis (9.5 percent for female sexual minority students and 8.2 percent for male sexual minority students) (Taylor et al. 2011, 50).

One promising finding of the GLSEN survey was that the frequency of antigay comments in schools appears to be decreasing over time. The rate of such comments has dropped in the organization's annual survey from over 80 percent in 2001 to about 70 percent in 2011. The use of specific terminology to denigrate LGBT students also declined over that period (Kosciw et al. 2012, xviii). The overarching fact that remains, however, is that LGBTQ students cannot attend most public or private schools in the United States or Canada without constantly being exposed to the use of language by their peers and their teachers that embarrasses and denigrates their very existence. One wonders about the consequents for LGBT students who simply survive in an environment of this kind.

As bad as the use of offensive language may be, it is only the mildest form of harassment to which most LGBT youth are exposed in schools. Indeed, some observers say that the data on the use of the language presented earlier in this discussion is an attempt to "make a mountain out of a molehill." So what if adolescents use language that offends some of their peers. Teenagers tend to be cruel in their relationships with other teenagers, and simply using unpleasant words does not cause any real harm to a young lesbians, gay men, bisexuals, or transgenders. Whether that argument is true, most harassment of LGBT students goes far beyond unpleasant language.

The next level of homophobia to which LGBT students are exposed is verbal harassment, which refers to a direct "in-your-face" use of offensive words and phrases to specific individuals, rather than more general use of offensive language to the general school population. For example, in the GLSEN 2011 survey, more than nine out of 10 LGBT students reported having had a peer call them an offensive name or threaten them with violence in the previous year. For 17.3 percent of those surveyed, this experience occurred "frequently"; for 16.5 percent, it occurred "often"; and for 26.7 percent, it occurred sometimes (with the remaining fraction reporting such experiences "rarely") (Kosciw et al. 2012, Figure 1.14, 24). The Egale survey found somewhat similar results with just over half (50.8 percent) of all LGBTQ students reporting that they had been verbally harassed at least once because of their sexual orientation, in comparison with 8.0 percent of non-LGBTQ students reporting that they had been harassed for the same reason (Taylor et al. 2011, Figure 3, 58).

Both U.S. and Canadian studies have found that LGBTQ students are both verbally and physically harassed not only for their sexual orientation, but also for other characteristics, such as their gender expression, gender, race or ethnicity, or physical or mental disability. In none of these categories, however, is the level of harassment as frequent as it is for sexual orientation. For example, in the GLSEN study, a total of 63.9 percent of all LGBT students reported being verbally harassed for their gender expression (the gender one chooses to present in public), 11.3 percent reported being harasses "frequently," 13.3 percent "often," and 20.5 percent "sometimes" (Kosciw et al. 2012, Figure 1.14, 24). In the Canadian study, just over half (55 percent) of gay, lesbian, and bisexual students reported having been verbally harassed because of their gender expression, 74 percent of transgender students reported verbal harassment, and 26 percent of non-LGBTQ students reporting such harassment (Taylor et al. 2011, 15).

The GLSEN study distinguishes between physical *harassment* and physical *assault*, which the Egale study does not. Both terms refer in general to a physical attack by one person on another person (a LGBTQ student, in this case), with varying degrees of severity and potential and actual damage. They may refer to such actions as pushing, shoving, slapping, kicking, grabbing, hair pulling, shaking, choking, hitting, biting, and using weapons such as knives and guns. Legal systems usually reserve the term *physical assault* for more serious instances of this range of actions, a pattern followed by the GLSEN researchers.

The GLSEN report found that about a third (38.3 percent) of LGBT students had been physically harassed during the previous school year because of their sexual orientation, 6.2 percent "frequently," and 5.0 percent "often." About a quarter (27.1 percent) had been harassed because of their gender expression, 4.1 percent "frequently," and 3.8 percent "often" (Kosciw et al. 2012, Figure 1.15, 25). The rate of physical assault was less, at 18.3 percent for sexual orientation and 12.4 percent for gender expression. When compared with verbal harassment, these numbers may seem small, but they still indicate that a significant number of LGBT students are not uncommonly at risk simply because of their sexual orientation or gender expression (Kosciw et al. 2012, Figure 1.16, 24).

Many of the actions against LGBT students are categorized as forms of *bullying*. That term is generally defined as "unwanted, aggressive behavior among school aged children that involves a real or perceived power imbalance" ("Bullying Definition" 2013). Bullying can occur in almost any school or out-of-school setting between two individuals or groups of any age through adolescence among boys and girls, young men and women of any sex, sexual orientation, gender expression, race, ethnic group, religion, or other social category. According to the most recent data available from the federal government, about one in five students in grades 9 through 12 had been bullied on school property during the 12 months prior to the survey (Eaton 2012, Table 14). Table 2.1 shows the breakdown by race and ethnicity and by grade for these data.

While bullying has probably occurred since time immemorial among children and adolescents, a new form of bullying

Table 2.1   Bullying in U.S. Schools in 2011, by Race/Ethnicity and Grade Level
(percentage of students who have experienced bullying)

Race/Ethnicity	Female	Male	Total
White	25.2	20.7	22.9
Black	12.2	11.1	11.7
Hispanic	19.3	16.0	17.6
Grade	**Female**	**Male**	**Total**
9	27.1	21.5	24.2
10	24.6	20.4	22.4
11	17.5	16.7	17.1
12	17.2	13.4	15.2

Source: Danice K. Eaton et al. 2012. "Youth Risk Behavior Surveillance: United States, 2011; Surveillance Summaries." *Morbidity and Mortality Weekly Report (MMWR)*. 61(SS04): 1–162, http://www.cdc.gov/mmwr/preview/mmwrhtml/ss6104a1 .htm#Tab14. Accessed on April 23, 2013.

has appeared in recent years, cyberbullying or electronic bullying. The term *cyberbullying* or *electronic bullying* refers to bullying that takes place by electronic means, rather than through face-to-face contact. The electronic devices most commonly used for cyberbullying include cell phones, computers, tablets, and any other medium that allows the transmission of social messages such as emails, Facebook or Twitter postings, websites, or text messages. Cyberbullying differs from physical bullying in a number of ways. For example, cyberbullying can be anonymous, with the person being bullied never knowing who it is that has posted harmful comments about her or him. Cyberbullying can also take place at any time or any place for any period of time. Messages that have been posted via cyberbullying become part of the permanent electronic media and are difficult, if not impossible, to remove from someone's personal history. Finally, messages sent via electronic sources may or may not be completely or even partially true. When one person attacks another person directly, there is seldom any question as to who the individuals are that are involved or what happens in the action. During cyberbullying, none of these factors may be known, and an anonymous person may attack

Table 2.2   Cyberbullying in U.S. Schools in 2011, by Race/Ethnicity and Grade Level (percentage of students who have experienced cyberbullying)

Race/Ethnicity	Female	Male	Total
White	25.9	11.8	18.6
Black	11.0	6.9	8.9
Hispanic	18.0	9.5	13.6
Grade	**Female**	**Male**	**Total**
9	22.6	8.9	15.5
10	24.2	12.6	18.1
11	19.8	12.4	16.0
12	21.5	8.8	15.0

Source: Danice K. Eaton et al. 2012. "Youth Risk Behavior Surveillance: United States, 2011; Surveillance Summaries." *Morbidity and Mortality Weekly Report (MMWR)*. 61(SS04), Table 16. http://www.cdc.gov/mmwr/preview/mmwrhtml/ss6104a1 .htm#Tab16. Accessed on April 23, 2013.

someone else with all types of information that is completely false.

Cyberbullying has now become at least as common as physical bullying in U.S. schools. Table 2.2 shows the frequency of cyberbullying reported in the Centers for Disease Control and Prevention (CDC) 2011 Youth Risk Behavior Surveillance System.

Directly comparing the frequency of physical bullying among LGBT youth and their non-LGBT peers is somewhat difficult because of differences in the way researchers use terms like *bullying, verbal harassment, physical harassment,* and *physical assault.* Experts who have studied the question, however, tend to suggest that the rate of bullying among LGBT youth is significantly greater than it is for non-LGBT youth. In a paper prepared for the 2010 White House Conference on Bullying Prevention, for example, Dorothy L. Espelage of the University of Illinois at Urbana-Champagne summarized the available research and concluded that "[b]ullying and homophobic victimization occur more frequently among LGBT youth in American schools than among students who identify as heterosexual" (Espelage 2013, 65).

Comparisons of cyberbullying among LGBT and non-LGBT youth are somewhat easier to find. In its 2011 national survey, for example, GLSEN found that 55.2 percent of LGBT youth reported having been the subject of cyberbullying at least once during the 12 months preceding the survey. Of that number, 9.1 percent had been so treated "frequently," 8.4 percent "often," and 16.4 percent "sometimes" (Kosciw et al. 2012, Figure 1.17, 26). These data rather closely match a survey conducted a year earlier by researchers at Iowa State University, who found that 54 percent of their sample of 350 self-identified nonheterosexuals and 94 allies of LGBT youth aged 11 to 22 reported having been cyberbullied in the preceding year (Blumenfeld and Cooper 2010).

Responses to Bullying

One of the first questions one might ask about the problem of bullying in schools is what options children and young adults have when they are being bullied by their peers. The most likely answer to that question might seem to be to report the problem to parents, other family members, teachers, school administrators, or other responsible adults. Interestingly enough, that "logical" response seems to occur far less commonly than one might expect or hope. In an overall summary of the situation, the federal government's antibullying campaign, StopBullying .com, has reported that somewhere between half and three quarters of all children and young adults who are bullied fail to report that action to any adult at all ("Bullying Prevention & Response Base Training Module" 2013, 50). The most common trend seems to be for very young children to report bullying primarily to parents, siblings, and friends (about half of all cases), somewhat fewer (about 35 percent of all cases) to teachers, and a smaller fraction (about 20 percent) do not report the bullying to anyone. Over time, those numbers change significantly so that by twelfth grade, only about one in five individuals being bullied says anything to parents and teachers, and half report their problem to no one at all (Olweus and Limber 2010).

Data for LGBT children and youth apparent to be largely similar to those for the general school population. In its 2011 survey, for example, GLSEN found that about one in six LGBT children and youth reported bullying to family members always (7.9 percent) or most of the time (9.2 percent) and to school staff always (5.9 percent) or most of the time (7.8 percent). By contrast, well over half of those being bullied never mentioned the problem to family members (55.8 percent) or to school staff (60.4 percent) (Kosciw 2012, Figure 1.18, 28).

The reasons that individuals do not report bullying to authority figures has been the subject of considerable research. For example, researchers at the University of Toronto reported in 2005 on seven major reasons for nonreporting. First, most bullying occurs in settings that make the action a "private" event between the bully (or bullies) and the bullied. Such settings are likely to be locations where adults are seldom present, so aggressors can carry out their actions without fear of being observed or interrupted. Second, the very essence of the bullying act is the interaction between someone who has greater power and someone who has lesser power. Almost by virtue of this definition, the powerless individual is less likely to seek assistance for escaping from a bullying situation. Third, some individuals who are bullied may actually feel that they deserve the action. In the case of LGBT children and young adults, for example, societal messages about same-sex relationships may be so strong that they may feel that it is their own fault if they are picked on by others.

Fourth, a person being bullied may see that the only practical consequence of reporting the action is for it to become worse. They may believe (perhaps correctly) that adults are not likely to want to correct the situation or, if they did want to, that they could do much of anything to prevent the bullying from continuing. Fifth, individuals who are bullied may hold on to the hope that their relationships with those doing the bullying may eventually improve and that, perhaps, they will eventually be accepted as equals by their tormentors. Sixth, as an extension of that belief, friendships sometimes do exist between the bully and the bullied, and the latter individual is reluctant to risk whatever remains of that positive relationship. Seventh, someone who is being bullied may fear that an adult to whom he or she reports the action will simply do nothing, which will serve to increase the severity and frequency of the bullying (Whitted and Dupper 2005).

The 2011 GLSEN survey found that LGBT youth provided broadly similar explanations as to why they do not report bullying to adults. The most common response was that LGBT youth thought that adults would not really do anything to make the bullying problem any better. A quarter of all respondents said that "nothing would be done to address the situation," and another 12 percent said that reporting simply was not worth the effort because, for example, doing so in the past had not produced any results.

The next most common reason for LGBT youth not reporting bullying was that they feared that doing so would only make the situation worse (28.7 percent of all responses), that is, those being bullied feared that the bullying would continue, it would get worse, or it would result in a person's sexual orientation being outed to others. A small number of respondents were also concerned about being labeled a "snitch" or a "tattle-tale."

Quite remarkably, the third most common reason for not reporting bullying was that those being bullied really did not perceive the action as a "big deal." They had become accustomed to bullying as a "normal" part of their lives, or it was much less significant than other problems in their lives. Finally, about one in six respondents (15.5 percent) were concerned about how reports of bullying would affect their relationship with school staff. They worried that staff would begin to think of them differently, would lose respect for them, would begin to judge them differently, or would develop other negative feelings toward them. A small number of respondents also noted that members of the staff were themselves homophobic and that reporting bullying would not produce any real action on their part (Kosciw 2012, Table 1.1, 29; 30–32).

To some extent, children and young adults appear to be at least partially justified in doubting the value of reporting bullying to adults. Research has shown that adults do not respond to and/or intervene in bullying situations nearly as often as might be desirable. A number of reasons explain this fact. In the first place, many adults do not seem to be aware of the extent to which bullying is occurring in the world around them (compare to reason number one earlier in this discussion that students do not report bullying) ("Education Forum on Adolescent Health" 2013, 12). In addition, a number of adults feel that bullying is a normal and natural part of childhood and adolescence and that they have no responsibility or role in preventing or dealing with bullying. According to one report, as many as a quarter of all teachers hold this view, with the consequence that fewer than 5 percent of this group of teachers intervene in bullying even when they are aware that it is occurring (Cohn and Canter 2013).

Perhaps the most common reason that young people do not report bullying to adults is that they do not believe those adults will take any action to ameliorate the situation. In one group of studies, children and young adults reported that teachers intervened in bullying events "almost never" or "once in a while" in about 40 percent of all cases (for elementary students) and 60 percent of all cases (for secondary students) (Charach, Pepler, and Ziegler 1995; Olweus 1993). LBGT youth in the 2011 GLSEN survey reported similar experiences. In more than a third of instances, respondents to the survey said that teachers and other staff members took no action to deal with the bullying situation, sometimes being told just to ignore the problem and sometimes being told that they, the reporting students, were responsible for the bullying's having taken place. The next most common response among educators

(25.0 percent of instances) involved the educator's telling the perpetrator to stop his or her actions. Some of the actions that might have represented a somewhat different view of handling the situation were rare. In about 5 percent of all cases, the educator specifically offered support to the reporting student; in 1.6 percent of cases, the educator recommended that the bully and person being bullied try to talk through their differences; and in just less than 1 percent of all case, the educator himself or herself spoke with the bully in an attempt to educate him or her about the nature of the problem (Kosciw 2012, Table 1.2, 34).

The anecdotal comments made by respondents to the GLSEN survey sometimes provide a better sense of what it must be like to be someone who is constantly being bullied but who receives little or no support from adults to whom she or he turns for help. One ninth grade girl, for example, remembers that the assistant principal she talked to told her, "I can't help you, you chose what you want to be. We can't help you because you chose to be this." A twelfth grade boy reported that the adults in his school suggested that he "should drop out and get my GED or 'be less gay' " (Kosciw 2012, 34).

Effects of Bullying

How does the bullying experience affect youngsters who have to go through that experience? Some answers to are fairly obvious. For one thing, individuals who are bullied are sometimes physically injured by bullies' actions. They may also experience a range of health problems, from inability to sleep to digestive disorders to headaches. In many cases, the person being bullied is also likely to experience a range of negative emotional and psychological reactions, including anger, depression, anxiety, reduced sense of self-worth, increased thoughts of suicide, feelings of hopelessness, and reduced academic achievement (see, for example, Dombeck 2013). In many cases, the response of a person being bullied is simply to avoid school and the opportunity for peers to bully him or her. As a result, the rate of absenteeism from school is directly related to the degree of bullying that a person feels. Some experts estimate that as much as 15 percent of all school absenteeism results from students' fears of being bullied (Bullying Statistics 2013).

Data from the 2011 GLSEN survey provides some quantitative data about the relationships between the degree of bullying experienced by LGBT youth and various physical, psychological, and emotional effects. Those data show, for example, that the level of academic achievement ranged on a linear scale from a grade point average (GPA) of 3.2 among students who experienced a low level of harassment to a GPA of 2.9 among those who experienced a high level of harassment. Other comparisons can be seen in Table 2.3.

As undesirable as these outcomes might be, one could hope that after a person leaves school, the effects of bullying might fade into the past and that one might take up a normal life again. Such is not necessarily the case, as an increasing body of research is beginning to show that bullying has significant long-term effects. In 2013, for example, researchers at the Duke University Medical Center reported on a 20-year study of individuals who either bullied or were bullied during their childhood and teen years to see what long-term effects they could discover. They found that victims of bullying were at higher risk for agoraphobia, generalized panic, and anxiety disorders, while those who had been both bullies and victims of bullying were at even greater long-term risk. These individuals scored high for risks such as young adult depression, agoraphobia, panic disorder, and suicidality (Copeland et al. 2013, 419). Interestingly enough, bullies themselves came off relatively unscathed by their earlier experiences, tending to be at higher risk only for antisocial personality disorder, a condition the researchers noted would be consonant with their behavior as youths.

A number of other studies have produced comparable findings about the long-term effects of bullying. A summary of those studies mentioned effects such as anxiety, loneliness, low self-esteem, poor social self-competence, depression, psycho-somatic symptoms, social withdrawal, refusal to attend school, school absenteeism, poor academic performance, physical health complaints, running away from home, alcohol and drug use, and suicide (McDougall, Hymel, and Vaillancourt 2013).

One of the most interesting commentaries on the long-term effects of bullying on victims was a long article on the topic by psychologist Mark Dombeck, who was bullied as a child. In think-ing about his own experiences and reviewing the literature on the topic, Dombeck concluded that a number of long-term mental and emotional conditions can be associated with early bullying, including reduced occupational opportunities; lingering feelings of anger and bitterness; desire for revenge; difficulty in trusting people; interpersonal difficulties, such as fear and avoidance of new social situations; increased tendency to be a loner; perception of self as someone who is easy to victimize, overly sensitive, and thin-skinned; reduced self-esteem; and an increased incidence of continued bullying and victimization (Dombeck 2013).

Among the most troubling findings reported in the past de-cade are those that deal with neurological changes that may be associated with bullying. That is, researchers are discovering from both animal and human studies that physical changes in the brain can be detected among individuals who have been subjected to bullying early in their lives. For example, a group of researchers led by Tracy Vaillancourt at McMaster University reported in 2008 that they had found variations in brain function between 12-year-old Caucasian boys and girls who had and had not been bullied (Vaillancourt et al. 2008, 294; also see Anthes 2013 for a summary report on this research).

The School's Role in Controlling Bullying

Experts on bullying in general, and bullying of LGBT youth in particular, agree that schools can have an important role in reducing the harm caused by bullying. They suggest that schools need to develop specific policies that outline policies about bullying, indicating the actions that constitute bullying and the responses schools intend to make to reduce bullying. They then need to develop mechanisms by which those policies are actually put into practice.

One example of the type of action a school can take involves creating a committee specifically for the purpose of dealing with bullying issues. The committee can establish school policies on bullying (if they do not already exist), conduct surveys to discover the extent and nature of bullying occurring in the school, talk with students who are being bullied or who are bullying other students, and design activities that will call the bullying problem to the attention of teachers and students and suggest ways of dealing with the problem. Some school systems have already developed system-wide programs for putting ideas such as these into practice at all schools in a town, city, or county (see, for example, "Anti-Bullying Resources" [2013]).

Individual teachers can also incorporate antibullying lessons into their own classrooms. A number of online resources now provide such lessons for use by elementary through senior high school teachers (see, for example, "Anti-Bullying Activities/Anti-Bullying Lesson Plans" [2013]; Burns [2013]; "Elementary School Bully Lesson Plans" [2013]).

Bullying Laws

There are no federal laws that deal specifically with the issue of bullying in U.S. public schools. Bullying activities may be prohibited, however, by laws that deal with discrimination on the basis of a number of characteristics, such as race, national origin, color, sex, age, disability, and religion. A person who bullies someone on the basis of any of these characteristics may be subject to prosecution for such actions. Sexual orientation is not one of the characteristics currently covered by federal law, although bullying based on sexual orientation may be covered by other considerations, such as picking on a person because of a sex-related issue ("Federal Laws" 2013). Senator Bob Casey (D-PA) has on at least three occasions introduced federal legislation dealing with bullying in American schools that receive some form of federal funding. This legislation has three major parts:

- Schools and school districts must adopt codes of conduct that ban harassment and discrimination based on a number of characteristics, including sexual orientation and gender identity.
- States must collect data on bullying in schools and report those data to the U.S. Department of Education.
- States must make these data available to the general public. (S.403 2013)

As of the end of 2013, no action has been taken on Senator Casey's bill beyond its referral to the Committee on Health, Education, Labor and Pensions.

The legal situation of antibullying legislation is very different at the state level. As of the end of 2013, 49 states had some form of antibullying legislation, with Montana being the only exception. While these laws have many elements in common, they also differ in a number of ways. For example, most state laws require individual school districts to develop and adopt policies on bullying, although the precise way in which that term is defined differs somewhat from state to state. The types of requirements that appear in state laws include assigning school districts the responsibility of tracking, investigating, and reporting on incidents of bullying; establishing consequences for students who bully; educating students on the importance of eliminating bullying and ways in which that goal can be accomplished; and communicating with school personnel and students the goals and mechanisms of the antibullying programs.

State laws also differ widely as to how they treat lesbian, gay, bisexual, and transgender youth. Fifteen states and the District of Columbia have passed antibullying laws that specifically mention sexual orientation and gender identity as protected categories. Those states are Arkansas, California, Colorado, Connecticut, Illinois, Iowa, Maine, Maryland, New Jersey, New York, North Carolina, Oregon, Rhode Island, Vermont, and Washington. Another 13 states and the District of Columbia have adopted laws that prohibit discrimination against students based on sexual orientation and gender identity in addition to or in place of antibullying laws. Wisconsin is the one state with laws that protect students on the basis of sexual orientation, but not gender identity ("States with Safe Schools Laws" [2013]; for an excellent, if slightly outdated, review of bullying laws, see Sacco et al. [2013]).

A question that one might well ask is whether state antibullying laws are effective, that is, does their existence actually reduce the rate of bullying in that state? At this point, the evidence is somewhat mixed. A 2007 review of state laws by researchers at Georgia State University, for example, found that such laws appear to have little or no impact on the rate of bullying. One possible reason for this finding, they said, was that bullies have high self-esteem and probably see little or no advantage in adopting antibullying behaviors. The researchers acknowledged that their findings were likely to be "disappointing for policy makers and the general populace given the increased interest in targeting bullying and other violence in the schools" but that scarce resources would probably better be spent on efforts to support at-risk students who are the primary targets of bullying (Ferguson et al. 2007, 410–411).

Other researchers have drawn similar conclusions and, as of late 2013, perhaps the most generous conclusion that can be drawn is that the effectiveness of antibullying programs in general is uncertain. At least one reason for this conclusion, as it turns out, is that many of the studies conducted to measure the effectiveness of such programs are themselves conceptually flawed, so any results obtained are *ab initio* doubtful (Ryan and Smith 2009).

Given this somewhat disappointing result, it is perhaps somewhat hopeful that at least some data suggest that antibullying policies and programs can be helpful in reducing the risk faced by LGBT youth from bullying. In the 2011 GLSEN study, for example, respondents were asked to comment on and assess antibullying programs in their own schools. Responses to that question were then compared to the rates of harassment, aggression, bullying, and other negative behaviors reported by respondents. Some clear trends appeared. For example, when respondents were asked how often they heard biased remarks about same-sex relationships, the number of "often" and "frequently" responses was inversely proportional to the severity of the school's antibullying policy. For specific types of comments, those rates ranged from a high of 87.3 percent in schools with no antibullying policy to a low of 45.8 percent in schools with strong antibullying policies (these rates differed depending on the specific comment mentioned) (Kosciw 2012, Figure 1.49, 68). Similarly, the percentage of LGBT youth who were subjected to victimization because of their sexual orientation ranged from as much as 36.0 percent in schools with no antibullying policy to a low of 21.7 percent in those with strong policies. Comparable data for victimization because of gender expression were 37.8 percent and 25.1 percent. The extent of intervention by school personnel also followed similar lines, with personnel intervening "all" or "most of the time" only 8.8 percent of the time in schools with no antibullying policy and 28.3 percent of the time in schools with strong policies. Comparable data for intervention for remarks about gender expression were 8.4 percent and 19.0 percent (Kosciw 2012, Figures 1.50 and 1.51, 70). Results obtained from the comparable Canadian study on the climate for LGBT youth in schools found similar results (see Taylor et al. 2011, Figure 25, 117).

Thus, although some questions may remain about the overall effectiveness of antibullying legislation and programs, there is some reason to believe that such programs may be of value for LGBT youth in both the United States and Canada.

Homelessness

The National Alliance to End Homelessness (NAEH) regularly conducts a national survey in the United States to collect data on the number of individuals and families who are homeless nationwide, the characteristics of those individuals and families, and social, economic, political, and other factors that affect changes in these data. The 2013 report estimated that on a given night in January 2012, there were 633,782 homeless people in the United States. The number represented a decrease of less than 1 percent from a comparable evening in January 2011 and a continued decrease over the preceding years from a high of 763,010 in January 2005 ("The State of Homeless in America" 2013, Box 1.1, 9). The report indicated that it had not yet begun collecting data specifically about homeless youth but that it would begin to do so in 2013.

Other organizations and agencies have collected firm data or good estimates, however, as to the number of homeless youth in the United States and the characteristics of that population. The U.S. Conference of Mayors' 2012 report on its Hunger & Homelessness Survey, released in December 2012, for example, found that 25 participating cities reported a total of 390 homeless youth (called *unaccompanied youth*) on the streets on an average night, 398 homeless youth in emergency shelters, and 143 in transitional housing (comparable data for homeless individuals in general were 22,652; 21,076; and 13,847) (U.S. Conference of Mayors 2012, 26).

A considerable amount of data is available about homeless youth from a wide variety of federal and state agencies, nonprofit organizations, and individual researchers. Among the conclusions that can be drawn from these sources are:

- An estimated 1.7 million teenagers are homeless in the United States.
- Nearly four out of 10 homeless individuals (39 percent) are teenagers.
- The average age at which homeless teenagers turn to the streets is 14.7 years.
- As many as 5,000 homeless young adults die on the streets each year because of physical assaults, illness, or suicide.
- The most common reason for becoming homeless is problems at home that caused parents to throw their children out or to take no action when a child decided to leave home.
- About 40 percent of all homeless teenagers identify as LGBT youth. ("11 Facts about Homeless Teens" 2013)

The last item on this list reflects what some people regard as the most serious problem facing LGBT youth: homelessness. Although estimates suggest that lesbian, gay, bisexual, and transgender children and teenagers make up no more than about 5 to 10 percent of the general population, they account for between 20 and 40 percent of all homeless teenagers ("Gay and Transgender Youth Homelessness by the Numbers" 2013; for a range of estimates of the LGBT homeless population, see Quintana, Rosenthal, and Krehely 2010, Table 1, 6). And they also represent a disproportionate share of homeless youth who experience a host of problems on the streets. For example, nearly six out of 10 (58 percent) of LGBT homeless youth report being sexually assaulted on the streets, compared to 33 percent of non-LGBT youth; 44 percent are propositioned for sexual encounters, compared to 26 of non-LGBT youth; 62 percent attempt suicide at least once, compared to 29 percent of their non-LGBT peers; and 42 percent abuse alcohol, compared to 27 percent of heterosexual homeless adolescents ("Gay and Transgender Youth Homelessness by the Numbers" 2013; also see Cochran et al. 2002).

A number of studies have found that by far the most important factor in forcing adolescents into homelessness is family problems of one type or another. For example, a study by the Williams Institute at the UCLA School of Law in 2012 found that 46 percent of homeless LGBT youth ran away from home because their family rejected their sexual orientation or gender identity. Forty-three percent were forced out of their homes by their parents for the same reason. And about a third of homeless LGBT youth left home because they were being physically, sexually, or emotionally abused at home (Durso and Gates 2012, 4; Milburn et al. 2006; Ray 2006, 2, 16–19).

Homelessness in and of itself is a traumatic experience. However, that experience tends to be magnified with a host of consequent problems for LGBT youth. In an extensive and comprehensive study on homelessness among LGBT youth, the National Gay and Lesbian Task Force (the Task Force) noted five areas on which homeless LGTB youth were particularly at risk: mental health issues, substance abuse, risky sexual behavior, victimization, and issues with the juvenile and criminal justice systems. A number of studies have shown, for example, that LGBT youth are more likely to become depressed, lonely, anxious, and withdrawn, and they are more likely to develop psychosomatic illnesses and social problems than are their non-LGBT peers. The Task Force points out that evidence also suggests that homophobia within helping agencies may limit the concern about and effectiveness with which various public and private agencies attack these issues among LGBT youth (Ray 2006, 2).

Research also shows that substance abuse tends to occur at very high rates among homeless LGBT youth. One of the most thorough studies on this topic was reported in 2006 by a research team led by James H. Van Leeuwen, at the University of Colorado at Denver. The Van Leeuwen team attempted to assess differences between LGB and non-LGB homeless youth on a number of risk factors, one of which was substance abuse. They found that alcohol use was more common among homeless LGB youth (42 percent of the sample) than among non-LGB youth, and 38 percent of LGB youth had been in substance abuse treatment programs compared to 27 percent of non-LGB youth (Van Leeuwen et al. 2006; for more on this topic, also see Ray [2006, 49–52]).

Risky sexual behavior is almost a given for homeless LGBT youth, who often have no other means of survival than selling their bodies for sexual activities to older men and women. Formal research on this issue has produced results that tend to confirm this assumption. For example, a study reported in 2011 found that GLB youth (in addition to African American homeless youth) tend to have engaged in so-called *survival sex* significantly more often than had their heterosexual white homeless counterparts (Walls and Bell 2011). The latest research shows that this trend is clear for young gay males but not necessarily for young lesbians or bisexuals (Walls and Bell 2011; see also Gangamma et al. [2008]). This pattern has also been observed in Canada, where a 2004 study found that homeless LGBT youth were about three times as likely as their heterosexual peers to engage in survival sex (Gaetz 2004).

A considerable body of research has demonstrated over the past two decade that homeless gay male youth experience physical and sexual victimization at a rate significantly greater than their heterosexual counterparts and than homeless lesbian and bisexual youth. For example, a study that was reported in 2004 of 63 homeless LGB youth and 366 heterosexual homeless youth in the Midwest noted that the former group tended to score higher on a variety of measurements of victimization, including physical abuse, sexual abuse, neglect, physical victimization, and sexual victimization. These differences were especially large for all categories except physical abuse for gay males and their heterosexual peers and for physical and sexual victimization for lesbians and their heterosexual peers (Whitbeck, et al. 2004, Table 1, 334). A recent review of existing studies on the rates of victimization among LGB homeless youth and their heterosexual counterparts concluded that available evidence showed beyond a doubt that "[e]ven accounting for overrepresentation amongst the homeless population, LGBT youth are more often victims of a range of crimes compared with their heterosexual counterparts" (Ventimiglia 2012, 441).

Interestingly enough, this same review argued that "the increased risk for all crimes that LGBT homeless youth face point [sic] to the problem of bias and inequality embedded within cultural and governmental systems" (Ventimiglia 2012, 442–443). This argument is somewhat difficult to defend empirically because there are virtually no studies on the way in which the criminal justice and juvenile systems deal specifically with LGBT youth, let alone homeless LGBT youth. (For a discussion of this point, see Ray [2006, 73–82].) Still, there may be reasons that mindsets of both homeless LGBT youth and members of the criminal justice and juvenile systems may treat crimes against the former in a somewhat different manner than is the case for their heterosexual peers.

For example, many LGBT youth appear to be aware of strong homophobic feelings in the general community, and those feelings may, after all, be the reason that they are homeless in the first place. In such circumstances, they may be reluctant to report victimization or other criminal or legal problems to police officers, social workers, and other individuals to whom they would otherwise be expected to appeal. In one study of homeless LGB youth in Toronto, the lead researchers found that respondents reported a reluctance to report even the most serious crimes to which they had been exposed (Gaetz 2004, 440).

On the other, hand police officers and other law enforcement personnel may not be particularly willing to hear about and act on complaints of crimes against LGBT youth. In one of the few studies of law enforcement officers' attitudes toward lesbians and gay men, researchers found that most officers did not specifically intend to apply the law differently to LGBT individuals compared to heterosexuals, but a majority of those interviewed did enthusiastically accept negative stereotypes about homosexuals and feelings of superiority for the law enforcement profession. Perhaps more revealing was the finding that between 30 and 40 percent of those police officers interviewed acknowledged that it was unlikely that gays and lesbians would be treated equally with their heterosexual peers (Bernstein and Kostelac 2002; also see Davies, Rogers, and Whitelegg 2009).

Communities across the nation have searched for ways of dealing with the unique problems faced by LGBT homeless youth outlined here. One example is the Ruth Ellis Center, located in Highland Park, Michigan. The center claims to be the only agency in the Midwest whose specific mission it is to work with lesbian, gay, bisexual, transgender, and questioning youth. The agency provides a wide range of services to homeless youth, including educational tutors; a cyber center for use of electronic resources; an HIV testing and counseling service; a laundry; mailbox service; job and school application counseling service; art group; clothing supplies; a creative writing program; and an individual, family, and group counseling program. The Ruth's House residential program consists of two elements, a live-in housing program for 12- to 17-year-olds and a transitional living program for older men and women age 18 to 21 years (Ruth Ellis Center 2013; also see Ray 2006, 91–103).

One of the most ambitious programs designed to deal with homelessness among LGBT teens is the Forty to None Project. The project was launched in 2012 as an offshoot of the True Colors Fund, which was established in 2008 by entertainer Cyndi Lauper. The Forty to None Project gets its name from its primary goal of reducing the rate of homelessness among LGBT youth from about 40 percent to 0 percent. The project's mission is to raise public awareness of the problem of LGBT youth homelessness, with the aim of developing policies and practices that will lead to the reduction, and eventually elimination, of the problem. One of the project's most valuable services is a listing of centers around the United States that have made their primary goal the provision of services for LGBT homeless youth. Some examples of these services are the Ruth Ellis Center (described earlier in this text); Triad House, in Ewing, New Jersey; Outright Vermont, in Burlington; Oasis Youth Center, in Tacoma, Washington; SunServe, in Manors, Florida; Ozone House, in Ann Arbor, Michigan; and HATCH, in Houston, Texas. The Forty to None listing can be found on the organization's website at http://fortytonone .org/support-your-local-service-provider/find-a-local-provider/.

Suicidal Ideation and Suicide Attempts

Perhaps the single most serious problem faced by LGBT youth involves thoughts about committing suicide (suicidal ideation)

Table 2.3   Data on Suicidal Thoughts and Behaviors among LGB and non-LGB Youth (percentage)

Thought/Behavior	Non-LGB	Lesbian or Gay	Bisexual
Seriously considered suicide			
median	11.7	29.6	40.3
range	9.9–13.2	18.8–43.4	35.4–46.2
Made plan to commit suicide			
median	10.0	21.2	35.7
range	8.0–11.9	15.8–37.1	30.0–37.7
Attempted suicide			
median	6.4	25.8	28.0
range	3.8–9.6	15.1–34.3	20.6–32.0
Suicide attempt requiring medical attention			
median	2.2	12.6	11.3
range	0.9–3.4	7.0–15.7	4.4–16.8

Source: Laura Kann et al. 2011. "Sexual Identity, Sex of Sexual Contacts, and HealthRisk Behaviors among Students in Grades 9–12: Youth Risk Behavior Surveillance, Selected Sites, United States, 2001–2009." *Mortality and Morbidity Weekly Report (MMWR)*. 60(SS07), http://www.cdc.gov/mmwr/preview/mmwr html/ss6007a1.htm#Tab3, Tables 20–23. Accessed on May 1, 2013.

and/or attempts to end one's life. For a number of gay, lesbian, bisexual, and transgendered youth, the very thought of having to survive on a day-to-day basis in the face of verbal and physical harassment from so many different people, ranging from total strangers to one's family and closest friends, is more than one can take. The only remaining option may seem to be to commit suicide. As a result, suicide is a very common cause of death among LGBT youth. (The claim is sometimes made that suicide is *the* leading cause of death within the population, although that claim is difficult to confirm. See Suicide Prevention Resource Center [2008, 13].)

A vast amount of research data now confirms the severity of this problem in the LGBT community. Probably the most comprehensive summary of those data is available in a research report published by the Suicide Prevention Resource Center in 2008. That report begins by pointing out some of the problems involved in obtaining reliable and valid data about suicidal behavior among LGBT youth (the definition used for *suicidal behavior* in the paper is "suicidal thinking, suicide attempts, and completed suicides") (Suicide Prevention Resource Center 2008, 11). For example, national surveys of health and risk behavior among adolescents and children seldom, if ever, include separate categories for sexual minorities. Many studies rely, therefore, on samples of varying sizes and compositions that may be difficult to compare with each other.

Nonetheless, some trends seem clear from the available research. For example:

- A 1998 study of gay, lesbian, and bisexual students in seventh through twelfth grades found that 28.1 percent of all gay and bisexual males and 20.5 percent of lesbian and bisexual females had attempted suicide at least once, compared to 4.2 percent and 14.5 percent of their heterosexual peers, respectively.

- A review of data from the National Longitudinal Study of Adolescent Health in 2001 found that LGBT youth are approximately twice as likely as non-LGBT youth to attempt suicide.

- A survey of 21,927 sexually active adolescents in Minnesota in 2006 found that the rates of attempted suicide among gay male and female students were 29.0 percent and 52.4 percent, respectively, compared to rates of 12.6 percent and 24.8 percent for their non-LG counterparts.

- Data from the National Health and Nutrition Examination Survey reported in 2000 showed that rates of suicidal ideation among gay men was 41.2 percent, compared to 17.2 percent for nongay men in the same age range.

- A study by the Massachusetts Department of Education in 2006 found that LGB youth were more than three times as likely as their heterosexual peers to have had suicidal thoughts in the year preceding the study. (All findings reported in Suicide Prevention Resource Center 2008, 14–15, 18, with citations of original research. Studies more recent than the Suicide Prevention Resource Center report appear to confirm the general conclusions of that document. See, for example, Almeida et al. [2009]; Hatzenbuehler [2011]; Liu and Mustanski [2012].)

A recent study focused on more detailed information about suicidal ideation and behavior among LGB youth. The study summarized data obtained from Youth Risk Behavior Surveys conducted in seven states (Connecticut, Delaware, Maine, Massachusetts, Rhode Island, Vermont, and Wisconsin) and six cities (Boston, Chicago, Milwaukee, New York, San Diego, and San Francisco) for gay, lesbian, bisexual, and heterosexual youth on a variety of measures related to suicidal thoughts and acts. The results of this study are summarized in Table 2.3.

The high rate of suicidal ideation and behaviors among LGBT youth has prompted experts to ask what actions can be taken to deal with this problem. The most obvious suggestion is that schools attempt to provide environments in which LGBT youth feel less at risk, safer, and generally more comfortable. Such conditions are unlikely to exist, for example, in schools where teachers and administrators openly and consistently ignore harassment of LGBT students or themselves have been heard to make homophobic comments. Research makes it clear that the presence of teachers who simply affirm the validity of a same-sex orientation vastly improves an LGBT youth's self-esteem, thereby reducing the likelihood of suicidal ideation and possible suicide attempts (see, for example, Hansen 2007; Jordan, Vaughan, and Woodworth 1998). In fact, one study has quantified that benefit, showing that LGBTQ students who believe that they have only a single staff member at their schools to whom they can talk about their problems are only a third as likely to report suicidal ideation or suicidal behaviors than are LGBTQ students who do not have even that modest level of support (Goodenow, Szalacha, and Westheimer 2006).

The Trevor Project claims to be the nation's leading national organization for suicide prevention services for LGBT youth. It has developed a set of guidelines for schools that want to work to reduce the risk for suicidal ideation and suicidal behaviors among their LGBTQ students. The first step in those guidelines is for school administrators and teachers to be on the lookout for warning signs of suicidal thoughts and actions among LGBT/Q students such as revealing comments ("I don't deserve to live" or "It will all be over soon") and risky behaviors (such as a reduced interest in otherwise popular activities and a tendency to give away prized possessions). Educators also need to be aware of risk factors that are known to be associated with thoughts of suicide, such as feelings of depression, anxiety, and other types of mental and emotional distress. Lack of access to school and community resources to whom an LGBT student can turn may also increase the risk of suicide faced by LGBT youth (Suicide Prevention 2013).

In addition to these reactive behaviors, school personnel can take proactive steps to decrease the risk of suicide among LGBT youth, such as ensuring that physical, mental, emotional, and other forms of support are available at schools and in the community. One of the most helpful forms of support is a gay-straight alliance (GSA) club. Such an organization provides at least one dependable ally to whom troubled LGBT youth can turn in their deepest moments of despair ... or it can simply be a place to go for daily support and friendship (Bishop and Casida 2011; Dessel 2010; Robinson 2009).

An indication of the growing interest in dealing with suicidal ideation and suicide acts by LGBT youth was the announcement in 2010 of the creation of the new National Action Alliance for Suicide Prevention (NAASP). The organization is an agency created to carry out the goals of the National Strategy for Suicide Prevention, originally adopted in 2001 and originally facilitated by the Suicide Prevention Resource Center. At a very early stage in its operations, the NAASP decided to focus on the special problems faced by three groups especially at risk for suicide: American Indians and Alaskan Natives, military service members and veterans, and LGBT youth. A special task force within NAASP was created to deal with each of these populations ("Task Forces" 2013). In its earliest phases, the primary objective of the Lesbian, Gay, Bisexual, and Transgenders Population Task Force will be to collect the data necessary to provide an understanding of the scope and nature of issues faced by LGBT youth dealing with suicide issues.

A number of state and local agencies and organizations have also begun to organize to deal more effectively with the challenges posed by LGBT suicide issues. One example is the OutLoud program of the Washington State Youth Suicide Prevention Program (YSPP). YSPP began operating in 1995 as a program under the Washington State Department of Health at the University of Washington School of Nursing. The program now delivers its suicide prevention programs to more than 30,000 young people between the ages of 10 and 19 throughout the state. It provides a wide variety of information and services about suicide prevention to educators, counselors, public health workers, parents, community leaders, and students. It often delivers its messages in concert with local GSA clubs.

Conclusion

Throughout much of history, LGBT youth have been a "lost population" of individuals who have been harassed and abused because of their sexual orientation or gender expression. While adult gay men and lesbians were battling for a host of new civil rights, such as the right to work and the right to marry, many LGBT were living lives characterized by constant torment. Little wonder, then, that homelessness, mental and emotional problems, and suicide were the common lot of many LGBT youth. However, that situation has begun to change rapidly and dramatically in the past few decades. More and more educators, counselors, public health workers, government officials, parents, and the general public have become conscious of the issues that LGBT youth face in their everyday lives. And at last, actions are being taken, organizations are being formed, and services are being provided to help these young gay men, lesbians, bisexuals, and transgendered individuals live happier and more productive lives.

References

"11 Facts about Homeless Teens." Do Something.org. http://www.dosomething.org/actnow/tipsandtools/11-facts-about-homeless-youth. Accessed on April 28, 2013.

"About the OutLoud Project." Youth Suicide Prevention Program. http://www.yspp.org/lgbtq/outloud_overview .htm. Accessed on May 2, 2013.

Almeida, Joanna et al. 2009. "Emotional Distress Among LGBT Youth: The Influence of Perceived Discrimination Based on Sexual Orientation." *Journal of Youth and Adolescence*. 38(7): 1001–1014.

"Ann Coulter's National 'Disown Your Son' Day Tweet Slammed by LGBT Rights Advocates." Huffpost Gay Voices. http://www.huffingtonpost.com/2012/10/16/ ann-coulter-national-coming-out-day-tweet-glaad-_n _1970502.html. Accessed on April 19, 2013.

Anthes, Emily. "Inside the Bullied Brain: The Alarming Neuroscience of Taunting." Boston.com. http://www .boston.com/bostonglobe/ideas/articles/2010/11/28/inside _the_bullied_brain/. Accessed on April 27, 2013.

"Anti-Bullying Activities/Anti-Bullying Lesson Plans." Education World. http://www.educationworld.com/ a_special/bully.shtml. Accessed on April 27, 2013.

"Anti-Bullying Resources." Boston Public Schools. http:// www.bostonpublicschools.org/antibullying. Accessed on April 27, 2013.

Arnett, Jeffrey Jensen. 1999. "Adolescent Storm and Stress, Reconsidered." *American Psychologist*. 54(5): 317–326.

"At What Age Were You Sure That You Were Gay/Lesbian/ Bisexual and It Wasn't a Phase?" Empty Closets. http:// emptyclosets.com/forum/coming-out-advice/13446-what -age-were-you-sure-you-were-gay-lesbian-bisexual-wasnt -phase-2.html. Accessed on April 19, 2013.

"Average Coming Out Age Has Fallen by over 20 Years." Stonewall CYMRU. http://www.stonewallcymru.org.uk/ cymru/english/media/current_releases/4878.asp. Accessed on April 19, 2013.

Be Yourself: Questions and Answers for Gay, Lesbian, Bisexual, and Transgender Youth. Washington, DC: Parents, Families and Friends of Lesbians and Gays, 1999, 2002.

Bembrey, Julie et al. "How to Come Out to Your Best Friend without Giving Her the Wrong Idea." WikiHow. http://www.wikihow.com/Come-Out-to-Your-Best-Friend-Without-Giving-Her-the-Wrong-Idea. Accessed on April 22, 2013.

Bernstein, Mary, and Constance Kostelac. 2002. "Lavender and Blue: Attitudes about Homosexuality and Behavior Toward Lesbians and Gay Men among Police Officers." *Journal of Contemporary Criminal Justice.* 18(3): 302–328.

Bettcher, Tallia. "Homosexuality and Morality: Part I." http://www.calstatela.edu/faculty/tbettch/homomoralityI.htm. Accessed on April 19, 2013.

Bishop, Holly N., and Heather Casida. 2011. "Preventing Bullying and Harassment of Sexual Minority Students in Schools." *Clearing House: A Journal of Educational Strategies, Issues and Ideas.* 84(4): 134–138.

Blumenfeld, Warren J., and R. M. Cooper. 2010. "LGBT and Allied Youth Responses to Cyberbullying: Policy Implications." *International Journal of Critical Pedagogy.* 3(1): 114–133.

Board on the Health of Select Populations. *The Health of Lesbian, Gay, Bisexual, and Transgender People: Building a Foundation for Better Understanding.* Washington, DC: National Academies Press, 2011.

"Bullying Definition." StopBullying.gov. http://www.stop bullying.gov/what-is-bullying/definition/index.html. Accessed on April 23, 2013.

"Bullying Prevention & Response Base Training Module." StopBullying.gov. http://www.stopbullying.gov/prevention/in-the-community/community-action-planning/training-module-speaker-notes.pdf. Accessed on April 26, 2013.

"Bullying Statistics." http://www.bullyingstatistics.org/content/bullying-statistics-2010.html. Accessed on April 26, 2013.

Burns, James H. "Great Anti-Bullying Activities and Lesson Plans." Bully Proof Classroom. http://bullyproofclassroom.com/great-anti-bullying-activities. Accessed on April 27, 2013.

Charach, Alice, Debra Pepler, and Suzanne Ziegler. 1995. "Bullying at School: A Canadian Perspective." *Education Canada* 35(1): 12–18.

Cochran, Bryan et al., 2002. "Challenges Faced by Homeless Sexual Minorities: Comparison of Gay, Lesbian, Bisexual, and Transgender Homeless Adolescents with Their Heterosexual Counterparts." *American Journal of Public Health*. 92(5): 773–777.

Cohn, Andrea, and Andrea Canter. "Bullying: Facts for Schools and Parents." NASP Resources. http://www.nasponline.org/resources/factsheets/bullying_fs.aspx. Accessed on April 26, 2013.

"Coming Out." LGBT Youth Scotland Green Light Project. https://www.lgbtyouth.org.uk/files/documents/guides/Coming_out_guide_-_LGB.pdf. Accessed on April 22, 2013.

"Coming Out Stories." AVERT. http://www.avert.org/coming-out-stories.htm. Accessed on April 22, 2013.

"Coming Out to Your Parents." Gay Lesbian Bisexual & Transgender Resource Center, Colorado State University. http://glbtss.colostate.edu/coming-out-to-your-parents. Accessed on April 21, 2013.

Copeland, William E. et al. 2013. "Adult Psychiatric Outcomes of Bullying and Being Bullied by Peers in Childhood and Adolescence." *JAMA Psychiatry*. 70(4): 419–426.

Davies, Michelle, Paul Rogers, and Lisa Whitelegg. 2009. "Effects of Victim Gender, Victim Sexual Orientation,

Victim Response and Respondent Gender on Judgements of Blame in a Hypothetical Adolescent Rape." *Legal and Criminological Psychology*. 14(2): 331–338.

Denizet-Lewis, Benoit. 2009. "Coming Out in Middle School." *New Yorker*. September 27, 2009, 36–44.

Dessel, Adrienne. 2010. "Effects of Intergroup Dialogue: Public School Teachers and Sexual Orientation Prejudice." *Small Group Research*. 41(5): 556–592. Also available as a doctoral thesis at http://etd.utk.edu/2008/August2008 Dissertations/DesselAdrienneBrodsky.pdf. Accessed on May 2, 2013.

Dombeck, Mark. "The Long Term Effects of Bullying." American Academy of Experts in Traumatic Stress. http://www.aaets.org/article204.htm. Accessed on April 26, 2013.

Dungca, Nicole. 2013. "Transgender Students Get Unisex Restrooms." *Oregonian*. 163(54,822): A1, A4.

Durso, Laura E., and Gary J. Gates. *Serving Our Youth: Findings from a National Survey of Service Providers Working with Lesbian, Gay, Bisexual, and Transgender Youth Who Are Homeless or at Risk of Becoming Homeless*. Los Angeles: Williams Institute with True Colors Fund and The Palette Fund, 2012.

Eaton, Danice K. et al. 2012. "Youth Risk Behavior Surveillance: United States, 2011; Surveillance Summaries." *Morbidity and Mortality Weekly Report (MMWR)*. 61(SS04): 1–162, http://www.cdc.gov/mmwr/preview/mmwrhtml/ss6104a1.htm#Tab14. Accessed on April 23, 2013.

"Education Forum on Adolescent Health: Bullying." American Medical Association. http://www.ama-assn.org/ama1/pub/upload/mm/39/youthbullying.pdf. Accessed on April 26, 2013.

Egregiously Homosexual et al. "How to Come Out to Your Friends." WikiHow. http://www.wikihow.com/Come-Out-to-Your-Friends. Accessed on April 22, 2013.

"Elementary School Bully Lesson Plans." http://www.iu1.k12.
pa.us/iss/bullying/eslessons.shtml. Accessed on April 27,
2013.

Elias, Paul. "California Gay Conversion Therapy Ban Upheld
by Federal Court." Huffington Post. http://www.huffington
post.com/2013/08/29/california-gay-conversion-therapy
-ban_n_3837922.html. Accessed on October 26, 2013.

Elliott, Leland, and Cynthia Johnson. *Sex on Campus: The
Naked Truth about the Real Sex Lives of College Students.*
New York: Random House, 1997.

Ergun, Damla. "Strong Support for Gay Marriage Now
Exceeds Strong Opposition." ABC News. http://abcnews
.go.com/blogs/politics/2012/05/strong-support-for-gay
-marriage-now-exceeds-strong-opposition/. Accessed on
April 22, 2013.

Espelage, Dorothy L. "Bullying & the Lesbian, Gay, Bisexual,
Transgender, Questioning (LGBTQ) Community," 65–72.
http://www.stopbullying.gov/at-risk/groups/lgbt/white_house
_conference_materials.pdf. Accessed on April 23, 2013.

"Fact Sheet: Lesbian, Gay, Bisexual and Transgender Youth
Issues." The Body. http://www.thebody.com/content/
art2449.html. Accessed on April 20, 2013.

"Family and Coming Out Issues for Latinas and Latinos."
Human Rights Campaign. http://www.hrc.org/resources/
entry/family-and-coming-out-issues-for-latinas-and-latinos.
Accessed on April 21, 2013.

"Federal Laws." StopBullying.gov. http://www.stopbullying.
gov/laws/federal. Accessed on April 27, 2013.

Ferguson, Christopher J. et al. 2007. "The Effectiveness of
School-Based Anti-Bullying Programs: A Meta-Analytic
Review." *Criminal Justice Review.* 32(4): 401–414.

"The First Person You Told." Empty Closets. http://
emptyclosets.com/forum/coming-out-advice/86663-first
-person-you-told.html. Accessed on April 21, 2013.

Friedrichs, Ellen. "Who Did You Come Out to First?" About.com. http://gayteens.about.com/od/experiences/a/ Who-Did-You-Come-Out-To-First.htm. Accessed on April 21, 2013.

Gaetz, Stephen. 2004. "Safe Streets for Whom? Homeless Youth, Social Exclusion, and Criminal Victimization." *Canadian Journal of Criminology and Criminal Justice.* 46(4): 423–455.

Gangamma, Rashmi, et al. 2008. "Comparison of HIV Risks among Gay, Lesbian, Bisexual and Heterosexual Homeless Youth." *Journal of Youth and Adolescence.* 37(4): 456–464.

"Gay, but Scared to Come Out to My Parents." Give a Damn Campaign. http://www.wegiveadamn.org/2010/10/gay -but-scared-to-come-out-to-my-parents/. Accessed on April 21, 2013.

"Gay and Transgender Youth Homelessness by the Numbers." Center for American Progress. http://www.american progress.org/issues/lgbt/news/2010/06/21/7980/gay-and -transgender-youth-homelessness-by-the-numbers/. Accessed on April 28, 2013.

Goodenow, Carol, Laura Szalacha, and Kim Westheimer. 2006. "School Support Groups, Other School Factors, and the Safety of Sexual Minority Adolescents." *Psychology in the Schools.* 43(5): 573–589.

Gross, Larry P., and James D. Wood, eds. *The Columbia Reader on Lesbians and Gay Men in Media, Society, and Politics.* New York: Columbia University Press, 1999.

Growing Up LGBT in America. Washington, DC: Human Rights Campaign, 2012. http://www.hrc.org/youth# .UmwAyvkqh8E. Accessed on October 26, 2013.

Hansen, Anastasia. 2007. "School-Based Support for GLBT Students: A Review of Three Levels of Research." *Psychology in the Schools.* 44(8): 839–848.

Hatzenbuehler, Mark L. 2011. "The Social Environment and Suicide Attempts in Lesbian, Gay, and Bisexual Youth." *Pediatrics.* 127(5): 896–903.

Lesley V. et al. "How to Come Out as a Gay or Lesbian Teen." WikiHow. http://www.wikihow.com/Come-Out-As-a-Gay -or-Lesbian-Teen. Accessed on April 21, 2013.

"How Do I Know if I'm Gay?" Gay Menno. http:// gaymennonite.wordpress.com/resources-for-gay-mennonite -youth/how-do-i-know-if-im-gay/. Accessed on April 20, 2013.

"How Do I Know if I'm Gay or Lesbian?" Seventh-Day Adventist Kinship. http://sdakinship.org/en/faqresources/ resource3.html. Accessed on April 20, 2013.

"I Think I Might Be Gay. Now What Do I Do?" Advocates for Youth. http://www.advocatesforyouth.org/index.php ?option=com_content&task=view&id=726&Itemid=336. Accessed on April 20, 2013.

Jordan, Karen M., Jill S. Vaughan, and Katharine J. Woodworth. 1998. "I Will Survive: Lesbian, Gay, and Bisexual Youths' Experience of High School." *Journal of Gay & Lesbian Social Services.* 7(4), 1998: 17–33.

Kinsey, Alfred C., Wardell Baxter Pomeroy, and Clyde E. Martin. *Sexual Behavior in the Human Male.* Philadelphia: W.B. Saunders, 1948.

Kitts, Robert Li. 2005. "Gay Adolescents and Suicide: Under-standing the Association." *Adolescence.* 40(159): 621–628.

Kosciw, Joseph G. et al. *The 2011 National School Climate Survey: The Experiences of Lesbian, Gay, Bisexual and Transgender Youth in Our Nation's Schools.* New York: Gay, Lesbian & Straight Education Network, 2012.

Laursen, Brett Paul, Todd D. Little, and Noel A. Card, eds. *Handbook of Developmental Research Methods.* New York: Guilford, 2012.

"LGBT: Who Do You Trust the Most?" Yahoo! Answers. http://answers.yahoo.com/question/index?qid=200905 16160935AAF7pVR. Accessed on April 20, 2013.

"The Lies and Dangers of Reparative Therapy." Human Rights Campaign. http://www.hrc.org/resources/entry/the-lies-and -dangers-of-reparative-therapy. Accessed on April 21, 2013.

Liu, Richard T., and Brian Mustanski. 2012. "Suicidal Ideation and Self-Harm in Lesbian, Gay, Bisexual, and Transgender Youth." *American Journal of Preventive Medicine.* 42(3): 221–228.

McDougall, Patricia, Shelley Hymel, and Tracy Vaillancourt. "What Happens Over Time to Those Who Bully and Those Who Are Victimized?" Education.com. http://www.education .com/reference/article/Ref_What_Happens_Over/. Accessed on April 27, 2013.

Milburn, Norweeta G. et al. 2006. "Discrimination and Exiting Homelessness among Homeless Adolescents." *Cultural Diversity and Ethnic Minority Psychology.* 12(4): 658–672.

Mirk, Sarah. "Nonprofit Works with Transgender Kids: Long Before Puberty." Blogtown. http://www.portlandmercury. com/BlogtownPDX/archives/2011/12/13/nonprofit-works -with-transgender-kidslong-before-puberty. Accessed on April 18, 2013.

Montemayor, Raymond, and Eric Hanson. 1985. "A Naturalistic View of Conflict between Adolescents and Their Parents and Siblings." *Journal of Early Adolescence.* 5(1): 23–30.

Morales, Lymari. "Knowing Someone Gay/Lesbian Affects Views on Gay Issues." Gallup. http://www.gallup.com/poll/ 118931/Knowing-Someone-Gay-Lesbian-Affects-Views -Gay-Issues.aspx. Accessed on April 22, 2013.

Morgan, Glennisha. " 'Trans 100,' Annual Event Honoring Transgender Rights Advocates, Launches In Chicago."

Huffington Post.http://www.emergence-international.org/
articles/page/3/. Accessed on April 18, 2013.

Neece, Randy. "The Parent Crap: 10 Tips for Coming Out."
Huffpost Gay Voices. http://www.huffingtonpost.com/
randy-neece/the-parent-crap-10-tips-for-coming-out_b
_2104164.html. Accessed on April 21, 2013.

Nicolosi, Joseph. *Reparative Therapy of Male
Homosexuality: A New Clinical Approach.* Northvale,
NJ: J. Aronson, 1991.

Nicolosi, Joseph. "You Don't Have to Be Gay." Thomas
Aquinas Psychological Clinic. http://josephnicolosi.com/.
Accessed on April 21, 2013.

Olweus, Dan. *Bullying at School: What We Know and
What We Can Do.* Oxford, UK; Cambridge, MA:
Blackwell, 1993.

Olweus, Dan, and Susan P. Limber. 2010. "Bullying in School:
Evaluation and Dissemination of the Olweus Bullying
Prevention Program." *American Journal of Orthopsychiatry.*
80(1): 124–134.

Padawer, Ruth. "Boygirl." 2012. *New York Times Magazine.*
August 8, 2012, 19–23+.

Payne, Ed, and Ashley Fantz. "Parents of Transgender First
Grader File Discrimination Complaint." CNN US. http://
www.cnn.com/2013/02/27/us/colorado-transgender-girl
-school. Accessed on April 18, 2013.

Penzel, Fred. "How Do I Know I'm Not Really Gay?" Western
Suffolk Psychological Services. http://www.wsps.info/index
.php?option=com_content&view=article&id=65%3Ahow
-do-i-know-im-not-gay-homosexuality-obsessions
&catid=0%3A&Itemid=64. Accessed on April 20, 2013.

"Position Statement on Reparative Therapy." International
Society of Psychiatric-Mental Health Nurses. http://www
.ispn-psych.org/docs/PS-ReparativeTherapy.pdf. Accessed
on April 21, 2013.

Quintana, Nico Sifra, Josh Rosenthal, and Jeff Krehely. *On the Street: The Federal Response to Gay and Transgender Homeless Youth*. Washington, DC: Center for American Progress, June 2010.

Ray, Nicholas, ed. *Lesbian, Gay, Bisexual, and Transgender Youth: An Epidemic of Homelessness*. Washington, DC: National Gay and Lesbian Task Force Policy Institute and National Coalition for the Homeless, 2006.

Robinson, Malila N. 2009. "A Pathway to Equality for Queer-Friendly Student Groups in U.S. Public Schools." *Journal of LGBT Youth*. 6(2/3): 325–327.

Ruth Ellis Center. http://www.ruthelliscenter.org/. Accessed on April 29, 2013.

Ryan, Caitlin et al. 2009. "Family Rejection as a Predictor of Negative Health Outcomes in White and Latino Lesbian, Gay, and Bisexual Young Adults." *Pediatrics*. 123(1): 346–352.

Ryan, Wendy, and J. David Smith. 2009. "Antibullying Programs in Schools: How Effective Are Evaluation Practices?" *Prevention Science*. 10(3): 248–259.

S. 403: Safe Schools Improvement Act of 2013. Govtrack.us. http://www.govtrack.us/congress/bills/113/s403/text. Accessed on April 27, 2013.

Sacco, Dena T. et al. "An Overview of State Anti-Bullying Legislation and Other Related Laws." http://cyber.law .harvard.edu/sites/cyber.law.harvard.edu/files/State_Anti _bullying_Legislation_Overview_0.pdf. Accessed on April 27, 2013.

Savin-Williams, Ritch C. *Mom, Dad, I'm Gay: How Families Negotiate Coming Out*. Washington, DC: American Psychological Association, 2001.

Seba, Jaime. *Coming Out: Telling Family and Friends*. Broomall, PA: Mason Crest, 2011.

Shilo, Guy, and Riki Savaya. 2011. "Effects of Family and Friend Support on LGB Youths' Mental Health and Sexual Orientation Milestones." *Family Relations.* 69(3): 318–330.

Siciliano, Carl. "Family Rejection of LGBT Youth Is No Joke." Huff Post Media. http://www.huffingtonpost.com/carl -siciliano/family-rejection-of-lgbt-_b_875841.html. Accessed on April 19, 2013.

Signorile, Michelangelo. *Outing Yourself: How to Come Out as Lesbian or Gay to Your Family, Friends, and Coworkers.* New York: Random House, 1995.

Spack, Norman P. "Puberty Inhibitors." Trans Youth Family Allies. http://www.imatyfa.org/permanent_files/puberty blockers101.html. Accessed on April 18, 2013.

The State of Homelessness in America 2013. Washington, DC: National Alliance to End Homelessness, April 2013.

"States with Safe Schools Laws." GLSEN. http://www.glsen .org/cgi-bin/iowa/all/library/record/2344.html. Accessed on April 27, 2013.

"Suicide Prevention." Trevor Project. http://www.thetrevor project.org/warningsigns. Accessed on May 2, 2013.

Suicide Prevention Resource Center. *Suicide Risk and Prevention for Lesbian, Gay, Bisexual, and Transgender Youth.* Newton, MA: Education Development Center, 2008.

Talbot, Margaret. 2013. "About a Boy." *New Yorker.* April 18, 2013, 56–65.

"Task Forces." National Action Alliance for Suicide Prevention. http://actionallianceforsuicideprevention.org/ taskforces. Accessed on May 2, 2013.

Taylor, Catherine et al. *Every Class in Every School: The First National Climate Survey on Homophobia, Biphobia, and Transphobia in Canadian Schools; Final Report.* Toronto: Egale Canada Human Rights Trust, 2011.

"To the Gay/Lesbian/Bi Society?" Yahoo! Answers. http://
answers.yahoo.com/question/index?qid=201110131
85749AAfr2J9. Accessed on April 19, 2013.

"Today's Gay Youth: The Ugly, Frightening Statistics."
PFLAG Phoenix. http://www.pflagphoenix.org/education/
youth_stats.html. Accessed on April 19, 2013.

"Tracy Morgan Goes on Anti-Gay Tirade at Nashville Show."
Hollywood Reporter. http://www.hollywoodreporter.com/
news/tracy-morgan-goes-anti-gay-196697. Accessed on
April 19, 2013.

"Trans Parent Journeys." Trans Youth Family Allies. http://
www.imatyfa.org/transparentjourneys/index.html. Accessed
on April 18, 2013.

U.S. Conference of Mayors. *Hunger and Homelessness Survey.*
Washington, DC: United States Conference of Mayors,
December 2012.

Vaillancourt, Tracy et al. 2008. "Variation in Hypothalamic–
Pituitary–Adrenal Axis Activity among Bullied and Non-
Bullied Children." *Aggressive Behavior.* 34(3): 294–305.

Van Leeuwen, James M. et al. 2006. "Lesbian, Gay, and
Bisexual Homeless Youth: An Eight-city Public Health
Perspective." *Child Welfare.* 85(2): 151–170.

Ventimiglia, Nusrat. 2012. "LGBT Selective Victimization:
Unprotected Youth on the Streets." *Journal of Law in Society.*
13(2): 439–453.

Walker, Jesse. "The Death of David Reimer." Reason.com.
http://reason.com/archives/2004/05/24/the-death-of-david
-reimer. Accessed on April 18, 2013.

Walls, N. Eugene, and Stephanie Bell. 2011. "Correlates of
Engaging in Survival Sex among Homeless Youth and
Young Adults." *Journal of Sex Research.* 48(5): 423–436.

"What Age Did You Come Out?" Yahoo! Answers. http://au
.answers.yahoo.com/question/index?

qid=20090329045134AAenDd5. Accessed on April 19, 2013.

"What Is Intersex?" Intersex Society of North America. http://www.isna.org/faq/what_is_intersex. Accessed on April 18, 2013.

"When Did You Realize You Were Gay?" Topix. http://www.topix.com/forum/news/gay/TAPU12KSJM9UHDAD6. Accessed on April 20, 2013.

"When I Came Out." http://whenicameout.tumblr.com/. Accessed on April 21, 2013.

Whitbeck, Les B. et al. 2004. "Mental Disorder, Subsistence Strategies, and Victimization among Gay, Lesbian, and Bisexual Homeless and Runaway Adolescents." *Journal of Sex Research*. 41(4): 329–342.

Whitted, Kathryn S., and David R. Dupper. 2005. "Best Practices for Preventing or Reducing Bullying in Schools." *Children & Schools*. 27(3): 167–175.

Introduction

This chapter provides contributors with an opportunity to present their own personal views on a variety of issues related to LGBT youth. Some essays describe a person's own individual experience in coming out and dealing with one's own sexual orientation, while others provide additional information on resources on which one can draw and organizations that deal with issues of importance to LGBT youth.

Andy's Coming Out: Andy Barlow

After recently celebrating my twenty-fifth birthday and being asked to reflect on my coming out, I can't help but feel as if it were so long ago. Truth is, it's been barely three years. It feels so distant because my life didn't truly start until that day three years ago. That afternoon in early June was the day I was reborn, the day I was finally allowed to live as me. Being honest about oneself is so vital to being happy, and to be honest about right now, I've never been happier nor more proud of who I am, but that wasn't always the case.

James Oliver, left, hugs his brother and fellow Eagle Scout, Will Oliver, who is gay, as Will and other supporters carry boxes filled with petitions to end the ban on gay scouts and leaders in front of the Boy Scouts of America headquarters in Dallas, Texas. (AP Photo/Tony Gutierrez, File)

Growing up I always knew I was attracted to boys, but at the time I had no idea what being gay was. As I got older and started to realize what the word meant, I knew that it was something I didn't want to be. I told myself I wasn't gay, but jealous of the guys who were so good looking and popular—I just wanted to look like them and that was why I was so interested in their bodies. I wouldn't even allow myself to think the word "gay" in my head.

This confusion and deep denial left me feeling different and alone. I had a good number of friends, but I was always very quiet. I often found myself depressed because even though I had girlfriends, it never felt complete and never satisfied me mentally or physically. I thus found myself overly attached to my male friends, which led to many bouts of worsening depression when they wouldn't return the feelings I had for them.

One year after high school graduation, and after a severe episode of depression from my first attempted relationship with a guy who outed me way before I was ready, I packed up my stuff and moved 2,300 miles to Oregon. I instantly made new friends and found myself very happy, on the outside at least. I started at the University of Oregon with more friends than I ever imagined and stronger friendships than I had ever had.

But that secret I hid kept on creeping back to me. I had gotten over the depression, but I still felt alone and lost, even surrounded by everyone I now had. I knew that I was missing out on so much, and not letting anyone know the real me made me feel like a bad friend.

It was about this time that my depression arising out of having this horrible secret changed to a depression that no one knew the real me. I had started to allow myself to say the word "gay" (only in my head of course) and as I did that I started to pay attention to anything gay around me—that season on MTV's *The Real World* featured a guy coming to terms with coming out, which really touched me. That also led me to learn more about Matthew Shepard. I secretly bought his mom's book and read it in two nights, crying through most of it.

I became saddened and angered by his story, and it made me want to make a stand and be true to myself. I didn't want kids to face what I had and especially to face what Matthew had. For the first time, I wanted to be gay.

Now the problem was, how to come out. Who to come out to first? When? Where? I instantly knew I first wanted to tell my parents, who also lived in Oregon now. I was pretty sure they would accept me, yet my attempts to tell them left me shaking and emotionally drained.

Finally one night I came home and they instantly knew I had something on my mind. My dad paused the TV and I sat down and said, "I don't know if you know this, but I'm gay." As I said this I felt as though I left my body—my head was spinning, yet I somehow got those words out. They sat for a minute to take it in, and then quickly started to ask questions. Was I sure? Gay not bi? Was it a phase? I answered honestly and asked them to accept me. I told them I was afraid because many kids get kicked out and punished for coming out.

It was that last statement that really awakened my dad. His voice became loud and firm, "That is NOT going to happen. We LOVE you and that would NEVER happen." We talked a little more and then just went on with the night.

Now, how to tell my friends? This really perplexed me. As a result of moving around, I had good friends in three different states and had so many friends that I knew I couldn't tell them all in person, nor did I really want to. But I also didn't want it to spread as a rumor—as someone who likes being in control and having power, I wanted control and power over how I came out.

My first thought was to write a post on Facebook that everyone could read, but I saw flaws in this approach. Next I thought about a video. A video would mean they had to look at me, in the eyes, and see my expression. That gave me the power. In the video, I would write out what I wanted to say on cards and then hold them up—this gave me control as they had to read each card and wait until I was ready to show the next one.

I went to work quickly, feeling completely numb the entire time. I was so immersed that all fears left me. I was on a mission now. I finished the video and posted a link to Facebook asking everyone to watch it. Within a minute, it got its first "like." This is the moment at which I came back to life. It was like slamming on the brakes, and all my feelings returned to me. I had done it, and people had seen it. There was no turning back.

I was so ready at this point to live a true life that I didn't care if I lost all my friends. I knew that I would make new ones and that it would be okay. I broke down in tears and called a friend of mine (she was also gay) and told her what I had done. She cried with me and told me everything would be okay. She was right.

I got nonstop messages that day, all with words of love and support. I felt so free. What was most touching and unexpected was the amount of support I got from my straight male friends. They were so happy and proud of me, telling me I was more brave than anyone they knew. These guys became a great support for me over the next few years—they even loved playing my wingman at the bar.

As the next few months passed, I finally was able to be me. My fears of losing friends proved to bring the exact opposite: my friends and I were closer than ever before. I became more open and outgoing, and all my friends and family took notice of how happy I had become.

I admit I was lucky in many ways. I had supportive and loving friends and family, helped by the fact that I attended college in a very liberal and gay-friendly city. However, I think it is important to understand that as lucky as I was, the internal struggle of being gay and coming out is still an extremely emotional and difficult task. And the fact remains that I will never stop coming out. With every new job and new friend, I must come out again.

Andy Barlow is a recent graduate from the University of Oregon with a degree in political science. His academic career focused on issues of race, gender and sexuality. He currently lives in Eugene, Oregon, with his ragdoll cat Cavanaugh.

Scouts for Equality: Justin Bickford

The Boy Scouts of America (BSA) has a long tradition of help-ing youth to become upstanding citizens and leaders in American society through its unique, youth-led outdoor pro-gram. The BSA has a much shorter tradition of barring mem-bership to LGBT youth, parents, and leaders.

The BSA's antigay policy first surfaced internally in 1978 and was widely publicized in the early 1990s with the expulsion of two young Eagle Scouts, Tim Curran and James Dale. James Dale's removal went to the Supreme Court in 2000 in a case known as *Boy Scouts v. Dale*, in which the Court ruled 5–4 that the BSA had the right to discriminate as a "private" organization despite state nondiscrimination laws. While many people still debate the status of the BSA as private (it was established by a federal congressional charter and has streamlined access to federal lands), many Scouts and Scout leaders began a movement for inclusion. In 1993, Dave Rice, a scoutmaster with over 50 years of experience, founded Scouting for All and was removed from the BSA for his advocacy. In 2000, the Inclusive Scouting Network emerged, founded by several gay Eagle Scouts who were expelled by the BSA immediately after the *Boy Scouts v. Dale* deci-sion. A primary function of this network was to create safe space for LGBT youth through the Inclusive Scouting Award, an unofficial knot worn by supporters so that LGBT youth could identify allies.

In 2012, a critical point was reached when Jennifer Tyrrell was ousted as a den leader of her son's Cub Scout Pack because she is a lesbian. With the country increasingly understanding and embracing LGBT individuals, plus a growing list of people working to make the BSA more inclusive, the time had come for change. Scouts for Equality was born, founded by four straight Eagle Scouts. With the help of allied groups like GLAAD and Change.org, Scouts for Equality made sure that Jenn's story was heard.

Despite the growing outcry from both within and without, the BSA acted again that same summer and expelled a young man, Ryan Andresen, from scouting simply for being gay. Ryan had just completed the requirements to earn his Eagle Scout Award, the highest achievement in Boy Scouts, but instead of an Eagle award, the BSA presented him with an expulsion letter. Even as public criticism mounted, the BSA maintained its hard-line position, announcing that it just finished a two-year review of the antigay policy and decided to keep it unchanged. On the heels of this announcement, the membership of another leader and parent, Greg Bourke, was revoked though he received accolades from his troop, church, and state.

Scouts for Equality and its allies opened dialogues with the public about this issue. We spoke to senators and members of Congress. We spoke to businesses, donors, and chartering partners. We spoke to scouting professionals and volunteers. Everywhere we looked, we found support. Every group had members who had been in scouting. Many individuals we spoke to had a father, brother, son, or friend who was an Eagle Scout. Everyone had witnessed the benefits of scouting, yet so many people now distanced themselves from the BSA because of its continued discrimination. The BSA needed to change for its own survival, in addition to the harm its policies were inflicting on LGBT youth and the hurtful lesson that its antigay discrimination was teaching to everyone else.

In August 2012, leading up to the U.S. presidential election, candidates Mitt Romney and Barack Obama both stated their support to end the ban. From September through December, multiple donors, notably Intel, UPS, and Merck, all announced that their donations to the BSA would cease until the ban was lifted. The internal and external pressure reached a tipping point in January 2013, when the BSA announced that the policy was being reconsidered. The BSA's board and volunteer representatives from across the country would vote on a policy change at the BSA's National Annual Meeting in May.

The BSA surveyed its membership to determine where they stood and decided that the only change offered for a vote would be an end to the ban on gay youth. Although our goal remains full equality for all ages, we embraced any available change that moved the BSA closer to equality and improved the environment for LGBT youth within scouting. Scouts for Equality set the ambitious goal of reaching out to the voting members to open a dialogue about this issue before the vote. This effort succeeded. In May 2013, the BSA voted 61–34 to lift the ban on gay youth—the first step toward LGBT equality in its history.

The new policy, which will be implemented on January 1, 2014, eases the fear and discrimination felt by gay youth in scouting, but it puts a time limit on their acceptance while still preventing LGBT adults and parents from participating, so it is far from perfect. With much more work left to be done, Scouts for Equality and the Inclusive Scouting Network have joined forces and are dedicated to the long campaign for a full end to all discrimination in the BSA.

Why did all these Eagle Scouts and Scout leaders, LGBT and allies, set out to fix the BSA's membership policies? It helps to remember that scouting is an international movement and is larger than just the BSA. The oath we took as Scouts compels us to help everyone and to stand by our moral convictions. The law we live by as Scouts tells us to be loyal, helpful, friendly, courteous, and kind. Discriminating against our fellow Scouts is none of these things. Scouting also aims to develop good citizens, but a democracy requires the ability to work together with people who are different in some way.

In the end, it's the very fact that we are Scouts that put us on this path. We cannot call ourselves Eagle Scouts and ignore everything that scouting stands for. With the increased risk of bullying, depression, and suicide among LGBT youth, the BSA has the opportunity to save lives. Instead, it maintains a policy that amplifies these risks. Even if the policy does not affect us directly, we all feel its impact. Discrimination is a huge problem, but it's one we can fix.

And Scouts always leave a place better than we found it.

Justin Bickford is a co-founder of Scouts for Equality. He is an Eagle Scout who spends his days as a molecular biologist and his nights making sure that he leaves the world a better place for his son.

Our GSA Journey: Alison Colby

Was this a dream? Less than 48 hours before, we had been at our graduation ceremony for the Class of 2013—yet here we stood in New York City to be honored as the national GLSEN GSA (Gay-Straight Alliance) of the Year. For Jonah and Malia, our student representatives, it was indeed a dream . . . come true.

We waited backstage as Janet Mock, renowned transgender activist, writer, and proud graduate of Farrington, began introducing us; in the next moment, Jonah and Malia were approaching the podium and teleprompter, slightly jet-lagged but fully prepared to accept the award on behalf of our school and GSA members back home in Honolulu.

Some background about the origins of the Farrington High School GSA might be in order. Hawaii is a special place—but not just because of its physical beauty. "Aloha" may sound cliché to some, but genuine efforts are made every day to live the spirit expressed by the word. Perhaps because of our diversity, we try to be respectful, humble, and accepting of one another's differences. However, like anywhere else, there are fissures. And while much has changed for the better in the last 20 years, adamant antigay voices still surround us. It is sometimes difficult to know who is and isn't supportive of LGBT rights, and I am often pleasantly—and sometimes unpleasantly—surprised.

W. R. Farrington High School, home of the school mascot Governors, is one of the oldest and largest schools in the state. Located in the heart of a tough area called Kalihi, most of our students are first- or second-generation immigrants, and the majority qualify for free or reduced-price lunches. Many of our students live in one of several housing projects surrounding our campus. But while our youth may not have many tangible resources, they have big and loving hearts.

It is within this "Gov Luv" environment that our GSA has flourished due to a core group of students who embraced the idea from the start. We have received an outpouring of assistance from our larger LGBT community, as well as uncommon support from our administrators. Our current principal, Alfredo Carganilla, a former school counselor, has great empathy for our LGBT students. And his predecessor, the progressive and visionary Catherine Payne, paved the way for us, beginning in the mid-1990s. Not only did she fully support our Teen Center social work and nursing services—such as peer mediation, anger management, and youth gang outreach—she gently pushed us to offer group programs specifically for LGBT youth. But it hasn't been easy to create or sustain. Today, I co-advise our GSA with fellow social worker Gwen Murakami, and for me, it is my third attempt at building this group.

Over the years, I have worked with many LGBT students individually, in the privacy of my office. Then, in 1998, a wonderful woman from the Life Foundation reached out to us to address the needs of our relatively large transgender student population. We collaborated to run a support group called Chrysalis (in which Janet participated). However, after about four years, we disbanded when key students graduated and participation waned. A few years later, partnering with a school counselor, we organized and advised a club we called BLEST Gs (Bisexual, Lesbian, Exploring, Straight, Transgender, Gay Governors). While active for a while, that effort also fizzled, for similar reasons. But providing an LGBT program remained on my "back burner."

In early 2011, several forces in the Farrington universe converged. The state Department of Education's HIV prevention specialist coordinated an excellent workshop related to LGBT youth and encouraged us to start a GSA. The Life Foundation started a GSA-Hawaii program. On the mainland, there was a tragic rash of suicides and incidents of violence directed at LGBT youth. These high-profile cases brought the problem of bullying and harassment to the forefront, and legitimized our GSA's vision of a safe school for all. In the midst of this changing atmosphere, a team of graduate students from the University of Hawaii chose as their semester project the resurrection of our GSA. Over 40 students showed up that first day, and our GSA was reborn.

The following school year, buoyed by that energetic start, we forged ahead under the continuous guidance of law student and mentor Adam Chang, who facilitated LGBT lessons every Friday after school. Then a nationwide contest challenged us to sponsor an event in our community to raise LGBT visibility and promote safe schools. Adam said, "Let's do it!"—so how could we not? Our GSA spent the next three months planning: mapping out the logistics and budget; securing diverse speakers, which included one of Hawaii's supreme court justices, our students, our principal, and a local comedian; arranging for student musical entertainment and food; creating a large mosaic mural; soliciting donations; and much more. The centerpiece of our event was *Out in the Silence*, a documentary film by Joe Wilson and Dean Hamer. That December, to our surprise and delight, the *Huffington Post* announced that we were the Grand Prize winners of the 2011 Out in the Silence Award for Youth Activism. The filmmakers presented us with the prize check at a pep rally in front of the entire student body, where we also received a congratulatory certificate from the state Senate and coverage in a local magazine.

We have since been riding a wave of energy, honors, and activity: Youth Grand Marshal at the 2012 Honolulu Pride Parade; the E Ola Pono award; an appearance on a local public television show; a GSA display for our library; and participation in the AIDS Walk, Gay Prom, and National Day of Silence. We were the first public school to host *Hawaii Family Portraits*, a traveling professional photo exhibition of diverse LGBT families. Also, GSA students wrote and produced a short video, which won first place in its category at our school's annual film festival. Our challenge now is to keep our momentum going. We have been fortunate in myriad ways, and we sometimes wonder how we will top these past two years!

In the days following the GLSEN Respect Awards, we explored the Big Apple together to add to our trove of memories. A thunderstorm and bitter cold hampered our efforts to see Stonewall Inn, but that was all right. Just being in New York gave us a chance to reflect: Our Farrington GSA is but one part of a bigger movement—of people all over the world, past and present, interconnected by common values of fairness, justice, and peace. We are grateful to those who have made it possible for us to continue on this journey together.

Alison Colby was born and raised in Hawaii, and has been a social worker since 1983. She received her bachelor's degree from Pomona College and her master's degree from the University of Hawaii. In addition to her work at the Farrington Teen Center, she is a member of a training team that provides violence prevention workshops in the community.

Athlete Ally: Brian Healey

In order to have a basic understanding of the plight of the LGBT community in the world of athletics, it is important to recognize just how far that community has come in the past few years. The work of organizations like GLAAD, the Human Rights Campaign, Athlete Ally, and You Can Play has made it possible for professional athletes not to only voice their support for the LGBT community, but to even come out themselves. In sports, soccer player Robbie Rogers and basketball player Jason Collins made waves with their own revelations, and the recent repeal of DOMA [the Defense of Marriage Act] made the climate in our nation even more welcoming for LGBT individuals. For athletes, the path to living a fully realized, open life was paved by past starts like Martina Navratilova and Billie Jean King from the world of tennis, baseball player Glen Burke, and football player Dave Kopay.

But as we look to the future, and to the next generation of leaders who will further bridge the equality gap for LGBT athletes, it truly is young men and women who hold the power.

When considering the most important developmental phase for athletic prowess, most coaches will point to the early years, when technique, drive, and skill are worked into the very framework of the lives of young athletes. Unfortunately, bad habits can be learned at this stage of life as well, so ensuring that youth coaches, physical education teachers, and parents create environments that are welcoming and inclusive for all is one of the most important things advocacy groups can work on for future generations. By instilling the values of respect and acceptance at a young age, we can avoid many of the problematic issues that currently complicate LGBT inclusion in athletics.

High school, it seems, can be a particularly challenging atmosphere for LGBT individuals, athletes included. Groupthink mentality among peers is oftentimes prevalent at this time in a young person's life, and standing up for those who are being marginalized is not always easy. But in finding vocal allies, we can support not only LGBT athletes, but also the entire community. Coaches, staff, and administrators must assert themselves as fervent backers of allies and LGBT students alike to show that sexual orientation and gender identity have no bearing on a person's ability to participate in sports.

Moving forward, advocacy and education in the K-12 age group is one of the best ways we can sustain progress for the LGBT community in athletics. Coaches and physical education teachers, many of whom help to shape the way young boys and girls treat each other in some of their most important developmental years, hold an enormous amount of power and responsibility. While many states are passing laws requiring youth educators to be trained about the importance of LGBT respect and inclusion, many part-time youth coaches still remain absent from this training. As a result, youth educators and coaches who need the training the most are still receiving it the least. If we are to truly change the sports climate for LGBT youth, we need to decipher the best ways to start educating and empowering these individuals as allies of the LGBT community.

Athlete Ally is a 501(c)(3) tax-exempt nonprofit organization focused on ending homophobia and transphobia in sports by educating allies in the athletic community and empowering them to take a stand. We recruit ambassadors in youth, collegiate, professional, and international sports who work to foster "allyship" in their athletic environments. Athlete Ally also provides public awareness campaigns, educational programming, and tools and resources to foster inclusive sports communities.

- Athlete Ally implements LGBT awareness and ally training and workshops at scores of colleges and high schools. Its programs often include meetings with athletic directors and staff and keynotes to groups ranging from entire student bodies to individual teams.

- Athlete Ally is a close partner of the National Basketball Association (NBA) and National Basketball Players' Association (NBPA) on player development and LGBT inclusion. Building on these partnerships, Athlete Ally delivers trainings at the NBA Pre-Draft Information Program, at the NBA/NBPA Annual Rookie Transition Program, and at workshops for Team Player Development Directors. It also produces training materials for these programs.

- Athlete Ally is a partner of the National Football League (NFL) Player's Association, and the two came together to support Pride in 2013 with shirts honoring some of the most vocal supporters of LGBT inclusion in the NFL.

- Founder and Executive Director Hudson Taylor worked with Pat Griffin to author the National Collegiate Athletic Association's (NCAA) first-ever handbook for college athletes, coaches and administrators on LGBTQ policies and best practices.

- Athlete Ally works with the NFL on player awareness and sensitivity on LBGT issues.
- Athlete Ally is a partner of the Yogi Berra Museum and Learning Center, where it supports a groundbreaking museum exhibit on allies in sports and builds educational programs for youth athletes, coaches and parents.

As you can see, there is a great deal of progress being made. With notable celebrities and athletes coming out to support LGBT rights, we come further and further with every new ambassador or league who pledges support.

With all this said, it is also important to look at the personal stories of athletes who have been able to make the most of their situations, and I happen to be able to say that I am one of those stories.

The following is an adaptation of a piece I wrote for the leading gay sports news source, OutSports.com.

I came out to two of my best friends on one most storied days of revelry at Saint Michael's College. P-Day at Saint Mike's is our answer to the traditional "Spring Weekend" before finals. It feels like a big music video shoot for one of those bands with a starlet of the moment's brother in it. Picture a lot of sweaty, boozed-up kids running around eating, drinking, and being merry in a way only the last party weekend of the year can inspire.

It was the end of my freshman year, and I finally figured it was time to tell my friends what most of them already knew. At last I'd worked up the courage to say it. Of course, there were a lot of tears and hugs, and one very well timed spin of that classic record "It's Raining Men" by a local radio station that I swear must have been listening to the conversation I was having. All the love and acceptance I received felt pretty nice, and as SMC is a very small community, the news gradually disseminated itself through my friends and acquaintances alike.

And it was fine. Even the friends I had worried about telling were respectful and kind. My best friend Amanda was a little disappointed, simply for the fact she had always thought I would come around and realize we were meant to be together, and that we would live happily ever after. She and I are still together in the sense that we are the closets of friends, there are just no delusions of marriage any more, at least on my part.

Telling my parents was difficult, but for the best, and today my relationship grows stronger all the time. I am from a very small town in Western Massachusetts called Ware, and it is fair to say that four-wheelin' and puttin'-down Bud heavies in the back of your pickup are the sort of activity that seem to define my generation's idea of a good time there. I would not exactly call Ware's climate "LGBT-friendly," though there are many accepting, loving people there. And even though my parents were born in "The Town That Can't Be Licked," (something about a flood in the 1920s) they are intelligent, loving people and have never given me anything but support.

For as long as I can remember I have known I was gay. I was also acutely conscious that this was not "ok," and that I needed to hide it. I could not even conceptualize the idea of coming out until college. I played soccer, basketball, and tennis growing up, and though I never was bullied in the way many LGBT youth are, I was always keenly aware that people were saying things about me behind my back. This certainly affected my confidence, but I was lucky enough to have a fantastic group of friends around me that were always there for support.

My experience as a gay athlete was overwhelmingly positive, especially during my final two seasons as a tennis player for SMC. The guys from the team remain some of my best friends today, and I am very thankful for this fact.

During my senior year, I was then lucky enough to be involved in a project at Saint Mike's as a part of the "It Gets Better" campaign that involved a lot of students, athletes, and administrators rallying around the cause. Though I'm sure there were and are other gay athletes at SMC, I did not happen to know any of them personally. I did not know any other gay athletes around the Northeast-10 Conference either, but I personally never experienced any negativity around the subject. It was one of the most rewarding activities I have ever been a part of, and I feel very lucky to have had my voice heard at SMC.

From there, I went on to begin interning for Athlete Ally, and today have worked my way up to the nonprofit's Program Coordinator. I feel right where I need to be, working for a cause I believe in with some of the LGBT space's most influential voices.

Brian Healey is program coordinator for Athlete Ally. If you ever need advice, or someone to speak with, contact me at brian.healey @athleteally.org.

Bi Youth Need Validation, Not Disbelief: Ellyn Ruthstrom

There is a common perception that the younger generation is much more accepting of sexual diversity than older generations, and there is a lot of evidence to back up that belief. Unfortunately, it doesn't always correspond to acceptance or understanding of bisexuality. As a member of the Massachusetts Commission on LGBT Youth for two years, I toured the state listening to youth in various communities—urban, rural, and suburban; middle and working class; youth of color and white—and I often heard bi youth express not only the usual problems about coming out to friends and family, but they also described peer pressure, sometimes even within their own Gay-Straight Alliance, to make a choice to be all-the-way gay. These experiences said for me that there is still much more to be done to broaden our understanding of the sexuality spectrum.

An important part of discussing sexuality and sexual orientation is to step away from the false binary concept of gay and straight. Learning about a continuum of sexual identity and experience at this formative stage of life is crucial so that later on we'll have adults who won't put everything into defined gay/straight boxes. Far too many of us don't fit into them, and far too often our existence is therefore denied rather than the mainstream ideas shifting to allow our inclusion.

Sadly, many youth who come out as bi are confronted with disbelief instead of validation. The claims made by noted gay adults like Dan Savage filter down to them. Savage has said things like, "When I meet a bisexual teenage boy ... I sometimes think to myself, 'Yeah, I was too at your age.'" This attitude clearly throws doubt on every teen, especially boys, about their ability to know and define their own feelings. In an episode of *Glee*, Kurt's first boyfriend, Blaine, questioned whether he was gay or bi after kissing Rachel at a drinking party. Kurt said to him, "Bisexual is a term that gay guys in high school use when they want to hold hands with girls and feel like a normal person for a change." Such comments voiced within positive gay media channels continue to endorse the wrongful supposition that bisexuals do not exist. Imagine what that feels like to teens who are coming to terms with their bisexual attraction.

I would never assert that every person who comes out as bisexual will always identify that way for the rest of his or her life. In fact, I've seen many people change the way they identify at different times of their lives. Even though a popular slogan of our community is "I was born that way," for many figuring out one's sexuality is much more complicated than that. Asserting a sexual determinism and absolutism may work politically (or not), but it doesn't always represent people's lived experience. Just in my own life, I thought I was straight until I was in college. All of my early attractions were for boys, so I didn't give it another thought. Surprise! And it was, believe me.

Some youth are not certain about how they want to define their identity and feel the bi label best captures an ambiguity that will later become more defined. And that's fine. I've known plenty of people who initially identified as gay or lesbian because their first relationship (or more than one) happened to be with someone of the same sex but later on fell for someone of another sex and realized that their sexuality was broader than what they had expected.

When you facilitate a bi support group or two, like I have, you learn that there is no one path to bisexuality, and many people experience fluidity at different points in their lives. Researcher Lisa Diamond points out in her book *Sexual Fluidity: Understanding Women's Love and Desire* that her own study as well as others have found it quite common for people's sexual attraction to change over time, even as adults. This pattern is more common for women on the whole, but it still happens for men as well. Diamond writes, "We simply need to shift from treating these orientations as rigidly fixed to viewing them as multidimensional and dynamic."

I think those terms really sum it up: multidimensional and dynamic! Wouldn't it be wonderful if we could capture that in our cultural understanding of sexuality! If that were true we would no longer have bi-erasure and biphobia.

Bi Youth Resources

One of the best books for someone who is wondering whether they are bisexual is *Getting Bi: Voices of Bisexuals around the World* (Robyn Ochs and Sarah Rowley, eds., 2nd ed. Boston: Bisexual Resource Center, 2009). Over 200 individual perspectives are shared that show how many different ways people define their bisexuality.

BiYouth.org is a site sponsored by the Bisexual Resource Center and has several pages of information and resources.

One of my favorites is the page called Quotes from Bi Youth, which has teens speaking honestly to other teens about how to feel comfortable about being bi, or really about being yourself. There is also a page called For Parents where a father talks through different issues that might arise when a child comes out as bisexual.

As the former editor in chief of *Teen Voices* magazine—a now-defunct print and online publication written by, for, and about teen girls—I am familiar with a lot of resources for teens. One of the best teen sexuality websites out there is Scarleteen.com. Their approach is supportive and accepting and gives voice to a wide range of teen perspectives. They have great content about bisexuality, this piece being one of the best to get a lot of the basic information out on the table: http://www.scarleteen.com/article/gaydar/bi_the_dozen_a_bisexuality_quiz.

And now for just a few final (and, I hope, not too cheesy) words of encouragement if you are a bi-identified youth:

- Accept and love yourself. You are fine the way you are.
- Find other people who accept and understand you. This makes all the difference!
- Life is unfolding—you will figure out what you need to as and when you need to.
- Don't listen to those who say you have to choose either a gay or straight identity. Rather, choose to be true to yourself and know that there are plenty of others who do not fit into the binary categories.

Ellyn Ruthstrom is the administrative director of the Bisexual Resource Center (BRC), the oldest national bi organization in the United States. Ellyn speaks at colleges, national conferences, and public forums about bisexuality and the bi movement. In 2012, Ellyn co-facilitated the first Bisexual Leadership Roundtable at Creating Change in Atlanta. Ellyn is also a writer and editor and has published in a variety of print and online publications, including the Women's Review of Books, The Review Review, Huffington Post, *and* Bilerico.com.

You're Not Straight and You're Not Gay: What's Up?: Jack Scott

When asked to contribute to this book, I jumped at the chance to participate in a project so important to me. I came of age when help with such issues was difficult, if not impossible, to find. Much has changed for GLBT people. The struggle for equal rights and protections under the law is essentially over for gays and lesbians. There is still work to be done, obviously; but the battle is won. Only the staunchest religious troglodytes still hold to past ignorance.

Unfortunately, for bisexuals and transgendered persons, the struggle continues. Because many straight men find bisexual women erotic, bisexual women are somewhat accepted. The story is different for bisexual men. A large segment of the population, including many gay men, don't think there is such thing as bisexual men. They see such men as simply unwilling to admit they are gay. They feel these so-called bisexual men are using their ability to pass for straight to avoid the struggles other gay men endure.

At age 10, I knew I was different from other boys. A few years later, I knew I was not straight. At age 16, I knew for sure I was not gay because I had a steady girlfriend; and I enjoyed straight sex very much. That begged the question, "What am I?" It took more years to figure out I am a bisexual man. I know it may sound strange, but in my early adult years, I'd never even heard the word "bisexual."

At 19, I married my girlfriend. From the beginning, our sex life was awesome. I assumed the years of sexual relationships with males was an adolescent thing, to be forgotten in the glow of satisfying and frequent sex with my wife; and it was, in the light of day. At night, things were different. In spite of the straight sex, now a part of my life, I often dreamed of same sex experiences, sometimes to the point of nocturnal emission. These dreams, and the physical results, disturbed me. I couldn't understand how I was so much in love with my wife, so drawn to straight sex, and yet would dream of male/male sex.

There seemed no satisfactory answers to my questions. Was I simply a monster? I felt no one would understand me if they knew my thoughts and fantasies. There seemed nowhere to turn for help or understanding.

I might have considered suicide at this point in my life; but the fact was, I was very happy in the straight side of my life. I had a loving and supportive spouse. By age 22, I had a family I loved as well. I had a great job that was challenging and important. I had it all, except for a basic understanding of the monstrous part of me I couldn't shake loose.

I was in my early thirties (the early 1970s) when I first came across an article about bisexuality. It was a transforming revelation for me. It was the first time in years that I thought, "Perhaps, I am not a monster after all."

I began searching for anything I could find about bisexuality. It's probably hard for those who have never known a time when "google" wasn't understood as a verb to realize, but it was difficult to find reading material on bisexuality in small-town libraries in Texas. The more I found and read, the more convinced I became of my own bisexuality.

Glad to still be a part of the human race, I was nevertheless scared. Where did I go from there? In the early 1990s I made the difficult decision to explore male/male sexuality as an adult, something I had not done since my marriage. I was lucky to come across a new friend who was also married. We began a friendship that has evolved and changed over the past 20 years. It was a turning point in our lives. It is much too long a story for the space I have here. Suffice it to say, he determined through our relationship that, in spite of his 25 years of marriage and three children, he was a homosexual man. I determined, in spite of my ability to be sexually attracted to men and to him, I was not homosexual. I had no desire to leave my spouse for a man. I wanted to be with her.

Bisexuals still have a difficult road today. They are often thought of as selfish, shallow, and untrustworthy. Gay men see them as gays afraid to come out of the closet. A bisexual man who comes out to his spouse after they are married often sacrifices the spouse's trust, if not marriage and family as well.

Fortunately, young contemporary bisexuals have often already acknowledged their bisexuality. That gives them opportunity, from the beginning, to be honest with those with whom they hope to build a relationship. True, not every potential spouse will want to chance a relationship with a bisexual spouse, but many will. Ground rules can be agreed upon early in the commitment. The relationship can be closed or open, with conditions agreed to by both spouses.

My experience convinces me that the path to happiness always lies in commitment to a monogamous relationship with a special person with whom one spends a lifetime. There is so much to gain from such a relationship. There is so much to loose in a life of anonymous sexual hookups with first one and then another and another person of both sexes. Even when spouses agree to such an arrangement, the losses still accrue.

At the same time, sex is much too important to leave to chance. I lucked out by finding the spouse who would stand by me at a very early age. For young bisexuals today, I think it is important to experiment with both sexes to determine where they will likely find lifetime happiness and fulfillment before any commitment is made. Only then can one make informed choices about a life partner, be the partner male or female.

In a monogamous relationship, one can still enjoy "eye candy." Just as a straight person who wishes to maintain a commitment to a spouse often looks at other persons of the opposite sex but doesn't touch, a bisexual person can maintain a spousal commitment while enjoying eye candy on both sides of the gender divide.

I have come to believe I was born bisexual for a purpose. My bisexuality brought friends into my life I would otherwise never have known. It has given me the opportunity to share the self-acceptance and peace I strived for over many years with other gay and bisexual people. Through thoughtful introspection and wise decision making, the same can be true for young bisexuals today.

Jack Scott is a retired public health professional who has blogged about sexuality for eight years. With the help of his spouse, who is a psychotherapist and private counselor, he has spent many years helping married gay and bisexual men reconcile their lives with their sexuality.

Survival Sex among Homeless LGBT Youth: Noelle Swan

For many LGBT-identified young people, home is not an option. According to a 2013 study conducted by the Williams Institute, 40 percent of homeless youth identify as lesbian, gay, bisexual, or transgender. With no means of filling basic needs, many young homeless LGBT individuals turn to sex for survival.

One young man who goes by the name Yoyo said in an interview that his parents kicked him out at the age of 14 for coming out as gay. A year later, he started turning tricks. He connected with clients at clubs and brought them back to a hotel room that he had rented. He was able to make more than enough cash to pay the hotel bill and still turn a profit. At first, it seemed like easy money.

"Being kicked out at 14, all I wanted was affection from someone ... I wasn't getting it from my own family, but I could get all the affection and love that I wanted from every client that I saw," he says. Soon, however, a different reality set in, one in which he was constantly looking over his shoulder for the police, and he started asking a friend to hide in the closet of his hotel room in case a client became violent.

Now 27, Yoyo talks about his time in "the life" from the comfort of an armchair at Boston Gay and Lesbian Adolescent Social Services (GLASS), where he mentors other young men who have been victims of sexual exploitation through the one-year-old program Surviving Our Struggle (SOS). Yoyo helps his mentees process their experiences on the streets and shares his own experiences with them.

Formal prostitution is just one way in which homeless LGBT youth turn to sex for survival. "When we talk about survival sex, we talk about actual prostitution, which is exchanging sex for money, but then there is also exchanging sex for a place to stay. Or we may have people staying with partners who are abusive, but they continue to stay with them because they have nowhere else to go," says Ayala Livny, a program manager for Youth on Fire (YOF), a drop-in day shelter for homeless and at-risk youth in Cambridge, Massachusetts.

During intake interviews, Livny and the staff at YOF ask all youth entering the shelter if they have exchanged sex for drugs, money, or a place to stay. Livny estimates that roughly 20 percent of the 550 youth who seek services at YOF each year disclose that they have employed some form of survival sex. "We see it not just with queer identified youth . . . but we see it most with the folks that are most marginalized," Livny says.

Unaccompanied youth exist on the fringes of society. Minors tend to avoid services entirely because providers are required by law to report them as runaways, Livny said.

Once they turn 18, these youth can theoretically access adult services, but emergency shelters can be dangerous places for young people. Other shelter guests may be intoxicated, have a mental illness, or be violent, and they may see young people as easy targets, she said. Services that specifically cater to young adults are limited.

New York City is often cited by social service providers as having one of the most robust networks for addressing youth homelessness. "The resources rival anywhere else in the country for serving homeless youth; however, the reality is that the services don't even come close to meeting the needs of the population," says Sassafras Lowrey, a Brooklyn-based author and educator who has worked with LGBT homeless youth since she was kicked out of her own family home when she was 17 years old. "There are 250 shelter beds in New York City, with an estimated 3,800 homeless youth on the streets on any given night," she said.

A decade after becoming homeless herself, Lowrey compiled, edited, and published *Kicked Out*, an anthology of stories of LGBT individuals who, like herself and Yoyo, were rejected by their family as young people for their sexual orientation. Several of the contributors revealed that they had resorted to some form of survival sex.

"Sex work, as well as survival sex, is not new . . . and it's naïve of advocates or service providers to think that they will leave sex work if they are lucky enough to make it off a waitlist into a shelter bed," she says.

While young people in general tend to avoid shelters, LGBT young people face additional concerns of discrimination and mistreatment, says Jessica Flaherty, the director of programs at the Boston Alliance for Gay Lesbian Bisexual and Transgender Youth (BAGLY). Many LGBT youths choose to take their chances on the street rather than endure homophobic slurs that frequently escalate into violence, she said.

Once on the street, the promise of a warm and dry bed for the night in exchange for having sex with a stranger can be tempting, despite the added risks. "People are going to make the choices that are going to keep them alive for the night and worry about the rest of their lives later," Flaherty said.

Around the country, the most successful youth programs seek to help youth minimize those risks rather than focusing on getting kids to change their behavior, Lowrey said. At YOF and SOS, outreach staff encourages youth to consider and take steps to minimize their risk.

At YOF, Livny asks young people how they plan to avoid assault, makes sure they have access to condoms and prophylactic treatments, and connects them to health services.

At SOS, Yoyo can administer STD [sexually transmitted disease] and HIV tests onsite and frequently accompanies mentees to doctor appointments for support. These efforts help to reduce but cannot eliminate the risks associated with survival sex.

"These kids need better options for meeting their basic needs," says Stephen Procopio, project coordinator for SOS. "No one wakes up in the morning and says, 'I want to be an escort.' Life circumstances bring [young people] to this life," Procopio says.

In an effort to help clients take control of some of those circumstances, outreach workers at places such as YOF and SOS connect youth with a variety of services, including help finding jobs, applying to schools, and applying for housing. However, those processes take time and patience. In the meantime, LGBT young people will continue to get by as best they can.

Noelle Swan is a freelance journalist based in Boston. She covers science, health, social services, and parenting. She has written for The *Christian Science Monitor,* Science *magazine, and National Public Radio affiliates.*

The Road to Transitioning: Danielle White

We thought we had a good idea when we offered my two year old, "Pee in the potty and we'll buy you underwear like Daddy wears," but the response was, "No thanks, I prefer pantyhose."

—Mom, circa 1976, about me

As a transgender individual who was assigned male at birth and identified as female, that statement was my first known expression of my gender identity, but it was far from my last. I grew up in Rural/Small town USA in Pennsylvania. It was an area that was conservative in about every sense of the word, particularly politically, religiously, and socially. It was a region that wasn't great for an LGBT individual.

As I grew up, I was aware that something wasn't right, but I lacked the language to describe it. That I was a girl informed so many of my thoughts, including my dreams. I learned that there are pink words and blue hobbies. I learned to play that role to survive.

In the early 1990s I began attending a small junior college in the same area. During lunch one day a group of students had a then-popular daytime talk show on in the lounge, and the topic was transsexuals. The show's treatment of the subject was abysmal, but the positive for me was that I finally had a word to describe who I was; I gained the start of having a vocabulary.

I graduated from that college and went on to another institution that had a slightly more expansive library and two books in their collection about the topic. One was a doctor's description of treating multiple trans patients. Written in the 1960s, its language and the treatment described left much to be desired, but it gave me the powerful notion that transition was possible.

After college, I decided to try to transition and began by seeing a therapist in my hometown. I had no idea that one needed to see a specialized therapist for this, and I paid for that mistake. My transition was effectively delayed for just over a decade, during which time I found a career in information technology (IT) and married. Still, I knew that I was a woman, if in the proverbial "sheep's clothing" of a man, and I was lesbian.

Finally, in 2008 after having moved to central North Carolina, I tried again. This attempt was vastly more successful but not without its troubles. I faced a lot of classic gatekeeping—the patriarchal approach of medical and mental health professionals toward transitioners in which the professionals set themselves up as absolute authorities on trans lives. My transition proceeded along an extremely slow path: more than a year to have estradiol prescribed, an additional nine months for an antiandrogen to be added, and years further to reach an effective dose, defined as one which would feminize my body.

There exists a concept of agency that an individual has, defined as the capacity for an individual to exert power in his or her life. In the context of transition, that power is heavily dependent on the providers' permission. The providers who treated me were not generally willing to permit me that power. My transition was heavily at their direction and not mine.

The most powerful effect of hormone replacement therapy (HRT) was emotional. I began to feel whole and complete as a person; not as though there was a chasm between my mind and body. Gradually, that chasm was bridged.

As I finally effected transition in my thirties, I was employed full-time and was working for what was likely one of the most accepting employers in the region: a certain large public university. In 2011 I was able to transition at work. It was an awkward proposition, reading a prepared statement to my coworkers to tell them that as of the next Monday I would be Danielle at work and would use female pronouns, and then the months of coworkers stumbling to get my name and pronouns correct and my trying to give them credit for trying.

The task of dealing with that awkward time was made easier due to the privilege I enjoy. I planned to leave that employer after transition was complete, and opportunity knocked four months later. In that time the U.S. government changed the policy about employment verification, which meant I did not have to worry about gender not matching letters anymore when a new employer verified my eligibility for employment in the United States. I was already feeling a sense of relief from that announcement when a recruiter for my present employer contacted me. Multiple interviews and a month later I had an offer and became an employee of a well-regarded software company a month after that. The benefit for me was being able to leave the history of my transition behind; I could simply be Danielle in that professional environment. This allowed me to define myself as an individual woman and not be constrained by others' ideas of what I am as a transgender woman.

With that came being a woman in technology. The part of the IT industry in which I work is heavily male dominated, and I experienced the sexism that comes with being a woman who is a new employee in such an environment, needing to prove my technical capability far beyond my male coworkers' to have my competence accepted. Call it a career in two genders—I definitely see that I had a much easier professional time when presenting as male than as female.

In the late spring of 2013, I traveled to Montreal, Canada, and had genital reassignment surgery (GRS). As far as work was concerned, I was out for an unknown medical absence. The rumor began as pregnancy and ended with hysterectomy. GRS brought me closer to a sense of being whole and complete as a person.

As I write this, in the summer of 2013, my transition draws to a close. I am planning facial feminization surgery (FFS) and breast augmentation for the summer of 2014. Generally, transition is becoming a closed chapter of my life. My marriage remains strong, and we join a small sorority of couples whose marriage survived transition. It's time to find my happily ever after.

Danielle White writes about transgender issues.

Introduction

This chapter focuses on individuals and organizations who have been and/or are active in the field of LGBT youth. The names included here are only a sample of the untold number of individuals and organizations involved in this field over the past half-century or more.

Advocates for Youth

2000 M St., NW, Suite 750
Washington, DC 20036
Phone: (202) 419-3420
Fax: (202) 419-1448
URL: http://www.advocatesforyouth.org/index.php

Advocates for Youth was formed in 1980 as the Center for Population Options. It was created for the purpose of advocating on behalf of adolescent reproductive and sexual health. Subsumed within that general role are activities designed to improve education on sexual issues for and about adolescents, working to prevent HIV/AIDS and other sexually transmitted

Members of Parents, Families & Friends of Lesbians and Gays (PFLAG) march with their signs in the St. Louis PrideFest 2005 Parade in 2005. (AP Photo/James A. Finley)

infections, preventing pregnancy among teenage girls, improving access to condoms and other contraceptive devices and techniques among adolescents, achieving equality among all adolescence in the whole range of health and medical issues, and expanding participation by youth in such fields.

Some of the highlights in its history cited by the organization are the development in 1983 of a Life Planning Education program, which includes units on sexuality, relationships, health, violence prevention, and community responsibility, a program that is still available in a revised and updated format; pioneering efforts to increase awareness of and provide programs for dealing with HIV/AIDS infection among teenagers; co-sponsoring the First Inter-Africa Conference on Adolescent Reproductive Health in 1992; establishing the first Internet intervention for LGBT youth, www.youthresource.com, and its Spanish-language sister site, www.ambientejoven.com; and creating the first online website for youth activism and youth-led grassroots movement building in the United States and around the world.

A key focus of Advocates for Youth activities and programs is the so-called Three R's approach. The three R's stand for the **R**ights that youth have to accurate and complete sexual health information, confidential reproductive and sexual health services, and a secure stake in the future; the **R**espect youth deserve that entitles them to be involved in decision making and participation in policies and practices involving their own health; and the **R**esponsibility that society has to provide young people with the knowledge and skills the properly care for their own reproductive and sexual health.

Advocates for Youth programs and activities are organized around about two dozen major themes that include abstinence, abstinence only until marriage, abortion, adolescent sexual behavior, condom efficacy and use, contraceptive information and access, cultural competency, developmental and intellectual disabilities, emergency contraception, European approaches, GLBTQ issues, growth and development, HIV/AIDS, Millennials, organizational development, parent-child communication, policy and advocacy, religion and spirituality, sex education, sexually transmitted infections, teen pregnancy prevention, violence and harassment, working with youth, youth in low- and middle-income countries, and youth of color.

The GLBTQ focus includes a wide range of activities that includes an overview of issues faced by LGBTQ young adults, resources for professionals who deal with LGBTQ youth, information for parents of LGBTQ youth, domestic and international policy issues regarding LGBTQ youth, and publications about and for LGBTQ youth. The publications list includes a number of pamphlets, fact sheets, brochures, and other print and electronic products on a variety of topics, such as "Creating Safe Space for GLBTQ Youth: A Toolkit;" "HIV/STD Prevention and Young Men Who Have Sex with Men;" "I Think I Might Be Bisexual, Now What Do I Do?;" "I Think I Might Be Gay, Now What Do I Do?;" "I Think I Might Be Lesbian, Now What Do I Do?;" "I Think I Might Be Transgender, Now What Do I Do?;" "The Impact of Homophobia and Racism on GLBTQ Youth of Color;" "Tips and Strategies for Addressing Harassment;" "Working with GLBTQ Youth;" "Young Men Who Have Sex with Men: At Risk for HIV and STDs;" and "Young Women Who Have Sex with Women: Falling through Cracks for Sexual Health Care."

Alliance School of Milwaukee

See Harvey Milk High School

American Civil Liberties Union

125 Broad St., 18th Floor
New York, NY 10004-2400
Phone: (212) 549-2500
Email: infoaclu@aclu.org
URL: http://www.aclu.org/

The American Civil Liberties Union (ACLU) was founded in 1920 in response to actions by then attorney general Mitchell Palmer, who ordered raids on a number of political activists whose views he deemed to be dangerous to the United States. Over the past century, the ACLU has been involved in most of the important civil rights issues in the nation, including the battle over the Scopes Trial of 1925 dealing with the teaching of evolution in public schools, the internment of Japanese American citizens by President Franklin D. Roosevelt at the beginning of World War II, the controversy over a parade of Nazi Party supporters in Skokie, Illinois, in 1978, and disputes over the adoption and enforcement of the Patriot Act after the destruction of the Twin Towers in New York City in 2001. The organization has grown to a membership of more than 500,000 with about 200 staff attorneys and hundreds more volunteer attorneys around the nation.

The ACLU organizes its work around about a dozen major themes, including the Bill of Rights and other Constitutional rights, racial justice, the rights of women, civil liberties in a time of national crisis, freedom of and from religion, and GLBT and related rights. The main focus of ACLU's work on behalf of LGBT youth is its LGBT Youth & Schools project, whose primary objective is to defend the free speech rights of LGBT youth in their schools and communities and to support their right to organize gay-straight alliances in schools and colleges. An ongoing part of the Youth & Schools project has been the legal support provided by the ACLU in a number of court cases involving the rights or LGBT students, usually with regard to their right to form gay/straight clubs. Some of those cases have been *PFLAG v. Camdenton R-III School District*, *Sturgis v. Copiah County School District*, *Franks v. Metropolitan Board of Public Education*, *Gillman v. Holmes County School District*, *Morrison v. Boyd Co. Board of Education*, and *Gonzalez v. School Board of Okeechobee County*.

In August 2011, the ACLU published its report *Don't Filter Me* on efforts by antigay and lesbian groups to prevent teenagers from accessing websites that contain positive LGBT messages, such as the website of the Gay, Lesbian and Straight Educators Network. The organization also makes available reports and informational sections on topics such as discrimination in schools ("What's Your Problem?"); resources and links on GLBT issues as well as steps that can be taken to improve the school environment for GLBT youth ("Change Your School"); assistance for LGBT youth experiencing harassment, bullying, or other negative experiences in their schools ("Get Help"); information on the legal rights of LGBT students ("Know Your Rights! A Quick Guide for LGBT High School Students"); and information on the federal student nondiscrimination act.

Harry Benjamin (1885–1986)

Benjamin was a German-born American endocrinologist and sexologist who became one of the world's first and best-known experts on the topic of transgenderism and transsexualism. He first became interested in the topic in about 1948 when Albert Kinsey, probably the world's most famous expert on human sexuality at the time, asked him to meet with a young man aged 23, "Barry," who had expressed a desire to become a female. Benjamin was moved by the young man's mother, who reportedly told him, "Look at this boy, he's not a boy! You've got to do something to help my son be a girl!" A medical challenge of this kind was virtually unheard of at the time, when even wearing the clothing of the opposite sex could be considered a crime in some parts of the United States. So Benjamin decided to send the young man to Germany to have the genital surgery that would accomplish his objectives.

"Barry" turned out to be only the first of several hundred men and women who appeared before Benjamin with similar histories and similar complaints. As he slowly learned more about the medical and emotional issues involved, Benjamin became one of the first medical workers to care about and be willing to act on sex change procedures. In 1966, Benjamin published the first comprehensive treatment of the topic in his book *The Transsexual Phenomenon*. That book brought him fame both in the United States and worldwide, drawing him a host of new patients seeking sex change procedures. Benjamin even developed a theory to explain the phenomenon of trans-sexualism, a theory based on the assumption that on rare occasions, the human brain develops abnormally prior to birth in some individuals, resulting in babies whose reproductive and sexual physiology is clearly of one sex but whose brain function is characteristic of the opposite sex. That theory achieved some popularity for a while (as it has to a limited extent today) and is known as Harry Benjamin syndrome (HBS).

Harry Benjamin was born in Berlin on January 12, 1885, into a wealthy family that had converted from Judaism to Lutheranism, the religion in which Harry was raised. He originally attended the Königliches Wilhelm Gymnasium but transferred to another school at the age of 15, purportedly because his classmates could not figure out whether he was Jewish, so he was harassed from both sides of the religious divide. He decided early in life to pursue a medical career and received his MD from the University of Tübingen in 1912, with a dissertation on tuberculosis. At that point, he had had some moderate introduction to sexual issues, primarily as a result of reading the Swiss sexologist Auguste-Henri Forel's new book, *Die sexuelle Frage. Eine naturwissenschaftliche, psychologische, hygienische und soziologische Studie für Gebildete* (The Sexual Question: A Scientific, Psychological, Hygienic and Sociological Study for the Educated). After receiving his medical degree, however, he pursued a very traditional career, specializing in the study and treatment of tuberculosis.

Benjamin's life underwent a dramatic change in 1914, when he booked passage on the German passenger ship SS *Kronprinzessin Cecilie* for a return trip from New York City to Germany. The ship was intercepted in the middle of the

Atlantic by a British ship, and Benjamin was offered the option of being sent to Great Britain, where he would be interned at a prison camp, or returning to New York City. Not surprisingly, Benjamin chose the United States, where he eventually spent the rest of his life. He worked most of his life in New York City but spent many summers in San Francisco. In addition to his primary work on transsexualism, Benjamin was also interested in extension of life issues. He lived to the age of 101, dying in New York City on August 24, 1986. At the time, he had been married to his childhood girlfriend, Gretchen, for 60 years. In 1979, a group of researchers interested in the subject of transsexualism founded an organization for the study of that field, which they named the Harry Benjamin International Gender Dysphoria Association. The organization changed its name in 2006 to the World Professional Association for Transgender Health.

Bisexual Resource Center

PO Box 170796
Boston, MA 02117
Phone: (617) 424-9595
Email: brc@biresource.net
URL: http://www.biresource.net/

The vast majority of organizations providing services for gay and lesbian youth today also extend their services to bisexuals and transgendered people. In many cases, questioning, queer, and intersex individuals may also be included in an organization's mission. A relatively small number of organizations focus specifically and primarily on the needs and interests of bisexuals, perhaps the oldest and best known in the United States being the Bisexual Resource Center (BRC). BRC has its roots in two bisexual organizations founded in Boston in 1983 (the Boston Bisexual Women's Network) and 1984 (the Boston Men's Bisexual Network). The BRC itself actually had its origins in a broader movement, the East Coast Bisexual Network (ECBN), which held its first meeting in 1985.

The bisexual movement has a much older history, however, dating to the earliest years of the gay liberation movement with the formation of the National Bisexual Liberation Group (NBLG) in 1972. At its peak, NBLG had at least 5,500 dues-paying members. Other bisexual groups also formed during the 1970s in cities such as San Francisco (the San Francisco Bisexual Center), Minneapolis (One to Five and Bi Women Welcome), Detroit (Bi Married Men's Group), and Chicago (Bi Ways). One of the reasons the Bisexual Resource Center was formed was to provide a mechanism by which bisexual groups in the United States and other parts of the world could connect with each other and share resources, an objective that still informs many of the present-day organization's programs and activities.

One of BRC's major areas of concern is outreach to bisexual adolescents. The organization's message is that a person's sexuality is often in flux. It uses terms such as *queer, pansexual, heteroflexible, omnisexual* and *fluid* to describe the range of sexual feelings a person may legitimately have. BRC encourages young adults to recognize that bisexuality is one of many possible forms of a person's sexuality, that there is no reason to be ashamed or not admit that one is bisexual, and that bisexuality is not necessarily (or even usually) a "phase" through which one goes before achieving her or his "real" sexuality. The organization offers information and support on issues with which bisexual youth may have to deal, such as coming out as a bisexual, understanding what bisexuality means, learning to talk about bisexuality, and dealing with one's bisexuality with one's parents.

BRC sponsors activities for bisexuals in the Boston area and provides news about bisexual activities at other organizations throughout the United States and countries around the world. It also provides links to other bisexual groups in the United States, such as AMBI Los Angeles, the American Institute of

Bisexuality, the Bisexual Organizing Project in Minneapolis, Bisexuals United (Corpus Christi, Texas), Dallas/Fort Worth BiNet, and the Seattle Bisexual Women's Network, as well as bisexual organizations in Australia, Canada, Denmark, England, France, Germany, Israel, and Scotland.

Campus Pride, Inc.

PO Box 240473
Charlotte, NC 28224
URL: http://www.campuspride.org/

Campus Price, Inc., is a 501(c)3 nonprofit organization whose mission it is to work with local campus groups and student leaders to create safer college and university campuses for LGBT students in the United States. The organization was conceived of in the fall of 2001 by M. Chad Wilson, Sarah E. Holmes, and Shane L. Windmeyer, who now serves as its executive director. Initially operating under the name Campus PrideNet, the organization began functioning in October 2002. It soon formed important partnerships with two other organizations with similar objectives, the Lambda 10 Project National Clearinghouse for LGBT Fraternity & Sorority Issues and the Stop the Hate! National Bias and Hate Crime Prevention Program for colleges and universities.

In its first year of operation, Campus PrideNet developed and put into operation a national program of public service announcements and an educational campaign on issues of anti-gay hate and so-called internalized homophobia that aired on mtvU, a division of the Viacom MTV network. The announcements reached an estimated 5.5 million viewers on more than 700 campuses nationwide. The organization also began work on a new book, *Inspiration for LGBT Students & Their Allies*, co-sponsored with Collegiate Empowerment Company, Inc. In 2004, Campus PrideNet also developed the *Power of an Ally Action Guide* in cooperation with Kepplers On Campus, a group that provides educational and inspirational speakers for college and university campuses.

In 2005, the organization began work on what was to become one of its most popular publications, the *LGBT-Friendly Campus Climate Index*, which ranks more than 360 colleges and universities in eight categories and more than 50 self-assessment questions about an institution's "gay-friendliness." The eight categories are LGBT policy inclusion, support and institutional commitment, academic life, student life, housing, campus safety, counseling and health, and recruitment and retention efforts. Top-ranking institutions in 2012 ranged from smaller institutions such as the University of Maine at Farmington (with about 2,000 students) and Dartmouth College (with about 4,000 students), to large state universities such as The Ohio State University (with more than 50,000 students) and the University of Minnesota–Twin Cities (with more than 45,000 students).

In 2006, Campus PrideNet substantially increased its goals and programs and became incorporated as a nonprofit organization under its current name of Campus Pride, Inc. Over the years, it has absorbed or formed cooperative relationships with a variety of other organizations working for LGBT students at the college level, including Soulforce, an organization dedicated to changing the hearts and mind of religious leaders who are opposed to homosexuality (2006) and Stop the Hate Bias & Hate Crime Prevention program (2008). Campus Pride's current efforts are organized into 10 major categories: leadership and organizing, activism and advocacy, event planning and fundraising, trans advocacy, bias and hate crime prevention, fraternity and sorority life, athletics, historically black colleges and universities, religion and faith, and health and wellness. Examples of some of the specific activities that fall within these general categories are the Deaf Queer Men Only Gathering; the Northeast Two Spirit Conference; IGNITE, a conference for queer and trans youth of color; an Out for Undergraduate Business conference; a number of regional Campus Pride LGBT-Friendly College

Fairs; a conference on Translating Identity; and webinars on topics such as National Coming Out Day, How Campus Law Enforcement Can Create a Safe Place for LGBT Students and Staff, Strategies for Serving Trans Populations, and Creating a Bias Incident Response Team for Your Campus.

Campus Pride relies heavily on social media for getting the word out about its existence and activities. It also publishes regular news releases on important issues of the moment, such as protests at college campuses around the nation, meetings and other events of interest to college-age LGBT students, current legislative actions, and events and activities that are part of the 10-topic program mentioned earlier.

Diverse Harmony

1111 Harvard Ave.
Seattle, WA 98122
Phone: (206) 389-5858
Email: info@diverseharmony.org
URL: http://www.diverseharmony.org/

Diverse Harmony is thought to be the first gay-straight alliance youth chorus in the United States. It was established in 2002 in Seattle as a way of bringing together young men and women of both sexes, all genders, and all sexual orientations to make music. The group is a member of GALA Choruses (the Gay and Lesbian Association of Choruses) and was the first youth group to perform at a GALA Chorus Festival in 2004.

Diverse Harmony was founded by a high school music director, Rhonda Juliano, who realized that gay and lesbian youth with whom she came into contact often felt isolated and needed a place where they could be themselves and live a more normal life. As a lesbian and a mother herself, as well as a music teacher, Juliano felt that a chorus would be the perfect organization through which young women and men could join together regardless of differences that might exist among them.

The chorus currently consists of about three dozen young women and men between the ages of 13 and 22, some of whom have been with the organization since its founding and are now in college. In addition to being a pioneer LGBT youth musical group, Diverse Harmony has a number of other firsts to its credit. It opened the 2004 Seattle Gay Pride Week with a presentation of the choral piece *Let There Be Pride* along with the Seattle Women's Chorus. The group was also the first LGBT youth choir to perform at the Gay Games when they sang at Gay Games VII in Chicago in July 2006. In 2004, they released their first—and so far only—CD, *Our World* (produced by Queer Music Heritage). In 2008, Diverse Harmony participated in the production of an independent film, *Why We Sing*, which was screened at a number of LGBT film festivals and on PBS stations nationwide.

In 2007, Juliano was replaced as music director by Brent McGee, who has since been replaced by the current music director, Jared Brayton Bollenbacher. Examples of the concerts recently offered by the group are *Magical Thinking*, which included songs about the changes that occur as one passes through adolescence into adulthood; *Harmony vs. Dissonance*, which explored the positive and negative issues that youth deal with in their daily lives; *Human Nature*, which was dedicated to nature and to the ways in which individuals interpret their own emotional experiences; *Freak Show*, which examined both the public and private personas that all people have; and *Double Knots and Forget-Me-Nots*, which explored issues of acceptance and self-worth.

Family Acceptance Project

San Francisco State University
3004 16th St., #301
San Francisco, CA 94103
Email: fap@sfsu.edu
URL: http://familyproject.sfsu.edu/home

The Family Acceptance Project (FAP) was founded in 2002 by two faculty members at San Francisco State University (SFSU), Caitlin Ryan and Rafael Diaz. FAP operates under the aegis of the Marian Wright Edelman Institute at SFSU. The project was created to provide research-based educational materials and activities to help families understand and support their gay, lesbian, bisexual, and transgender children. FAP claims to be "the only community research, intervention, education and policy initiative that works to decrease major health and related risks for lesbian, gay, bisexual and transgender (LGBT) youth, such as suicide, substance abuse, HIV and homelessness—in the context of their families." The key to this objective is the emphasis on the role of the family in helping LGBT youth deal with the problems they face in their everyday lives.

One arm of the FAP program is an assessment of the current status of acceptance or rejection by families of their own LGBT youth, with an eye toward developing mechanisms by which this response can be more accepting. The program has also developed a community outreach arm in which parents, students, and community organizations work together to conduct the type of research needed to gain more information about the challenges faced by LGBT youth. Currently, the group's Community Research Council consists of staff and youth from the Berkeley and San Francisco school districts, the Good Samaritan Family Resource Center, Lavender Youth Recreation and Information Center, Stanford University, and the University of California at San Francisco Division of Adolescent Medicine, among other resources.

FAP also works with Child and Adolescent Services at San Francisco General Hospital to provide confidential family counseling and support services for families with LGBT youth or gender nonconforming children to help them deal with questions and issues that arise in their lives. Two of the organization's most important publications are a booklet, *Supportive Families, Health Children,* and a set of policy and practice guidelines, *Best Practice Guidelines for Serving LGBT Youth in*

Out-of-Home Care. The former publication has been endorsed by the American Foundation for Suicide Prevention as a best practices resource for parents and youth. In addition to these publications, FAP has produced a number of important research reports on physical, mental, emotional, and social issues faced by LGBT youth, including "School Bullying, Violence against LGBT Youth Linked with Suicide Risk, HIV & STDs in Young Adulthood" (*Journal of School Health*, 81(5): 223–230); "School Victimization of Gender-Nonconforming LGBT Youth Linked with Depression and Quality of Life in Adulthood" (*Developmental Psychology*, 46(6): 1580–1589); and "Gay-Straight Alliances in School Benefit Health, Education of LGBT Young Adults" (*Applied Developmental Science*, 15(4): 175–185).

GLAAD

Los Angeles Office:
5455 Wilshire Blvd, #1500
Los Angeles, CA 90036
Phone (323) 933-2240
Fax (323) 933-2241
New York Office:
104 West 29th St., 4th Floor
New York, NY 10001
Phone (212) 629-3322
Fax (212) 629-3225
Email: http://www.glaad.org/contact
URL: http://www.glaad.org/

GLAAD was originally known as the Gay & Lesbian Anti-Defamation League. It changed its name to the Gay & Lesbian Alliance against Defamation shortly after its creation in response to legal action threatened by the Anti-Defamation League, a Jewish group that felt its name was being appropriated by the new organization. The organization changed its name again to its present form in March 2013 to reflect a widening of its interests to include bisexual and transgender individuals. GLAAD's mission is to "amplif[y] the voice of the LGBT community by empowering real people to share their stories, holding the media accountable for the words and images they present, and helping grassroots organizations communicate effectively." These stories, the organization believes, promote understanding, increase acceptance, and advance equality for all LGBT people.

GLAAD was formed in 1985 in New York City by a group of activists that included Vito Russo, probably the most famous gay and lesbian film critic and historian; Gregory Kolovakos, an employee at the time of the New York State Arts Council; Jewelle Gomez, author, poet, and playwright; Darrell Yates Rist, author, actor, producer, director, and script writer; and author Allen Barrett. (The four men all died of AIDS-related causes at an early age.) The organization was founded to take action against blatantly homophobic reporting and statements made by a number of news media, most prominently the *New York Post*. The *Post* had gained a reputation as being particularly offensive in its reporting of HIV/AIDS-related issues, although the paper was by no means the only print, radio, or television outlet to do so. One of GLAAD's first successes was in convincing the *New York Times* to begin using the word *gay* in place of terms generally regarded by the gay and lesbian community as offensive and demeaning.

GLAAD's work is currently organized around a dozen major themes: Commentator Accountability Project, National News Media, Spanish-Language Media, Voices of Color, Transgender Voices, Entertainment Media, Religion Faith and Values, Spiritday, Advertising Media, Field Work and Community Media, Sports Advocacy, and Young Adults. The Young Adults program is an ambitious and vigorous program that monitors the treatment of LGBT youth in all forms of media and promotes opportunities for such individuals to speak out about their lives and their activities. Some of the topics in which GLAAD has been involved are the Ali Forney Center's program on religious intolerance for LGBT homeless youth, efforts to increase openness among college admissions officers to the needs and concerns of transgender youth, activities to deal with homophobia in sports programs at all levels in both amateur and professional leagues, lobbying on behalf of efforts to get the Boy Scouts of America to change its anti-LGBT policies and practices, and campaigning against state and local legislation that seeks to discriminate against young lesbians, gay men, bisexuals, and transgenders.

GLAAD also maintains a special program, the GLAAD Media Awards Young Adults Program, which provides financial support for LGBT youth to attend the annual GLAAD Media Awards ceremonies in New York and Los Angeles each year. The organization notes that at least partly as a result of this program, more than 1,000 young people attended the awards ceremonies in 2012, where they had the opportunity to watch and in some cases meet LGBT men and women in the political, news, entertainment, and other fields who can serve as role models.

Christopher T. Gonzalez (1963–1994) and Jeff Werner (d. 1997)

Gonzalez and Werner were founders of the Indiana Youth Group (IYG), originally known as the Indianapolis Youth Group, in 1988. At the time, Gonzalez was working as a volunteer at the Indianapolis Gay and Lesbian Switchboard, where he received calls from teenagers who were confused about their own sexuality or who knew that they were gay or lesbians but were uncertain as to how to deal with the many problems they faced as a result of their orientation. In an interview with the *Indianapolis Star* at a later date, Gonzalez said that his work at the hotline made him realize that "The time has come for us as a society to stop teaching these kids to hate themselves. I have to deal with them on a daily basis. I hear the pain and see the pain. It's just not right. I can't understand it being right by anybody's value code."

Acting on these feelings, Gonzalez, his life partner Jeff Werner, and fellow volunteer at the hotline Pat Jordan decided to hold a meeting of gay and lesbian youth at the men's home. As with so many gay and lesbian groups at the time, the first meetings were largely semisocial events at which young men and women had the opportunity—often for the first time in their life—to talk with other lesbians and gay men about their common experiences and common problems. Political action was not a major focus of the meetings at that point, as participants were primarily interested in trying to better understand themselves and the consequences of issues related to their common sexual orientation.

Eventually, the meetings moved from the Gonzalez/Werner home to the Damien Center, Indianapolis's primary support organization for gay men and lesbians with HIV/AIDS. In 1989, the youth group was formally organized as a nonprofit organization and in 1997, it changed its name to the Indiana Youth Group. The organization remains in existence today. In 1991, the organization received funding from the Health Foundation of Greater Indiana that allowed it to purchase a private home for use as its offices and meeting space.

Chris Gonzalez was born on October 28, 1963, in Griffith, Indiana. He understood as early as his high school years at Griffith High School that he was "different" and that he was attracted more to men than to women. He kept this realization to himself, however, concerned about the effect of informing his "very traditional Hispanic family" and his peers at school. He dated girls and played an active part in the school's social life, serving at one point as president of the school's student council. By the time he had matriculated at Franklin College, however, he had decided to come out to his parents, who received his news with equanimity and support. He also began dating men and fell in love with his future partner, Werner.

Gonzalez also began to commit himself to political activism and volunteered at the Indianapolis switchboard.

Gonzalez began to imagine a variety of ways in which LGBT Indiana teenagers could begin to receive the attention and service they needed in their lives. For example, in 1993, he worked with members of the Indiana State Department of Health to develop a program called the Indiana Youth Access Project (IYAP) as a mechanism for applying for and administering grants to IYG that allowed hiring staff and expanding services of the organization. Gonzalez was also active in a variety of other political events, including campaigns against local Ku Klux Klan groups and activities of Gays and Lesbians Working against Violence.

Gonzalez died on May 5, 1994, of complications related to HIV/AIDS. Werner continued to be active in IYG, becoming executive director of the organization after Gonzalez's death, a post he held until October 1996. He then resigned because of ill health and died in January 1997. The two men are buried together at Indianapolis's Crown Hill Cemetery. The Chris Gonzalez Library and Archives on the Indiana LGBT group, Indy Pride, Inc., is a circulating library of LGBT documents and videos named in Gonzalez's honor that contains his personal papers and documents.

GSA Network

1550 Bryant St., Suite 800
San Francisco, CA 94103
Phone: (415) 552-4229
Email: info@gsanetwork.org
URL: http://gsanetwork.org/

GSA Network was founded as a coordinating group for 40 GSA clubs in the San Francisco Bay Area in 1998. The goal of the organization was to work with individual clubs and to establish new clubs for the purpose of fighting homophobia and transphobia in local schools. The organization grew rapidly and by 2001 had become a statewide organization and. By 2005, it had become a national organization with headquarters in San Francisco. In 2008, GSA Network was incorporated as a 501(c)3 nonprofit organization. Today, the organization has state chapters or affiliates in 38 states and is attempting to add such chapters in the 12 states currently without them.

Some of the achievements listed by GSA Network include the expansion of the number of GSA clubs in California from 40 to more than 900 over the past 15 years, extending the GSA program to more than 1.1 million students in the state, playing a leadership role in the passage of the California Student Safety and Violence Prevention Act of 2000 (AB 537), serving as plaintiff in the first lawsuit filed under that act, promoting the passage of 11 additional state laws protecting LGBT youth in schools, and developing a model of youth-led social justice programs for ending homophobia and transphobia in New Mexico, Texas, and other states.

GSA Network activities are currently organized into five major areas. Networking and Supporting GSAs involves working with individual GSA clubs throughout the country, providing resources and advice, and helping them become connected with other GSA clubs nationwide. The program also works to establish new GSA clubs and to provide the guidance needed to get those clubs up and running. The Training Student Leaders program offers conferences, leadership training sessions, activist camps, and other activities designed to teach LGBT youth how to take leadership roles in their local organizations. Local leaders may also become involved in leadership positions within the GSA Network through the organization's Youth Council and its Statewide Advocacy Council.

The Transforming Schools program of the GSA Network works with local GSA clubs to become more activist, working with local school administrations, school boards, and other parent, teacher, and student groups to make the goals of gay-straight alliances better known and help them reach attainment.

Changing Policies and Laws in California is a continuation of the GSA Network's long-term efforts to improve the state's policies and practices related to providing safer learning environments for all LGBT students in the state. An example of efforts in this program is Queer Youth Advocacy Day, in which LGBT youth and their allies participate in a rally at the state capital to make their goals and objectives better known to legislators and the general public.

The goal of the Building the National GSA Movement is clear from its title. The major focus of the program is the Change the Nation campaign, which has as its purpose making all schools safe for LGBT youth and having in place GSA Network chapters in all 50 states by 2020.

GSA Network sponsor an impressive variety of events throughout the year in addition to those outlined previously. For example, they sponsor an annual GSA Advocacy & Youth Leadership Academy (GAYLA), a three-day training program in the legislative process, policy and administrative advocacy, media activism, and other important leadership skills. The organization also holds the annual National Gathering that includes guest speakers, hands-on workshops, specialized training, a large group session, and social events. Some of the workshop topics included in recent meetings are racial justice; rural, suburban, and urban models for GSA organizing; youth leadership models; gender identity and expression; fundraising; developing organizational infrastructure; and safe schools advocacy and policy activism.

GSA Network provides a wide array of resources for GSA clubs and individuals who are involved in them. In addition to research reports, posters, videos, and other print and visual resources, the organization provides materials for use in establishing and maintaining a local GSA, and offers guidance in building coalitions with other groups with similar goals and objectives, working within the local community, finding and using legal resources, and calling on adults for guidance and advice. Resources in Spanish are also available.

Harvey Milk High School

2-10 Astor Place
New York, NY 10003
Phone: (212) 477-1555
URL: http://schools.nyc.gov/SchoolPortals/02/M586/default.htm
See The Alliance School of Milwaukee, following.

The Alliance School of Milwaukee

850 W. Walnut St.
Milwaukee, WI 53205
Phone: (414) 267-5400
Email: 042@milwaukee.k12.wi.us
URL: http://www5.milwaukee.k12.wi.us/projects/school/alliance
.html

For more than three decades, some educators and social activists have been arguing for the creation of separate schools for LGBT youth. The argument is that lesbian, gay, bisexual, transgendered, and questioning boys, girls, and young adults often experience severe social, physical, and emotional problems at traditional schools, where they are harassed for their sexual orientation or simply being "different."

The first program established to respond to these calls was the Harvey Milk School (HMS), created in New York City in 1985 under the auspices of the Hetrick-Martin Institute (HMI), an organization that provides support for at-risk youth, especially LGBTQ young people. The school opened with a single teacher, Fred Goldhaber; a two-room facility; and about a dozen students. It was funded and operated by HMI in collaboration with the State of New York Department of Education's Career Education Center. In 2002, HMS received full accreditation and became a part of the New York City Department of Education (NYCDOE), with no connection with HMI (although the school and the institute still share a common building).

The school has grown to become one of the most prestigious schools in the NYCDOE system, with an annual enrollment of between 75 and 100 students at its Greenwich Village campus, with a graduation rate of more than 90 percent (compared to a city average of 65 percent). In addition, more than 60 percent of HMS graduates go on to college or some other form of higher education.

Other cities have considered the possibility of opening special schools for LGBT youth, the best-known and largest having been Chicago and Toronto. Such efforts have generally not been successful. Perhaps the best-known exception to that rule has been the Alliance School of Milwaukee (Wisconsin), a charter school founded in 2005 to meet the special needs of LGBT youth. When the school opened, it had about 100 students in grades 6 through 12, and four years later, the Board of Education allowed the school to expand to include a middle-school component, the only such school in the United States. About half of the student body has come out publicly as LGBT, although others still regard themselves as being in the "Q" phase of evolution.

The Alliance School has garnered an impressive array of honors. In 2009, it received the Silver Award (second place) for High Achievement Charter School of the Year from the Wisconsin Charter Schools Association and in 2011, it was given that organization's Platinum Award as the best charter school of the year in the state. The school has also received recognition from institutions of higher education as a potential model for working with at-risk youth and from the public media. It was featured on an episode of ABC's *20/20* in October 2011 and in a feature article in *People* magazine in 2010. One of its students has posted an online comment on the Great Schools website calling Alliance "one of the three greatest schools in the history of the 20th century."

The most recent school designed primarily for LGBT youth is Q High in Phoenix, Arizona. After a number of years as a distinct program but not distinct school, Q High opened with

14 LGBT students. Its current facility is capable of handling twice that number, although plans for expansion have yet to be developed. Administrators, teachers, and students see Q High as a promising alternative to the constant bullying, harassment, and physical danger faced by LGBT students at traditional Phoenix schools.

The Hetrick-Martin Institute

2 Astor Place
New York, NY 10003
Phone: (212) 674-2400
Email: info@hmi.org
URL: http://www.hmi.org/

The Hetrick-Martin Institute (HMI) was founded in 1979 by life partners Dr. Emery A. Hetrick, chief of psychiatric emergency and crisis treatment services at Harlem Hospital, and Dr. A. Damien Martin, professor of speech pathology at the New York University School of Education. Hetrick and Martin had been told of the plight of a 15-year-old boy who had been physically abused and evicted from a homeless shelter because he was gay. The two men decided that such actions were reprehensible and impermissible, and that something needed to be done to prevent their reoccurrence. That something turned out to be the founding of a new organization, originally called the Institute for the Protection of Lesbian and Gay Youth (IPLGY). The organization was renamed the Hetrick-Martin Institute in 1988, a year after Hetrick's death. Martin himself died in 1991 as a result of complications related to HIV/AIDS.

HMI now claims to be the largest organization whose purpose it is to provide social support and programming for at-risk LGBT youth between the ages of 12 and 24 from more than 300 zip code areas in and around metropolitan New York City. Perhaps its most notable accomplishment in its almost 35 years of existence was founding the Harvey Milk High School in 1985 for LGBT youth who find it impossible to attend traditional public or private high schools. The city board of education has since taken over operation of the school, but it continues to share physical facilities with HMI in the Greenwich Village district of New York.

The institute's activities for LGBT youth fall into three general areas: after school programs, supportive services, and internships. After school programs focus on topics such as arts and culture, health and wellness, academic enrichment, and job readiness and career exploration. Youth attend classes in these areas after regular school hours, whether they are actually enrolled in a formal school program or not. Parents and other interested adults may also attend at least some of the classes. Annual attendance for the after school programs typically is about 2,000 young adults and their families.

The supportive services program provides trained counselors to meet with individuals to discuss specific problems and issues in their lives and ways of dealing with them. They help youth deal with a wide variety of topics ranging from physical safety to provision of food and clothing (the former at the on-site Café HMI) to counseling sessions to referrals to city, state, and private agencies willing and able to deal with LGBTQ issues.

HMI clientele are also provided with an opportunity to become interns at organizations and agencies where they can receive training for a variety of jobs and occupations. Among the agencies that offer internships are CHANGE (Challenging Houses and Networks to Get Educated), which works toward safer sex practices, antiviolence, and risk reduction for youth; CHAT (Curbing HIV/AIDS Transmission); Women's Task Force; Street Smart, an HIV/AIDS and STD prevention for transgender youth; and a host of LGBT organizations, such as Gay Men's Health Crisis, Callen-Lorde Health Center, and Lambda Legal. In addition to these services, the institute also provides a wide variety of social activities throughout the year, such as the annual Fall Fest fundraiser for the institute, the Summer Camp at Fire Island Pines, Jeffrey Fashion Cares charity fashion show, and the annual Women's Award Ceremony.

Human Rights Campaign (HRC)

1640 Rhode Island Ave. NW
Washington, DC 20036-3278
Phone: (202) 628-4160
TTY: (202) 216-1572
Toll-Free: (800) 777-4723
Fax: (202) 347-5323
URL: http://www.hrc.org/

The Human Rights Campaign (HRC) was founded in 1980 by political activist Steve Endean, who had created the Gay Rights National Lobby two years earlier. The purpose of both organizations was to work for the civil rights of all gay men and lesbians in the United States. In 1986, the HRC board of directors established the HRC Foundation, a nonprofit organization that would research and educate on GLBT issues. The foundation was created at least in part as a response to the rapid and aggressive growth of right-wing evangelical Christian groups that had formed to oppose the extension of basic civil liberties to LGBT individuals.

Today, HRC claims to have a membership of more than 1.5 million members and supporters nationwide, making it the largest organization devoted primarily to gay and lesbian civil rights issues. The work of the Human Rights Campaign is currently organized into 12 major areas: coming out, federal advocacy, hate crimes, health and aging, marriage, parenting, religion and faith, state advocacy, straight supporters, transgender, workplace, and youth and campus. The youth and campus program is designed to provide young LGBT individuals with the tools they need to work for equal rights and fight oppression in their educational and workplace settings and to make connections with LGBT youth groups throughout the country. A major feature of the HRC youth and campus program is Generation Equality, a campaign to expand the organization's outreach to LGBT youth. Generation Equality has sponsored a series of national conference for LGBT youth, offered leadership training sessions, and, for a period of time, provided scholarships for promising LGBT leaders to attend institutions of higher education. News about the Generation Equality campaign is available through a free electronic newsletter, GenEQ News, for which information is available at the organization's youth and campus website at http://www.hrc.org/resources/category/youth-campus.

HRC publishes a variety of resources aimed at LGBT individuals who want to learn more about becoming politically active consumers in the United States. These resources include a Buyer's Guide that rates businesses on their attitudes and policies on LGBT issues; the Corporate Equality Index (11th edition in 2013) that lists hundreds of U.S. corporations' policies related to LGBT issues; Find Your Legislator, which provides contact information for all U.S. senators and representatives and their stand on federal LGBT legislation; Healthcare Equality Index, which ranks hundreds of U.S. hospitals and clinics on the basis of their policies related to dealing with LGBT individuals; the Municipal Equality Index, which lists 137 U.S. municipalities and summarizes their laws, regulations, and policies related to LGBT topics; State Laws; and State Maps, an interactive resource through which one can find out about state policies on a host of issues, such as hospital visitation laws, statewide housing laws and policies, parenting laws, statewide employment laws and policies, marriage equality and other relationship recognition laws, statewide marriage prohibition laws, state hate crimes laws, statewide school anti-bullying laws and policies, and statewide school nondiscrimination laws and policies. The HRC website also provides an interactive map that allows users to click on a specific state and view the organization's activities in that state.

IMPACT

Feinberg School of Medicine
Northwestern University
Center on Halsted
3656 N Halsted
Chicago, IL 60613
Phone: (773) 661-0742
Email: impact@impactprogram.org
URL: http://www.impactprogram.org/

The IMPACT program operates in the Feinberg School of Medicine at Northwestern University. It was established in 2009 for the purpose of conducting so-called translational research on LGBT health and development. The term *translational*, as used here, is meant to include researching health issues that impact on LGBT youth, identifying factors that put people at risk or that protect them from potential harm, and translating that knowledge into programs that can actually be used for the benefit of LGBT youth. The term is also used in the sense of explaining for the general public the sometimes esoteric or confusing results produced by research on the health and development of lesbians, gay men, bisexuals, and transgendered individuals.

Some examples of the types of research being conducted at IMPACT include the following:

Keep It Up! is a multimedia, Internet-based HIV prevention program for 18- to 24-year-old men who are HIV negative and who have sex with other men. The goal of the program is to help such individuals maintain their HIV status.

Project Q2 is an ongoing research project on LGBT youth between the ages of 16 and 20 to obtain information on their mental health, substance abuse, HIV risk, and resilience.

CREW 450 is a research program designed to identify the factors involved in co-occurring disease epidemics, that is, diseases that tend to occur simultaneously within a particular cohort of subjects, in this case, 16- to 20-year-old young men who have sex with other men.

The Internet as a Setting for Sexual Health Development among LBG Youth is an effort to determine the ways in which the Internet impacts the sexual health of GLBT youth and attempts to find ways in which it can be used to promote sexual health.

Developmental Infrastructure for Population Research is an attempt to build a national network of experts in the field who will work toward developing specialized knowledge and skills to deal with health issues faced by LGBT youth.

Intervention Development: Reducing HIV Risk for At-Risk Youth is a pilot program designed to develop an HIV and substance abuse prevention program for young men who have sex with men.

Guy2Guy (G2G) is an experimental program designed to use text messaging as a way of reaching young men who have sex with men ages 14 to 18 with information about disease and substance abuse prevention.

IMPACT provides useful resources on its website, including a blog that deals with issues of importance and interest to LGBT youth and interested adults. It also contains a set of quizzes on topics such as HIV knowledge, women's health issues, and transgender health. The site provides useful links to other websites and organizations with information on HIV/AIDS, sexually transmitted infections, and questions related to sexuality in general. The organization also jointly sponsors the Chicago LGBTQ Health and Wellness Conference to foster the engagement and education of students, faculty, and providers in the field of LGBT health in the Chicago area.

International Lesbian, Gay, Bisexual, Transgender, Queer Youth and Student Organization

Rue de la Charité 17
B-1210 Brussels

Belgium
Email: info@iglyo.com
URL: http://www.iglyo.com/

The International Lesbian, Gay, Bisexual, Transgender, Queer Youth and Student Organization (IGLYO) was created after a series of three international meetings in 1984 through 1986. The first meeting was held in Amsterdam under the auspices of the Dutch Gay Youth Platform (LHJO) and was followed by a second meeting in Dublin in 1985 and a third meeting in Oslo in 1986. At that third meeting, participants decided to establish a permanent organization for gay and lesbian youth, with the later addition of bisexual, transgender, and queer youth. The organization is funded by the European Commission Programme for Employment and Social Solidarity PROGRESS (which runs from 2007 to 2013), the Government of the Netherlands, and the Council of Europe European Youth Foundation. IGLYO's mission is to "empower and enable its members to ensure representation of LGBTQ youth and student issues. IGLYO's approach promotes cooperation and joint strategies, and often advocates on behalf of members to international bodies, institutions and other organisations."

IGLYO consists of 78 LGBT youth organizations in 40 countries, primarily in Europe, with associated groups in Brazil, Israel, Nicaragua, and Pakistan.

IGLYO organizes its activities around five major themes: capacity building, advocacy, focus areas, working in partnerships, and external representation. The purpose of capacity-building activities is to increase the knowledge and skills of individuals and LGBT groups in their home nations to recognize and deal with specific problems faced by LGBT youth. This goal is achieved by a variety of international conferences and training sessions that deal with topics such as health, education, volunteering, monitoring, using modern technology, and conducting intercultural dialogues. The organization is increasingly moving toward the use of electronic and Internet resources to accomplish these objectives.

IGLYO's advocacy arm aims to increase the visibility of LGBT youth among a variety of policy- and decision-making organizations in Europe, including the European Commission, members of the Intergroup on LGBT Rights at the European Parliament, and certain permanent representations to the Council of Ministers of the European Union. The organization is currently working toward the adoption of the proposed Horizontal Anti-Discrimination Directive, which would ban discrimination throughout Europe on the basis of various characteristics, including sexual orientation. It was also active in the drafting and adoption of Recommendation CM/Rec(2010)5 of the European Committee of Ministers, which deals with measures to combat discrimination on the grounds of sexual orientation or gender identity.

The major field of concern within the focus area field is currently human rights, an effort that has motivated work on a number of projects. One such project is the Human Rights Working Group, established by IGLYO in April 2011 to study and make recommendations on ways in which the human rights of all LGBT youth can be recognized and respected. A human rights focus was also a major theme of the 2009 conference, during which discussions were held about the best ways to implement the Yogyakarta Principles on the Application of International Human Rights Law in relation to Sexual Orientation and Gender Identity, a set of guidelines adopted at a meeting of the International Commission of Jurists, the International Service for Human Rights, and human rights experts from around the world at the Indonesia city of that name in November 2006.

IGLYO's working partnership initiative focuses on improving and expanding contacts with other groups in Europe interested in issues relating to LGBT youth, such as the European Network Against Racism, ILGA-Europe, Fundamental Rights Platform, the European Youth Forum, the European

Students' Union, the Organising Bureau of European School Student Unions, UNITED for Intercultural Action, and IHLIA (Internationaal Homo/Lesbisch Informatiecentrum en Archief; International Gay/Lesbian Information Centre and Archives).

The field of external representation consists of IGLYO's efforts to send representatives to as many external meetings, conferences, training sessions, and other activities as possible to make its goals and activities better known to agencies that might have common interests with the organization. Some events in which IGLYO has participated in recent years include a workshop on LGBT youth activism at the Baltic Pride week in Riga, Latvia; Peer 2 Peer: Active Citizens and Youth Organizations, an event sponsored by the European Commission in Brussels; the European Pride Organizers Association Annual Conference in Brussels; Come Out & Play! at the LGBT Excellence Centre in Cardiff, Wales; the International Green Students Conference in Berlin; a panel entitled Friend Me, Don't Tag Me, Poke Me: LGBTQ Young People and Social Media, at EuroPride in Rome; BalticPride in Tallinn, Estonia; and a conference on LGBT in Education in Edinburgh.

Three major publications have been produced by and are available from IGLYO: The Age Project Report, which deals with the special problems of young LGBT people; LGBTQ-Inclusive Education Guidelines, a set of 10 suggestions related to ways in which schools can do a better job of dealing with discrimination against LGBT youth; and LGBT Social Exclusion, a report on the ways in which LGBT youth are routinely discriminated against throughout Europe.

It Gets Better Project

110 S. Fairfax Ave., Suite A11-71
Los Angeles, CA 90036
URL: http://www.itgetsbetter.org/

Many lesbians and gay men are distressed at the number of young LGBT youth who take their own lives every year because of a feeling of desperation, a feeling that life is miserable—even hopeless—and that it will never get any better. In September 2010, author and journalist Dan Savage wrote on his blog about this problem with regard to one specific young man, 15-year-old Billy Lucas. Lucas had hanged himself at his home on September 9, 2010, after an especially difficult day at school when some classmates had told him to "go hang your-self" for being gay. In his blog, Savage wrote that he wished he could have had five minutes with Billy at that difficult time and said to him just one thing: It gets better. In that phrase, Savage articulated what many gay men and lesbians have learned in their lives, often only after years of the same kind of harassment and bullying experienced by Billy. The fact is that for many gay men and lesbians, life does get better. The people who matter in a lesbian or gay man's life do accept one's sexual orientation, and life becomes more normal—and often more glorious.

In thinking more about this issue, Savage and his domestic partner and now husband, Terry Miller, decided to make a video in which they express just this idea, life does get better. Savage and Miller also encouraged others—gay men, lesbians, bisexuals, transgenders, nongays, or anyone else with a similar message to LGBT youth—to make their own videos on the same theme. Within a week, more than 200 such videos had been made and uploaded, and a week later, 650 more videos had been posted on YouTube. As of 2013, more than 50,000 videos had been uploaded to various sites, and viewership had passed 50 million worldwide. Creators of videos included average lesbians and gay men, politicians like Barack Obama and Nancy Pelosi, entertainers such as Anne Hathaway and Colin Farrell, and business leaders like Suze Orman and members of the Gap corporation.

It Gets Better has gone far beyond making its own videos and encouraging others to do the same. For example, it now has an international arm that works with local organizations to improve conditions for LGBT youth in many countries around the world. It has formal affiliates in Australia, Chile, Denmark, Italy, Jamaica, Monterrey (Mexico), Paraguay, Portugal, Puerto Rico, Spain, Sweden, and Switzerland.

Another function of the project is its BetterLegal program, through which It Gets Better videos are offered to organizations who request them for use in efforts to improve conditions for LGBT youth. The process involves an organization requesting such videos, volunteers putting together a collection of videos appropriate for the organization, and the organization then incorporating those videos in its own legal and/or advocacy programs and efforts. It Gets Better also has a link on its website to a variety of agencies and services that provide immediate and long-range assistance to LGBT youth who are in distress and require advice and support.

More than 2,700 It Gets Better videos are available for viewing on the program's website at http://www.itgetsbetter.org/video/.

Kevin Jennings (1963–)

Jennings was the founding sponsor of the first gay-straight alliance club in the United States. He created the organization at Concord Academy, a private secondary school in Concord, Massachusetts, in 1990. He later went on to found the first and now the largest LGBT school organization in the world, Gay, Lesbian and Straight Education Network (GLSEN).

Kevin Brett Jennings was born on May 8, 1963, in Fort Lauderdale, Florida. His parents were Chester Henry Jennings, an itinerant Baptist preacher, and Alice Verna Johnson Jennings, a homemaker. He was the youngest of five children and grew up in a very protective family, a situation created in part by a life-threatening disease he developed at the age of three. He was so closely watched by his family that he eventually became known as a "mama's boy," a nickname that stayed with him for the rest of his early years. (In fact, Jennings later took that term as the title of one of his six books, *Mama's Boy, Preacher's Son: A Memoir* [Beacon, 2006].)

Because of Chester Jennings's work, the family regularly moved throughout the South. Wherever they went, however, Kevin experienced homophobia and bullying that made his life so difficult that at one point, he refused to go to school because, as he later wrote, "I simply wasn't going to go back to a place where I was bullied every day." He did well academically at Paisley Magnet School in Winston-Salem, North Carolina, but was beaten regularly and once attempted to commit suicide. He finally graduated from Radford High School in Honolulu, where his mother had moved after the death of his father.

Jennings then matriculated at Harvard College, where he was awarded his bachelor's degree in history in 1985. He took a teaching job at the Moses Brown School in Providence, Rhode Island, where he remained until 1987. After leaving Moses Brown, he moved to Concord Academy, where he remained on the teaching staff until 1995. In addition to his teaching responsibilities at Concord, Jennings was active in the development of gay-straight alliances in Massachusetts and elsewhere and in the development of GLSEN and its predecessors, the Gay and Lesbian Independent School Teachers Network (GLISTN), Gay and Lesbian School Teachers Network (GLSTN), and the Gay, Lesbian and Straight Teachers Network (GLSTN).

In 1994, Jennings took a leave of absence from teaching to accept an appointment as Joseph Klingenstein Fellow at Columbia University's Teachers College. A year later, he was awarded his master's degree in interdisciplinary studies by Columbia. At that point, he decided to leave teaching to become full-time paid executive director of GLSEN at its national headquarters in New York City. After more than a decade in that position, Jennings was appointed assistant deputy secretary of education by President Barack Obama. In this position, he served as head of the Department of Education's Office of Safe and Drug-Free Schools (OSDFS), where he was responsible for federal efforts to promote the safety, health, and well-being of America's students. One of Jennings's primary accomplishments at OSDFS was the development of the Obama administration's antibullying initiative, whose landmark achievement was the White House Conference on Bullying Prevention held in October 2011.

In 2011, Jennings accepted an appointment as chief executive officer (CEO) of the Be the Change Foundation, an organization that helps create national campaigns for important social topics. The campaign on which he spent most of his time was Opportunity Nation, a national program to increase economic mobility in the United States. In July 2012, Jennings left Be the Change to become executive director of the Arcus Foundation, an organization that works for social justice and conservation issues worldwide.

Jennings is the author or editor of five books in addition to *Mama's Boy*, including *Becoming Visible: A Reader in Gay & Lesbian History for High School & College Students* (Alyson, 1994); *One Teacher in 10: Gay and Lesbian Educators Tell Their Stories* (Alyson, 1994; 2005); *Telling Tales out of School: Gays, Lesbians, and Bisexuals Revisit Their School Days* (Alyson, 1998); and *Always My Child: A Parent's Guide to Understanding Your Gay, Lesbian, Bisexual, Transgendered, or Questioning Son or Daughter* (with Patricia Gottlieb; Simon & Schuster, 2003). He has received honors, including his selection in 1997 by *Newsweek* magazine to its Century Club of individuals who are likely to make a difference in the twenty-first century, the Lambda Literary Award in 1998 for his book *Telling Tales out of School*, and the Virginia Uribe Award for Creative Leadership in Human Rights for 2004 of the National Education Association.

Jennings lives with his domestic partner, Jeff Davis, who is the managing director of Global Equities Business Strategy at Barclays Capital, and their two Bernese mountain dogs, Ben and Jackson.

Fred (Fritz) Klein (1932–2006)

Klein was a psychiatrist and sex researcher whose primary field of interest was bisexuality. Early in his professional career, Klein realized that what he regarded as his own sexual orientation, bisexuality, had been little studied by scientific professionals. The scientific literature was barren of research on the topic, and almost no organizations existed to provide support for people who felt that they were attracted in a roughly equal proportion to members of both the same and the opposite sex. He spent the greatest part of his career studying the subject of bisexuality and building those organizations that had been so lacking prior to his work. For example, he founded the American Institute of Bisexuality (AIB) in 1988 to encourage and support research on bisexuality. He also founded and became editor of the *Journal of Bisexuality* in 1997.

Fred Klein was born in Vienna, Austria, on December 27, 1932. His family fled to the United States while he was still a small boy because, like many Jewish families, they were concerned about the rising tide of anti-Semitism in central Europe. He attended Yeshiva University in New York City, from which he received his bachelor of arts degree in 1953 and then matriculated at Columbia University, which awarded his MBA two years later. Klein studied medicine at the University of Bern, Switzerland, from which he received his MD in 1961. He specialized in psychiatry and returned to the United States to establish a practice in New York City. While working in New York, Klein founded the city's first bisexual group, the Bisexual Forum, and published two books on the subject, *The Bisexual Option: A Concept of One Hundred Percent Intimacy* (Arbor House, 1978) and *The Male: His Body, His Sex* (with Alfred Allan and Eli Bauman; Anchor, 1978).

In *The Bisexual Option*, Klein introduced the concept for which he is probably best known today, a measurement of one's sexuality called the Klein Sexual Orientation Guide.

The guide is an attempt to measure the extent to which an individual is attracted to someone of the same or the opposite sex. It is, in that regard, similar to the Kinsey scale (which runs from one to six) as a measure of one's sexual orientation. But Klein took into consideration a wider variety of measurements in determining a person's sexual orientation. A 21-cell grid takes into consideration sexual attraction, sexual behavior, sexual fantasies, emotional preference, social preference, heterosexual or homosexual lifestyle, and self-identification at three different time periods—past, present, and future. From his research with the guide, Klein concluded that a person's sexuality is much more fluid among different measures and over time than most sex researchers had realized in the past.

Klein moved to San Diego in 1982, where he continued both his professional work and his political activism. He published his next book, *Bisexualities: Theory and Research* (Haworth) in 1985 and his last book of research, *Bisexual and Gay Husbands: Their Stories, Their Words* (Harrington Park) in 2001. Klein concluded that his sexuality could be classified toward the "gay" end of his scale and, at the time of his death, he was living with long-time domestic partner Tom Reise. His death occurred in San Diego on May 24, 2006. In 2008, the Lambda Archives in San Diego awarded Reise and Klein its first annual Lifetime Family Membership Award.

Lambda Legal

120 Wall Street, 19th Floor
New York, NY 10005
Phone: (212) 809-8585
Fax: (212) 809-0055
URL: http://www.lambdalegal.org/

Lambda Legal was established in 1973 by attorney William J. (Bill) Thom for the twofold purpose of providing legal assistance to gay men and lesbians and the organizations of which they were members and of educating the general public and the legal profession about the necessity of extending civil rights to lesbians and gay men and their organizations. Thom's first challenge was to convince the state of New York that such an organization qualified for legal status as a nonprofit organization, which a lower court refused to do. Only when the state supreme court overruled that court did Lambda become a reality.

One of Lambda's first successes came only a year after its founding in the case of *Gay Student Organization v. Bonner*, in which a group of gay students sued the University of New Hampshire for preventing it from forming a student group. With Lambda as its legal representative, the students eventually won that case. Much of the organization's efforts during the 1980s focused on antidiscrimination cases, especially cases involving the HIV/AIDS epidemic. In 1983, for example, Lambda won an important decision in *People v. West 12 Tenants Corp.* that prohibited discrimination in housing against people with the disease. During the 1990s, Lambda took up a number of cases dealing with the rights of LGBT youth. In 1996, for example, it won a decision in *Nabozny v. Podlesny* that held schools responsible for not taking action in cases of harassment against LGBT students. In *Colín v. Orange Unified School District* (2000), it won the right for LGBT students to form gay-straight alliance clubs in their schools. In the first decade of the twenty-first century, Lambda devoted much of its efforts to the fight for same-sex marriage. It represented the plaintiffs in the case of *Varnum v. Brien* that invalidated the state of Iowa's laws against same-sex marriage and was a lead counsel in two U.S. Supreme Court cases dealing with same-sex marriage in 2013. In June 2013, the court upheld Lambda's position in both of these cases, invalidating much of the U.S. Defense of Marriage Act and upholding the validity of same-sex marriage in the state of California.

Currently, Lambda organizes its work around 10 major themes: employment rights in the workplace; the fair courts project; government misconduct and support for discrimination; HIV/AIDS; health care fairness: marriage, relationships, and family protections; seniors; transgender rights; youth; and Proyecto Igualdad, Lambda's outreach project to the Latino/Latina community. In addition to its main offices in New York City, Lambda has regional offices in Los Angeles, Chicago, Atlanta, and Dallas. The organization has a senior staff of almost 100, including attorneys, legal assistants, development and finance staff, and support staff.

Lambda produces a wide variety of print and electronic publications dealing with legal issues relating to lesbians, gay men, bisexuals, and transgenders, including books, press releases, toolkits dealing with legal cases and issues, fact sheets, and videos. It also produces two online newsletters, *In Brief* and *Of Counsel,* in addition to a blog dealing with its ongoing work. Its *Impact* magazine is published three times a year in February, June, and October, and comes with membership in the organization.

Jeanne Manford (1920–2013)

Jeanne Manford was the founder of Parents and Friends of Lesbians and Gays (PFLAG), an organization created to foster the health and well-being of gay men, lesbians, bisexuals, and transgendered persons. Manford was inspired to establish this group as the result of an event that occurred in April 1972. She was called to a hospital in Manhattan because her son had been brought in after being severely beaten during a gay rights rally at the local Hilton Hotel. The young man, Morty Manford, was a member of the New York Gay Activists Alliance and had attended the rally as part of a protest against the neglect of gay rights issues by attendees at a dinner being held at the hotel. Mrs. Manford was later quoted as describing how angry she was at hearing about her son's beating. "I remember thinking," she said, "What right have they got to assault my son and the others? Why didn't the police protect them? What kind of a police force do we have in New York?"

At first, Mrs. Manford restricted her political activity to a single letter in the *New York Post*, but by the time of the annual gay rights parade in New York City in June, she decided to join her son in the march up Broadway. A year later, Mrs. Manford's anger was further transformed into political action when she and a group of parents of gay and lesbian children met to form PFLAG. The organization is now widely respected as spokespersons for the civil, social, and political rights of all lesbians, gay men, bisexuals, and transgenders.

Mrs. Manford was born Jean Sobelson on December 4, 1920, in Queens, New York. In later life, she changed her first name to Jeanne. She graduated from Queens College in 1964 and took a job teaching in the New York City public school system. She eventually taught mathematics in grades 5 and 6 at Public School 32 in Queens. Until the 1972 event, she had led a relatively quiet life, with her family and her job consuming most of her time and interests. All that changed with Morty's beating and the founding of PFLAG, however.

Manford's husband died in 1982, another son Charles died in 1966, and Morty died in 1992 from complications related to HIV/AIDS. She died on January 9, 2013, at the home of her daughter in Daly City, California, at the age of 92.

Matthew Shepard Foundation

1530 Blake St., Suite 200
Denver, CO 80202
Phone: (303) 830-7400
Fax: (303) 830-6952
URL: http://www.matthewshepard.org/

The Matthew Shepard Foundation was started in 1998 by Dennis and Judy Shepard in honor of their son, Matthew, who was murdered on the evening of October 7, 1998, by Aaron McKinney and Russell Henderson. McKinney and Henderson abducted Matthew at a bar in Laramie, Wyoming, drove him to a remote area of the region, tied him to a split-rail fence, and beat him severely. Matthew died five days later in Fort Collins as a result of his injuries. Both McKinney and Henderson were eventually found guilty of murder in the first degree and were sentenced to two consecutive life sentences. The story of the crime and the trial was later the subject of one of the most popular plays written in ensuing years, *The Laramie Project*. In addition, three films and a documentary, as well as a number of popular songs, were written to memorialize the Shepard murder.

In searching for an appropriate response to this horrendous event, Judy and Dennis Shepard decided to establish a nonprofit organization "to encourage respect for human dignity and difference by raising awareness, opening dialogues, and promoting positive change." The organization's work is organized into five major categories: speakers bureau, Matthew's Place, Laramie Project support, educator resources, and *Small Bear Big Dreams*. The speakers bureau program provides speakers from a variety of backgrounds—including journalists, activists, and public safety experts—who will appear before educational institutions, companies, and community groups to provide their perspectives on the lessons to be learned from Matthew's tragic death. Matthew's Place is an online community through which LGBT youth, their parents, friends, and others may exchange views on personal and public issues raised by homophobia and other antigay attitudes, as well as related issues. The Laramie Project works to distribute information about the two major theatrical events that were developed after Matthew's death, *The Laramie Project* and *The Laramie Project: Ten Years Later*. Producers of the shows estimate that they have been seen by over 30 million people worldwide, and even two decades after Matthew's death, they draw as much interest as they did when they were first produced.

Efforts related to educator resources aim to cooperate with local school personnel to develop policies and practices that make their institutions safer environments for all students.

Small Bear, Big Dreams is a book written to celebrate Matthew's life and to teach children how better to deal with issues of diversity. The book includes narrative, worksheets, and classroom supplements.

The Matthew Shepard Foundation has also been active in supporting the adoption of hate crime legislation on a federal, state, and local level. It was instrumental in working toward the adoption of the Matthew Shepard Act, which was eventually passed by the U.S. Congress in 2009 and signed by President Barack Obama on October 28, 2009, more than a decade after Matthew's death. As of late 2013, Wyoming has no hate crime legislation, and the state legislature rejected same-sex marriage and domestic partnership bills in its 2013 session.

In 2006, MSF announced that it would partner with the Point Foundation to award three $10,000 scholarships annually to high school graduates at the college or university of their choice. Scholarship winners are expected to serve on the MSF Youth Advisory Council.

National Gay and Lesbian Task Force

1325 Massachusetts Ave. NW, Suite 600
Washington, DC 20005
Phone: (202) 393-5177
Fax: (202) 393-2241
Email: info@TheTaskForce.org
URL: http://www.ngltf.org/

The National Gay and Lesbian Task Force (NGLTF; often referred to as the Task Force) was founded in 1973 by a group of gay and lesbian activists that included Bruce Voeller, formerly associate professor and researcher at Rockefeller University; Howard Brown, formerly administrator for City Health Services for New York City; Nath Rockhill; and Ron Gold. The founders felt that existing organizations had not been working aggressively enough on behalf of achieving civil rights for all lesbians and gay men in the United States. They wanted their new organization to become a major national force to lobby the federal government for nondiscrimination legislation for lesbians and gay men in housing, employment, public accommodation, and other areas.

In its 40-year history, the Task Force has helped achieve many of its original goals, including reversal of Internal Revenue Service (IRS) policies that did not recognize organizations that promoted gay and lesbian issues; a resolution from the National Council of Churches opposing antigay and antilesbian discrimination; introduction of the first antigay and antilesbian discrimination legislation in the U.S. Congress; convincing the American Bar Association to take a stand against sodomy laws in states where they existed; creating the Military Freedom Project that worked to overturn the ban on lesbians and gay men in the U.S. military; establishing the first national hotline for LGBT individuals; creating the Fight the Right project as a counterbalance against the increasing number of radical right organizations appearing in the 1980s; founding the Legislative Lawyer Project to provide legal advice on LGBT issues; and participating in many state and local government efforts to adopt antidiscrimination ordinances.

The Task Force currently organizes its efforts into about a dozen areas of concern: Aging, Anti-Gay Industry, Campus, Elections and Politics, Faith, Hate Crimes, Health and HIV/AIDS, Marriage/Partner Recognition, Nondiscrimination, Parenting and Family, Racial and Economic Justice, Transgender, and Youth. Some examples of the specific programs developed in some of these fields are as follows:

The Aging focus includes projects such as research on and publication of a report dealing with *The Aging and Health Report: Disparities and Resilience among Lesbian, Gay, Bisexual and Transgender Older Adults*, which studied LGBT health disparities among adults between the ages of 50 to 90; cosponsorship of national research on agencies that are providing services to older LGBT adults, resulting in the report *Ready to Serve? The Aging Network and LGB and T Older Adults*; a report on long-term care facilities for older LGBTs, *Stories from the Field: LGBT Older Adults in Long-Term Care Facilities*; and a state-by-state analysis of antidiscrimination laws, *Our Maturing Movement: State-by-state LGBT Aging Policy and Recommendations*.

The Campus project has produced a report on the status of LGBT young adults on college and university campuses in the United States entitled *Campus Climate for Gay, Lesbian, Bisexual and Transgender People: A National Perspective*.

Transgender programs deal with specific topics affecting transgender people, such as discrimination, health care, police and jails, identity documents, and homelessness. A general report on these topics was *Injustice at Every Turn: A Report of the National Transgender Discrimination Survey*.

The primary activity in the Youth emphasis at the Task Force is the annual Creating Change conference. The 2013 conference, held in Atlanta, was a five-day meeting that attracted more than 3,400 LGBT youth from across the nation for more than 300 workshops, training sessions, meetings, and other events.

Task Force publications fall into three major categories: issue maps, fact sheets, and reports. Examples of the last of these categories include reports such as "Caught in the Budget Battle: How the 'Fiscal Showdown' Impacts Gay and Transgender Americans"; "Movement Analysis: The Impact of the 2012 Presidential Election on the LGBT Policy Agenda"; "Movement Analysis: The Full Impact of the EEOC Ruling on the LGBT Movement's Agenda"; "A Gender Not Listed Here: Genderqueers, Gender Rebels, and OtherWise in the National Transgender Discrimination Survey"; "A La Familia: A Conversation about Our Families, the Bible, Sexual Orientation, and Gender Identity"; "Living in the Margins: A National Survey of Lesbian, Gay, Bisexual and Transgender Asian and Pacific Islander Americans"; "Bisexual Health:

An Introduction and Model Practices for HIV/STI Prevention Programming"; "Lesbian, Gay, Bisexual and Transgender Youth: An Epidemic of Homelessness"; "Same-Sex Marriage Initiatives and Lesbian, Gay and Bisexual Voters in the 2006 Elections"; and "Homophobia at 'Hell House': Literally Demonizing Lesbian, Gay, Bisexual and Transgender Youth."

Parents and Friends of Lesbians and Gays

1828 L Street NW, Suite 660
Washington, DC 20036
Phone: (202) 467-8180
Fax: (202) 349-0788
Email: info@pflag.org
URL: http://community.pflag.org/

The first formal meeting of the organization that was to become Parents and Friends of Lesbians and Gays (PFLAG) was held on March 26, 1973, at the Metropolitan-Duane Methodist Church in Greenwich Village, New York. About 20 people attended, one of whom was Jeanne Manford, who is generally acknowledged as the original moving force behind the group. Mrs. Manford had become active in an effort to speak up for LGBT youth when her son was beaten at a protest rally at a local hotel the previous year. Word of the organization spread slowly across the country over the next few years, with local groups eventually being established in more than a dozen cities. Representatives of those groups first met following the 1979 National March for Gay and Lesbian Rights in Washington, DC, at which time discussion was held about creating a national organization. That organization, first known as Parents FLAG, had by 1982 become incorporated as a non-profit organization, Federation of Parents and Friends of Lesbians and Gays, Inc., in the state of California. At that point, PFLAG had already garnered some national attention after being mentioned in a Dear Abby newspaper column, which brought more than 7,000 letters of inquiry to the national office.

In 1990, the organization moved its national headquarters to Washington, DC, and at the same time, solicited the support of then first lady Barbara Bush. Mrs. Bush responded, "I firmly believe that we cannot tolerate discrimination against any individuals or groups in our country. Such treatment always brings with it pain and perpetuates intolerance." PFLAG's official history notes that Mrs. Bush's comment was probably the first gay-positive comment ever to come from the White House.

Over the years, PFLAG has developed programs to address specific issues faced by lesbians, gay men, bisexuals, and transgendered individuals. One such program is Cultivating Respect: Safe Schools for All. The program works with school administrators, teachers, students, and parents to develop school environments that are safe and nurturing for all students, no matter their sexual orientation. The Straight for Equality program was created in 2007 to enlist nongay men and women in the campaign to provide equal rights for all LGBT individuals. The PFLAG National Scholarship program is underwritten by major corporations for graduating LGBT seniors to attend the college of their choice. Bringing the Message Home is a campaign aimed especially at the parents of LGBT youth to let them know what is going on at the legislative level nationally and in specific regions. Welcoming Faith Communities is an effort to draw on the resources of faith-based communities to provide support and nurturing for LGBT youth and adults who are faced with difficult religious issues. A Spanish-language program, De nuestra casa a la escuela, (From Our Home to School) is designed to bring the PFLAG message to Latina/Latino and Hispanic communities.

For all of its formal programs, many of PFLAG's most profound accomplishments have been achieved on the personal level, with concerned parents and friends of gays and lesbians reaching out to other parents who have learned for the first time that their own children are gay, lesbian, bisexual, or transgender. For such individuals, it is difficult to know how to respond to this news or where to go for support and information. PFLAG is that resource.

Robert Parlin (1963–)

Robert Parlin announced his sexual orientation in the spring of 1991 at a meeting of the South Newton (Massachusetts) High School Committee on Human Differences. He took this step after hearing a school administrator announce that homosexuality was not an issue for the committee because he had never met a gay or lesbian student or teacher in the system. Parlin felt that he could not allow that observation to pass unremarked and proceeded to share with committee members his own experiences as a gay man at South Newton and prior to his employment there. He described to his colleagues his sense of isolation as a high school student and the benefits he would have had in finding a role model at that stage of his life.

Later that same year, Parlin announced his sexual orientation to his students and went on to form the first Gay-Straight Alliance (GSA) in any public school in the United States. His action followed by less than a year a similar move by his former partner, Kevin Jennings, who founded the first GSA group at any school in the United States, the private Concord (Massachusetts) Academy. Parlin remains active in dealing with LGBT youth issues, including sponsoring the South Newton GSA and offering classes for other teachers in the CEFA (context, empathy, facts, action) program that he developed.

Robert Parlin was born in Grafton, Massachusetts, on August 1, 1963. He attended Harvard College, from which he received his bachelor's degree in history and literature in 1985. He continued his studies at the Harvard Graduate School of Education (HGSE), from which he received his MEd in 1987. Parlin came out as a gay man during his first year at Harvard. After graduating from HGSE, he accepted a job teaching history at Newton South, where he has remained ever since. In 1989, he was co-founder of the Gay and Lesbian School Teacher Network (GLSTN), which was later renamed the Gay, Lesbian and Straight Education Network (GLSEN). In addition to his regular teaching assignments at Newton South, Parlin helped write the ninth grade sexuality and health curriculum for the Newton school system. He has also been a trainer on lesbian, gay, bisexual, and transgender (LGBT) issues in the New England region and has worked for the Massachusetts Department of Education's Safe Schools Program for Gay and Lesbian Students.

Parlin was elected to the HGSE Alumni Council in 2004 and was appointed to the Cambridge (Massachusetts) GLBT Commission in 2005. In 2007, Parlin created and taught a course on the history of gay-straight alliances at Wheelock College in Boston through the Stonewall Center for Lifelong Learning. In 1998, Parlin and his partner, Bren Bataclan, had the first gay commitment ceremony ever held at Harvard University's historic Memorial Church. In 2004, they were legally married in Cambridge.

Point Foundation

5757 Wilshire Blvd., Suite 370
Los Angeles, CA 90036
Phone: (323) 933-1234
Toll free: (866) 33-POINT (337-6468)
Fax: (866) 39-POINT (397-6468)
Email: info@pointfoundation.org
URL: http://www.pointfoundation.org/

The Point Foundation was founded in 2001 by life partners Bruce Lindstrom and Carl Strickland as a way of reaching out to young leaders in the LGBT community. Their goal was to help young LGBTQ men and women achieve their maximum potential "despite the obstacles often put before them" and to help them make a significant impact on society. The core activity of the Point program is the provision of academic scholarships to young men and women who are academically capable of attending institutions of higher education but who, for one reason or another, are financially unable to do so. The foundation provided eight such scholarships in its first year of operation, and in 2013 was supporting 76 young women and men in colleges and universities throughout the United States. Overall, 145 Point alumni and alumnae have gone on to earn their degrees and begin professional careers in a variety of fields.

As of 2013, the foundation administered 28 named scholarships funded by individuals in honor or memory of specific persons (such as the Tyler Clementi Point Scholarship and the Allan Gilmour and Eric Jergens Point Scholarship) or by contributing businesses for general purposes (such as the Darden Restaurants Point Scholarship and the Wells Fargo Point Scholarship).

In addition to its scholarship program, the Point Foundation works to develop LGBT leaders in a variety of ways. For example, it provides a mentoring program in which each Point scholar is assigned a mentor from her or his field of interest. The foundation also operates a Community Service Program to which every scholar is expected to donate a year of her or his time to help build a stronger LGBT presence in some community. The foundation also sponsors an annual Scholar & Alumni Leadership Conference at which scholars, alumni, regents, trustees, and staff have an opportunity to meet and exchange ideas on ideas such as HIV/AIDS, White House Community Leadership Briefing, Legislative Perspectives on the LGBTQ Agenda, An Insider View of the 2012 Election, and Building Your Personal Brand. A version of the Scholar & Alumni Leadership Conference is the Regional Leadership Forum, which is held on a regular basis each year in various regions of the country. Finally, Point provides internships to its scholars and alumni as a way of providing training and experience in an individual's chosen line of work. The internships are arranged and operated in cooperation with cooperating for-profit and nonprofit businesses that hire interns for 10-week sessions at competitive wages.

The quarterly newsletter, *On Point*, is available at no charge online at the organization's website: http://www.pointfoundation .org/Newsletters.

Dan Savage (1964–)

Savage is an author, blogger, journalist, and newspaper editor perhaps best known for founding of the It Gets Better project, which he started with his husband Terry Miller in 2010. Savage and Miller were motivated to initiate the project as the result of suicides among gay and lesbian teenagers, specifically that of 15-year-old Billy Lucas. Lucas hanged himself in his family's barn in Greensburg, Indiana, on September 9, 2010, after being bullied by classmates, one of whom told the young man to "go kill yourself." Savage and Miller knew that the teen years are often the most difficult period in a young gay man or lesbian's life, and these young people need to know that life eventually gets easier and better as one grows older and, to some extent, as society becomes more understanding and accepting of lesbians, gay men, bisexuals, and transgenders. Their response to the spate of suicides among LGBT youth was to produce a video promoting the "it gets better" theme on YouTube and to encourage other individuals to create similar videos to express their own encouraging messages. More than 200 such videos were posted in the first week following Savage and Miller's initial work, and an additional 650 videos became available in the second week. As of late 2013, more than 5,000 such videos have been posted by both LGBT men and women and supportive nongays, including President Barack Obama; former secretary of state Hillary Clinton; former speaker of the House Nancy Pelosi; actors Anne Hathaway, Colin Farrell, Matthew Morrison, and Sarah Silverman; and employees of major corporations such as

Adobe Systems, Apple, Dream Works, Facebook, Gap, Microsoft, Thomson Reuters, and Yahoo.

Daniel Keenan Savage was born on October 7, 1964, in Chicago to William and Judy Savage in a devout Roman Catholic family. Dan attended Quigley Preparatory Seminary North, which he later described in an interview with *Oasis* magazine as "a Catholic high school in Chicago for boys thinking of becoming priests." Savage knew during his high school years that he was probably gay, but he was reluctant to tell his parents for fear of their rejection. Nonetheless, he finally took at step at the age of 18 and discovered that after a period of adjustment, his parents accepted his status and acknowledged their love for him.

After graduating from high school, Savage matriculated at the University of Illinois at Champagne-Urbana, where he majored in theater. After receiving his bachelor's degree, however, he became convinced that he had had enough of acting and decided to go no further in that field. However, he had no alternative plans and was working in a video rental store in Madison, Wisconsin, when a chance remark changed his life. One of his customers at the store was Tim Keck, one of the founders of the *Onion*, one of the oldest and most highly respected alternative news channels available on the Internet. Savage later told an interviewer for the online GLBTQ Encyclopedia that he told Keck that his new alternative newspaper, the *Stranger*, should contain an advice column. Keck embraced the idea and offered the job to Savage, which—after some hesitation—he accepted. Savage suggested the name *Hey Faggot!* for the column, which many subscribing papers refused to print, so he changed the name to *Savage Love*. The column turned out to be a highly popular part of many newspapers across the United States, similar in style to the long-running and enormously popular Ann Landers (Eppie Lederer, whose desk Savage bought at auction after that columnist's death in 2002). Observers have commented on the irony of heterosexuals writing to an out gay man (Savage) for advice about their sexual and personal problems, but it is an ongoing assignment that Savage obviously loves. In addition to personal advice, he includes more than a modest amount of political commentary from the liberal end of the spectrum.

Savage and Miller were legally married in Vancouver, British Columbia, in 2005 and again in Seattle, Washington, after same-sex marriage became legal in the state on December 9, 2012. The couple has an adopted son, D. J.

Mark Segal (1951–)

In 1976, Segal founded the *Philadelphia Gay News* (PGN) and is founder and former president of the National Gay and Lesbian Press Association. He was born in Philadelphia on January 12, 1951, and moved to New York City at the age of 18 shortly after the Stonewall riots that marked the beginning of the modern gay rights movement on the East Coast. He immediately became active in the movement, joining with three other gay men to form the Action Group, which organized demonstrations for three nights following the original riot. He was then one of the founding members of the first specifically gay and lesbian political action in New York City, the Gay Liberation Front (GLF). Less than a year later, he decided that GLF was not doing enough to meet the unique needs of gay and lesbian youth, and he founded a new organization for teenagers called Gay Youth, which is widely known simply as GY. Segal became the organization's first president at the age of 19. Gay Youth continues to work on behalf of LGBT youth in New York City today.

Early on in his activist days, Segal decided that local protests were not adequate to bring to the nation's attention issues in which GLBT youth were interested, and he decided to initiate a series of "zaps" to make this case better known. Zaps were unannounced appearances at important public events by gay and lesbian activists who brought their message of protest before wide public audiences. One of Segal's first zaps was planned because of his outrage that he and a boyfriend were evicted from a television dance program in 1972 for dancing together. A few days later, he barged in unannounced during a news broadcast at the same television station to protest against the action.

Segal and a group of his colleagues known as the Gay Raiders conducted zaps at such popular programs as the *Tonight Show* starring Johnny Carson and the *Mike Douglas Show*, although his best-known zap involved the famous news reporter and commentator Walter Cronkite in December 1973. Just as Cronkite began to report on a breaking story, Segal pushed his way in front of the television cameras and raised a banner that said "Gays Protest CBS Prejudice." The news program was immediately interrupted, and Segal was expelled from the studio. The story did not end there, however, as Cronkite and Segal later had an opportunity to discuss in more detail the reason for the young man's actions. In the process, Segal gained a new and unexpected ally in the veteran newsman. Less than six months later, Cronkite included a special segment on his show dealing with the gay rights movement that addressed many of the issues about which Segal had been concerned.

Segal was 23 at the time, and he had returned to Philadelphia to turn his attention to gay rights issues in his hometown and home state. In one of his first actions there, he requested a meeting with then governor Milton Shapp at which he convinced the governor to establish the Governor's Council for Sexual Minorities. Segal calls this "the first governmental body in the world to specifically look at the problems faced by the LGBT community." He was also able to get the governor to issue the first executive order banning discrimination in state government, an order that the Pennsylvania state police at first refused to enforce. Segal's response to this defiance was in his usual mode: He volunteered to become the state's (and the nation's) first openly gay state trooper.

Segal continues to be a prolific writer, speaker, and blogger in the twenty-first century, having reported on the gay and lesbian movement not only from Philadelphia, but also from far-flung regions that include Cuba, East Berlin, and Lebanon. In 1991, he lectured in Moscow and St. Petersburg at a series of events that has since become known to some as Russia's Stonewall. In one of the encomiums earned by Segal, a local colleague at the prestigious *Philadelphia Enquirer* wrote that "Segal and PGN continue to step up admirably to the challenge set for newspapers" by Finley Peter Dunne: "To afflict the comfortable and to comfort the afflicted."

Trans Youth Family Allies

PO Box 1471
Holland, MI 49422-1471
Phone: (888) 462-8932
Email: info@imatyfa.org
URL: http://imatyfa.org/

Trans Youth Family Allies (TYFA) was founded in 2006 by Kim Pearson after the youngest of her three children came out as a lesbian. To support her child, she decided to become actively involved in the campaign to support LGBT youth by founding a local chapter of Parents and Friends of Lesbians and Gays (PFLAG). Eighteen months later, when her child announced that she was actually transgender, Pearson founded Trans Youth Family Allies (TYFA) to provide additional and focused support and assistance to transgender youth and their families. The organization is now a nonprofit 501(c)3 organization located in Holland, Michigan.

One of TYFA's primary objectives is to provide information and support to parents whose children declare themselves as transgender and/or who seek hormonal, surgical, and/or other treatments for their status. The organization's website provides parents with an opportunity to write about their own experiences with transgender and gender nonconforming children, including suggestions for other parents facing a similar situation. Useful documents are also available on the TYFA website, such as a list of frequently asked questions; "Learning the Lingo," a guide to the language used in speaking about transgender issues; "Tips for Parents"; Spanish-language versions of these three documents; recommended readings in print and on the Internet dealing with transgender issues; and links to websites with additional information on transgenderism. A special page on the TYFA website, TransParent Journeys, allows parents to write about their own personal experiences with children who identify as transgender and, in some cases, have undergone gender and/or sex transition.

The TYFA website also provides general and technical information on transgenderism for health care professionals. Examples of the articles provided in this category are recommendations and statements of policy by professional organizations such as the American Psychological Association and the National Endocrine Society, guidelines for treatment of the transgendered child, and peer-reviewed articles on moral and technical aspects of transgenderism. An additional section of the TYFA website focuses on educational aspects of transgender issues. It includes questions that have been raised by a variety of educational institutions, as well as descriptions of policies, programs, and actions that various schools have taken to be more supportive of gender nonconforming and transgendered individuals.

A major TYFA publication, "Understanding through Education," describes the mission of the organization and provides a list of the services it provides for transgender youth, their parents and caregivers, health care practitioners, and educators and administrators. The organization also provides the names and addresses of health care professionals who specialize in transgender issues in specific regions of the country. It also has a speakers bureau, which provides individuals who can make presentations on the work of the organization and on issues related to transgender youth. TYFA also sponsors the Ian Benson Project, a program developed in memory of a

16-year-old transgender man who took his own life in October 2007. The project is a tax-deductible organization that works to educate the general public and health care professionals about the special emotional needs of transgendered youth.

For individuals who want to learn more about transgender issue, the TYFA website provides links to print, visual, and electronic programs that deal with this issue. They include episodes from news and commentary programs such as ABC News, CNN Prime News, ABC's *20/20*, the *Current Health* young adult news magazine, and articles from national and local newspapers such as the *Denver Post*, *Rocky Mountain News*, *XPress Magazine*, and *Advocate*, in addition to interviews on radio stations KQED and KALW in San Francisco, on NPR's *All Things Considered*, and Chicago Public Radio's *This American Life*.

The Trevor Project

Administrative Offices
8704 Santa Monica Blvd., Suite 200
West Hollywood, CA 90069
Phone: (310) 271-8845
Fax: (310) 271-8846
New York Office Phone: (212) 229-1510
The Trevor Lifeline: (866) 488-7386
Email: info@thetrevorproject.org
URL: http://www.thetrevorproject.org/

The Trevor Project was founded in 1998 by James Lecesne, Peggy Rajski, and Randy Stone, creators of the short film *Trevor*. The film tells the story of a 13-year-old boy who becomes attracted to the most popular boy at his school. When classmates learn about Trevor's feelings for the boy, they begin to make his life unbearable with taunts and physical abuse. Trevor considers committing suicide as the only way out of this "impossible" situation. As he thinks more about that option, however, he decides to battle back against bullying and harassment, and the story ends happily with Trevor finding a new life for himself. The film tied for Best Short Subject with *Franz Kafka's It's a Wonderful Life* at the Academy Awards ceremony in 1995.

Prior to the commercial release of the film on HBO, Lecesne, Rajski, and Stone considered the possibility that it would speak to a significant number of LGBT youth who would easily relate to the trials faced by Trevor. They realized that there were few resources to which these young women and men could turn for help in dealing with suicidal thoughts related to their sexuality, and they decided to create a resource of just that kind—hence, the Trevor Project. The project now describes itself as "the leading national organization providing crisis intervention and suicide prevention services to lesbian, gay, bisexual, transgender, and questioning youth." In addition to the Academy Award, *Trevor* was honored with the Golden Arrow Award (first prize) at the Hampton Film Festival, first prize at the Aspen Film Festival Shortsfest, the Teddy Award (Best Short Film) at the Berlin International Film Festival, Golden Gate Award for Best Short Film at the San Francisco International Film Festival, and Audience Award for Best Short Film at the San Francisco Gay & Lesbian Film Festival—all in 1995.

The Trevor Project offers a variety of resources for GLBT youth who have suicidal feelings or are otherwise conflicted and distressed by issues of their sexuality. These resources include the Trevor Lifeline, a 24/7 hotline that receives thousands of calls every year; Trevorchat, a confidential interactive chat site available through the Trevor Project website at http://www.thetrevor project.org/chat; and Ask Trevor, a non–time sensitive question and answer website through which LGBT youth can ask about nonurgent issues related to their sexuality.

The Trevor Project also sponsors other programs and activities designed to aid LGBT youth in dealing with personal and social issues related to their sexuality. Trevorspace, for example, is an online social networking resource through which LGBT youth and their allies from anywhere in the world can get in touch with each other and share concerns, solutions, and ideas about their lives. The project also sponsors the Trevor Ambassadors program, which is available in seven cities across the nation and through which volunteer organizations can provide face-to-face assistance for LGBT youth. The program is available in Atlanta, Chicago, Philadelphia, San Diego, San Francisco, Seattle, and Washington, DC. More information about the program is available on the project website at http://www.thetrevorproject.org/ambassadors.

The project also provides reference materials and resources for educators, parents, friends, and other individuals who work with LGBT youth and deal with suicide issues. These resources include conferences, workshops, webinars, and classroom toolkits available through the project website. Among its most useful general resources is a brochure on books and films for LGBTQ youth, available for downloading from the project website.

Zachariah Wahls (1991–)

Zachariah (Zach) Wahls has sometimes been called one of the best straight allies that LGBT youth have. In response, he has said that he does not consider himself an "ally" of the LGBT movement. Instead, he says that although he is himself a "straight cisgender man," he is, in his own mind, "a member of the LGBT community." He goes on to explain that "even though I'm not gay, I do know what its like to be hated for who I am. And I do know what its like to be in the closet, and like every other member of the LGBT community, I did not have a choice in this. I was born into this movement."

Wahls was born on July 15, 1991, in Marshfield, Wisconsin, to a lesbian couple, Terry Wahls, a physician, and Jackie Reger, a nurse practitioner at the Iowa City VA Medical Center.

The couple met in 1995, had a commitment ceremony a year later, and were legally married in 2009, shortly after the Iowa state supreme court ruled that the state's ban on same-sex marriage was illegal under the state constitution. Zach's last name reflects the fact that Dr. Wahl is his biological mother.

The Wahl-Reger family moved from Wisconsin to Iowa City in 2000, where Zach attended elementary school and Iowa City West High School, from which he graduated in 2009. He became aware of controversy surrounding his family structure while he was still in elementary school and by the time he was in high school, he had begun writing letters to the editor and newspaper articles about being the son of two lesbians. Among these was an op-ed piece in the *Des Moines Register* arguing that marriage should be redefined as strictly a religious ceremony, and civil unions be the legal state of affairs between two individuals, whether they be same- or opposite-sex couples. His YouTube video, Zach Wahls Speaks about Family, has been seen by more than 17 million viewers. Other than this political activity, Wahls was a fairly traditional high school student, taking part in speech and debate at West High and playing quarterback for the school's football team.

Upon completing high school, Wahls matriculated at the University of Iowa, where he majored in civil and environmental engineering. He also founded his own business, called Iowa City Learns, which offered tutoring services to secondary school students in the city. He withdrew from the university in the fall of 2011 to devote his time to activities on behalf of LGBT causes and to focus on writing a book about his family called *My Two Moms: Lessons of Love, Strength, and What Makes a Family*, which was published in April 2012 by Gotham Press.

After leaving college, he also took a position as co-chair of the Outspoken Generation, a program of the Family Equality Council for adult children of LGBT parents. In May 2012, he appeared before the National Annual Meeting of the Boy Scouts of America (BSA), where he presented a petition bearing 275,000 signatures in support of a Cub Scout den leader who was forced to resign because she is a lesbian. Wahl, an Eagle Scout himself, then went on to found Scouts for Equality, an organization that works to change BSA policies that ban gay boys from joining the scouts and gay adults from serving as scoutmasters in the organization. Wahls currently spends his time speaking to student and other groups around the nation about LGBT and related issues and working on Scouts for Equality projects.

The Williams Institute

UCLA School of Law
337 Charles E. Young Dr. East
Public Policy Building Room 2381
PO Box 951476
Los Angeles, CA 90095-1476
Phone: (310) 267-4382
Fax: (310) 825-7270
Email: williamsinstitute@law.ucla.edu
URL: http://williamsinstitute.law.ucla.edu/

The Williams Institute was founded at the University of California at Los Angeles (UCLA) Law School in 2001 through a grant made by businessman and philanthropist Charles R. ("Chuck") Williams. Williams owns a consulting business and has made generous gifts to the institute amounting to more than $13 million since it was created. The mission of the institute is to conduct research on sexual orientation and gender identity law and public policy. Some of the topics subsumed under this general subject are census and LGBT demographics, marriage and couples rights, economic impact reports, race and ethnicity, parenting, workplace, the military, safe schools and youth, transgender issues, health and HIV/AIDS, violence and crime, immigration, and international issues. The institute calls on a professional staff of nearly 50 academics to carry out and report on its research.

The institute sponsors a variety of programs designed to bridge the gap between academic research and public education and implementation of its findings. One such activity is its judicial training program, which is designed to provide in-service education to jurists on important LGBT issues, such as LGBT youth in the juvenile justice system, domestic violence in same-sex relationships, and judicial bias on LGBT issues. The institute also provides the Empirical Training Program, which is designed to educate academics about LGBT issues and methodologies that can be used to conduct research on those issues. The institute also holds an annual conference that addresses current topics in the nexus between gender and sexuality and law and policy. The topic of the 2012 conference was "Fair Play? LGBT People, Civic Participation, and the Political Process."

As part of its effort to improve and encourage research on LGBT issues, the institute annually awards prizes and recognition for outstanding work in the field, including the Dukeminier Awards for the Best Sexual Orientation and Gender Identity Law Review Articles, named in honor of long-time UCLA law professor Jesse J. Dukeminier; the Human Rights Essay Award Competition on LGBT Rights, sponsored by the Academy on Human Rights and Humanitarian Law at American University (Washington, DC) College of Law; the Sexual Orientation Public Policy Research Fellowship; the annual Williams Institute Moot Court Competition; and the Sexual Orientation Law Teaching Fellowship. Beginning in the fall of 2013, the institute offered a new LL.M. degree in law and sexuality for those interested in further specialization in the field. A number of press releases describing institute research are available on its website at http://williamsinstitute.law.ucla.edu/category/press/.

Introduction

The chapter includes data and statistics on issues of importance to those who deal with LGBT issues on topics such as bullying and homelessness among LGBT youth. This chapter also contains documents dealing with issues of concern to LGBT youth and their allies. Documents such as laws and court cases provide insight into the legal status of LGBT youth in American society, which in turn reflects social attitudes toward this portion of the American population.

Data

Estimates of the number of young men and women who self-identify as gay, lesbian, bisexual, or transgender are difficult to come by. One study that attempted to answer this question was conducted by researchers at the Centers for Disease Control and Prevention (CDC) in 2011. These researchers compiled data from a series of regular studies called the Youth Risk Behavior Surveys (YRBSs). Some results from that study are reproduced in Table 5.1.

Fresno High School senior Cinthia Covarrubias, the school's first transgender prom king candidate, is surrounded by mens' tuxedo's while waiting to try hers on in Fresno, California in 2007. (AP Photo/Gary Kazanjian)

Table 5.1   Estimate of Sexual Orientation of Young Women and Men

Survey Site	Percentage of Respondents Who Reported That They Are:			
	Heterosexual	Gay or Lesbian	Bisexual	Not Sure
Delaware	93.5	1.3	3.8	1.3
Maine	93.3	1.2	3.4	2.1
Massachusetts	93.6	1.2	3.2	2.1
Rhode Island	90.7	1.7	5.2	2.5
Vermont	93.0	1.0	3.7	2.3
Boston	93.4	1.1	2.9	2.5
Chicago	90.5	2.6	3.7	3.2
New York	91.2	1.4	4.3	3.2
San Francisco	90.3	1.4	3.7	4.7
Median	93.0	1.3	3.7	2.5
Range	90.3–93.6	1.0–2.6	2.9–5.2	1.3–4.7

Source: Laura Kann et al. 2011. "Sexual Identity, Sex of Sexual Contacts, and Health-Risk Behaviors Among Students in Grades 9–12: Youth Risk Behavior Surveillance; Selected Sites, United States, 2001–2009." *Mortality and Morbidity Weekly Report (MMWR)*. 60(SS07): 1–133, Table 3. http://www.cdc.gov/mmwr/preview/mmwrhtml/ss6007a1.htm#Tab3. Accessed on February 21, 2013.

An interesting research question about LGBT youth is how a person's self-identification as nongay, gay, lesbian, or bisexual compares with one's actual sexual experiences. Another phase of the YRSB review mentioned earlier in this chapter attempted to answer this question from five state studies and three urban studies, with the results shown in Table 5.2.

To what extent do lesbian, gay, and bisexual students engage in risky behavior at a rate greater than, less than, or equal to that of their heterosexual peers? The CDC attempted to answer that question by reviewing research studies on the question by a wide variety of scholars. The results they obtained are shown in Table 5.3.

In 2012, the Williams Institute at the UCLA School of Law published some of the most extensive and most recent data on homelessness among LGBT youth in America, along with information about agencies that provide services for such individuals. Table 5.4 summarizes some of these data.

Table 5.2   Sexual Behaviors of Non-Gay, Gay, Lesbian, and Bisexual Youth

	Sexual Experience	Heterosexual	Gay or Lesbian	Bisexual	Not Sure
Median	Opposite sex only	96.3	0.4	2.0	1.4
Range	Opposite sex only	94.9–97.7	0.0–0.8	1.2–3.3	0.6–2.1
Median	Same sex only	61.7	21.7	11.3	4.4
Range	Same sex only	17.0–77.8	10.8–60.0	6.6–22.3	0.7–6.6
Median	Both sexes	29.8	9.1	50.9	10.1
Range	Both sexes	17.3–63.4	2.3–14.7	24.9–61.9	6.1–15.9
Median	No sexual contact	94.7	0.7	1.7	2.7
Range	No sexual contact	93.1–96.3	0.5–2.0	1.4–2.6	1.7–3.5

Source: Laura Kann et al. 2011. "Sexual Identity, Sex of Sexual Contacts, and Health-Risk Behaviors Among Students in Grades 9–12: Youth Risk Behavior Surveillance; Selected Sites, United States, 2001–2009." *Mortality and Morbidity Weekly Report (MMWR)*. 60(SS07): 1–133, Table 4. http://www.cdc.gov/mmwr/preview/mmwrhtml/ss6007a1.htm#Tab3. Accessed on February 21, 2013.

Table 5.3   Prevalence of Certain Risk Behaviors among Lesbian, Gay, and Bisexual Students Compared to Heterosexual Students

Behavior	Number of Comparisons	Lesbian/Gay > Heterosexual (%)[1]	Lesbian/Gay < Heterosexual (%)[2]	Lesbian/Gay = Heterosexual (%)[3]
Unintentional injuries	32	25.0	0.0	75.0
Violence	79	88.9	0.0	11.1
Attempted suicide	43	80.0	0.0	20.0
Tobacco use	89	81.8	0.0	18.2
Alcohol use	43	60.0	0.0	40.0
Other drug use	101	84.6	0.0	15.4
Sexual behaviors	87	63.6	0.0	36.4
Dietary behaviors	36	0.0	0.0	100.0
Physical activity and sedentary behaviors	67	40.0	10.0[4]	50.0

(*continued*)

Table 5.3   (*continued*)

Behavior	Number of Comparisons	Lesbian/Gay > Heterosexual (%)[1]	Lesbian/Gay < Heterosexual (%)[2]	Lesbian/Gay = Heterosexual (%)[3]
Weight management	26	100.0	0.0	0.0
Total	603	63.8	1.4	34.8

[1]Prevalence among lesbian and gay students greater than that among heterosexual students.
[2]Prevalence among lesbian and gay students less than that among heterosexual students.
[3]Prevalence among lesbian and gay students equal to that among heterosexual students.
[4]Mathematical error in original table.

Behavior	Number of Comparisons	Bisexual > Heterosexual (%)[1]	Bisexual < Heterosexual (%)[2]	Bisexual = Heterosexual (%)[3]
Unintentional injuries	36	75.0	0.0	25.0
Violence	84	90.0	0.0	10.0
Attempted suicide	44	100.0	0.0	0.0
Tobacco use	98	81.8	0.0	18.2
Alcohol use	44	100.0	0.0	0.0
Other drug use	107	100.0	0.0	0.0
Sexual behaviors	97	54.5	0.0	45.5
Dietary behaviors	42	20.0	0.0	80.0
Physical activity and sedentary behaviors	67	50.0	0.0	50.0
Weight management	16	100.0	0.0	0.0
Total	645	76.0	1.3	22.7

[1]Prevalence among bisexual students greater than that among heterosexual students.
[2]Prevalence among bisexual students less than that among heterosexual students.
[3]Prevalence among bisexual students equal to that among heterosexual students.
Source: Laura Kann et al. 2011. "Sexual Identity, Sex of Sexual Contacts, and Health-Risk Behaviors Among Students in Grades 9–12: Youth Risk Behavior Surveillance; Selected Sites, United States, 2001–2009." *Mortality and Morbidity Weekly Report (MMWR)*. 60(SS07): 1–133, Table 83. http://www.cdc.gov/mmwr/preview/mmwrhtml/ss6007a1.htm#Tab3. Accessed on February 21, 2013.

Table 5.4   Data on LGBT Homeless Youth

Clients Served: LGBT and Non-LGBT Youth

Facility	LGBT Youth (%)	Non-LGBT Youth (%)
Drop-in centers	43	57
Street outreach programs	30	70
Housing programs	30	70
Estimate of LGBTQ youth in the general population[1]	6.4–9.7	90.3–93.6

[1]From Laura Kann et al. 2011. "Sexual Identity, Sex of Sexual Contacts, and Health-Risk Behaviors Among Students in Grades 9–12: Youth Risk Behavior Surveillance; Selected Sites, United States, 2001–2009." *Mortality and Morbidity Weekly Report (MMWR)*. 60(SS07): 1–133, Table 3. http://www.cdc.gov/mmwr/ preview/mmwrhtml/ss6007a1.htm#Tab3. Accessed on February 21, 2013.

Reasons that LGBT Youth Are Homeless or at Risk for Being Homeless

Ran away because of family rejection of sexual orientation or gender identity	46%
Forced out by parents because of sexual orientation or gender identity	43%
Physical, sexual, or emotional abuse at home	32%
Aged out of the foster care system	17%
Financial or emotional neglect from family	14%
Substance abuse by youth	12%
Lack of culturally competent services[2] available in the community	11%
Mental illness	10%
Unaffordable housing	7%
Parental or family substance abuse	6%
Other reason	4%
Released from juvenile justice system or prison	3%
Pregnancy	2%

[2]*serviced* in original

Homeless LGBT Youth with the Following History Serviced by Agencies

Family rejection	68%
Mental health issues (depression, anxiety, etc.)	65%
Family abuse (physical, sexual, emotional)	54%
Alcohol and substance abuse	53%
Sexual exploitation	42%
Sexual assault	39%
Foster care	33%
Domestic/partner abuse	31%
Contact with juvenile justice system	31%

(*continued*)

Table 5.4   (*continued*)

Biggest Barriers in Improving Efforts to Prevent or Address LGBT Youth Homelessness

Lack of state government funding	36%
Lack of local/city/county funding	34%
Lack of federal funding	32%
Difficult to identify LGBT youth homeless population	20%
Lack of foundation funding	19%
Lack of financial support from the public/community	17%
Other barriers	14%
Doing so is not central to our mission	14%
Lack of designated staff	9%
Lack of information and training on LGBT youth	9%
Lack of local/city/county government support	9%
Lack of community support	7%
Lack of access to others doing work in this area	7%
Lack of state government support	6%
Lack of federal government support	4%
Poor technology (client database, outdated computers, etc.)	3%
Lack of staff support	3%
Lack of board support	1%

Source: Laura E. Durso and Gary J. Gates. *Serving Our Youth: Findings from a National Survey of Service Providers Working with Lesbian, Gay, Bisexual, and Transgender Youth Who Are Homeless or At Risk of Becoming Homeless.* Los Angeles: Williams Institute with True Colors Fund and The Palette Fund, 2012, p. 3 and Figures 7, 8, 13. Used by permission of the Williams Institute.

Documents

Tinker v. Des Moines School District, 393 U.S. 503 (1969)

Perhaps the most important Supreme Court decision regarding student First Amendment rights in the United States is a case decided in 1969. The case arose when three high school students in Des Moines, Iowa, were suspended from school for wearing black armbands to protest U.S. military involvement in Vietnam. The students' parents filed suit on their behalf in district court, where they lost. They lost again in the court of appeals, after which the case reached the U.S. Supreme Court. On February 24, 1969, *the Supreme Court with a vote of 7–2 reversed the lower courts' rulings and found in favor of the plaintiffs. The major arguments offered by the Court were as follows (notes and references are omitted at points indicated by triple asterisks, ***).*

1. In wearing armbands, the petitioners were quiet and passive. They were not disruptive, and did not impinge upon the rights of others. In these circumstances, their conduct was within the protection of the Free Speech Clause of the First Amendment and the Due Process Clause of the Fourteenth. ***

2. First Amendment rights are available to teachers and students, subject to application in light of the special characteristics of the school environment. ***

3. A prohibition against expression of opinion, without any evidence that the rule is necessary to avoid substantial interference with school discipline or the rights of others, is not permissible under the First and Fourteenth Amendments. ***

The Court expressed the fundamental principle involved in this case in a now-famous paragraph:

First Amendment rights, applied in light of the special characteristics of the school environment, are available to teachers and students. It can hardly be argued that either students or teachers shed their constitutional rights to freedom of speech or expression at the schoolhouse gate. This has been the unmistakable holding of this Court for almost 50 years.

. . .

The school officials banned and sought to punish petitioners for a silent, passive expression of opinion, unaccompanied by any disorder or disturbance on the part of petitioners. There is here no evidence whatever of petitioners' interference, actual or nascent, with the schools' work or of collision with the rights of other students to be secure and to be let alone. Accordingly, this case does not concern speech or action that intrudes upon the work of the schools or the rights of other students.

Only a few of the 18,000 students in the school system wore the black armbands. Only five students were suspended for wearing them. There is no indication that the work of the schools or any class was disrupted. Outside the classrooms, a few students made hostile remarks to the children wearing armbands, but there were no threats or acts of violence on school premises.

The District Court concluded that the action of the school authorities was reasonable because it was based upon their fear of a disturbance from the wearing of the armbands. But, in our system, undifferentiated fear or apprehension of disturbance is not enough to overcome the right to freedom of expression. Any departure from absolute regimentation may cause trouble. Any variation from the majority's opinion may inspire fear. Any word spoken, in class, in the lunchroom, or on the campus, that deviates from the views of another person may start an argument or cause a disturbance. But our Constitution says we must take this risk, *** and our history says that it is this sort of hazardous freedom—this kind of openness—that is the basis of our national strength and of the independence and vigor of Americans who grow up and live in this relatively permissive, often disputatious, society.

In order for the State in the person of school officials to justify prohibition of a particular expression of opinion, it must be able to show that its action was caused by something more than a mere desire to avoid the discomfort and unpleasantness that always accompany an unpopular viewpoint. Certainly where there is no finding and no showing that engaging in the forbidden conduct would "materially and substantially interfere with the requirements of appropriate discipline in the operation of the school," the prohibition cannot be sustained.

Source: *Tinker v. Des Moines Sch. Dist.*, 393 U.S. 503 (1969). http://supreme.justia.com/cases/federal/us/393/503/case.html. Accessed on February 20, 2013.

Aaron Fricke v. Richard B. Lynch; 491 F. Supp. 381 (1980)

In the spring of 1980, Aaron Fricke, a student at Cumberland High School in Cumberland, Rhode Island, announced his *intention to invite a male friend to be his partner at the school's spring prom. Richard B. Lynch, principal of the school, notified Fricke that he would not be allowed to do so based on a number of reasons, one of which was the possibility of physical harm to Fricke and his guest. Fricke filed suit in the U.S. District Court for the District of Rhode Island, appealing Lynch's decision. Judge Raymond James Pettine eventually ruled in favor of Fricke who did, indeed, attend the prom with his friend Paul Guilbert. The core of Judge Pettine's reasoning was as follows (notes and references are omitted at points indicated by triple asterisks, ***).*

After considerable thought and research, I have concluded that even a legitimate interest in school discipline does not outweigh a student's right to peacefully express his views in an appropriate time, place, and manner. *** To rule otherwise would completely subvert free speech in the schools by granting other students a "heckler's veto," allowing them to decide through prohibited and violent methods what speech will be heard. The first amendment does not tolerate mob rule by unruly school children. This conclusion is bolstered by the fact that any disturbance here, however great, would not interfere with the main business of school education. No classes or school work would be affected; at the very worst an optional social event, conducted by the students for their own enjoyment, would be marred. In such a context, the school does have an obligation to take reasonable measures to protect and foster free speech, not to stand helpless before unauthorized student violence.

. . .

The present case is so difficult because the Court is keenly sensitive to the testimony regarding the concerns of a possible disturbance, and of physical harm to Aaron or Paul. However, I am convinced that meaningful security measures are possible, and the first amendment requires that such steps be taken to protect rather than to stifle free expression. ** Some may feel that Aaron's attendance at the reception and the message he will thereby convey is trivial compared to other social debates, but to engage in this kind of a weighing in process is to make the content-based evaluation forbidden by the first amendment.

As to the other concern raised by Tinker, some people might say that Aaron Fricke's conduct would infringe the rights of the other students, and is thus unprotected by Tinker. This view is misguided, however. Aaron's conduct is quiet and peaceful; it demands no response from others and in a crowd of some five hundred people can be easily ignored. Any disturbance that might interfere with the rights of others would be caused by those students who resort to violence, not by Aaron and his companion, who do not want a fight.

Source: U.S. District Court for the District of Rhode Island. 491 F. Supp. 381. http://www.aclu.org/FilesPDFs/fricke.pdf. Accessed on February 20, 2013.

Equal Access Act; 20 U.S.C. §§ 4071-74 (1984)

In 1984, the U.S. Congress passed the Equal Access Act, an act designed to guarantee the right of high school students to form school clubs on religion. The act was offered in response to efforts on the part of some secondary schools to prevent students from creating such clubs. The act is of relevance to LGBT students because the reasoning on which the original act is based turns out to be equally valid to other types of clubs, including those formed to support the interests and activities of LGBT students.

Title 20 - Education

Chapter 52 - Education for Economic Security

Subchapter Viii - Equal Access

Sec. 4071. Denial of equal access prohibited

-STATUTE-

(a) Restriction of limited open forum on basis of religious, political, philosophical, or other speech content prohibited.

It shall be unlawful for any public secondary school which receives Federal financial assistance and which has a limited open forum to deny equal access or a fair opportunity to, or discriminate against, any students who wish to conduct a meeting within that limited open forum on the basis of the religious, political, philosophical, or other content of the speech at such meetings.

(b) "Limited open forum" defined

A public secondary school has a limited open forum whenever such school grants an offering to or opportunity for one or more noncurriculum related student groups to meet on school premises during noninstructional time.

(c) Fair opportunity criteria

Schools shall be deemed to offer a fair opportunity to students who wish to conduct a meeting within its limited open forum if such school uniformly provides that -

(1) the meeting is voluntary and student-initiated;

(2) there is no sponsorship of the meeting by the school, the government, or its agents or employees;

(3) employees or agents of the school or government are present at religious meetings only in a nonparticipatory capacity;

(4) the meeting does not materially and substantially interfere with the orderly conduct of educational activities within the school; and

(5) nonschool persons may not direct, conduct, control, or regularly attend activities of student groups.

The remainder of the act deals with administrative issues and protection of the rights of schools not affected by the act.

Source: Public Law 98-377, Title VIII, Section 802, Statute 1302.

Board of Education v. Mergens; 496 U.S. 226 (1990)

One of the first efforts to implement the provisions of the Equal Access Act (see previous section) arose in 1988 when a group of students at Westside High School in Omaha, Nebraska, asked permission to form a Christian club as an extracurricular organization under the auspices of the school. The school administration—and later the school board—denied the students' request, claiming that they could find no faculty member who would serve as advisor for the group. The students sued the board of education, claiming that the school allowed other noncurricular groups to meet and its refusal to permit a Christian club violated their rights to equal treatment under the U.S. Constitution and the Equal Access Act. The case dealt with three fundamental issues: (1) Did the Equal Access Act violate the so-called establishment clause of the U.S. Constitution ("Congress shall make no law respecting an establishment of religion . . ."), in which case it would be unconstitutional? (2) Did the act promote religion in the public schools, which would also violate the Constitution? and (3) Would the school have been guilty of promoting religion if it permitted students to form a Christian club? The case reached the Supreme Court in January 1990 and was decided in June of that year. The case is of special interest to LGBT youth because the principle on which the court's decision was based has turned out to be applicable to efforts by LGBT youth to form noncurricular groups also. The case's impact for LGBT youth can perhaps best be appreciated by substituting LGBT *for* Christian *in the court's decision. The main features of the court's decision are as follows (notes and references are omitted at points indicated by triple asterisks, ***).*

[With regard to the first point above:]

. . . there is a crucial difference between government speech endorsing religion, which the Establishment Clause forbids, and private speech endorsing religion, which the Free Speech and Free Exercise Clauses protect. We think that secondary school students are mature enough and are likely to understand that a school does not endorse or support student speech that it merely permits on a nondiscriminatory basis. *** The proposition that schools do not endorse everything they fail to censor is not complicated.

[With regard to the second point above:]

. . . the broad spectrum of officially recognized student clubs at Westside, and the fact that Westside students are free to initiate and organize additional student clubs, *** counteract any possible message of official endorsement of or preference for religion or a particular religious belief. *** Although a school may not itself lead or direct a religious club, a school that permits a student-initiated and student-led religious club to meet after school, just as it permits any other student group to do, does not convey a message of state approval or endorsement of the particular religion. Under the Act, a school with a limited open forum may not lawfully deny access to a Jewish students' club, a Young Democrats club, or a philosophy club devoted to the study of Nietzsche. To the extent that a religious club is merely one of many different student-initiated voluntary clubs, students should perceive no message of government endorsement of religion. Thus, we conclude that the Act does not, at least on its face and as applied to Westside, have the primary effect of advancing religion.

[With regard to the third point above:]

Under the Act, however, faculty monitors may not participate in any religious meetings, and nonschool persons may not direct, control, or regularly attend activities of student groups. *** Moreover, the Act prohibits school "sponsorship" of any religious meetings, ***, which means that school officials may not promote, lead, or participate in any such meeting ***. Although the Act permits "[t]he assignment of a teacher, administrator, or other school employee to the meeting for custodial purposes," *** , such custodial oversight of the student-initiated religious group, merely to ensure order and good behavior, does not impermissibly entangle government in the day-to-day surveillance or administration of religious activities. Indeed, as the Court noted in Widmar *[a precedent case at the university level]*, a denial of equal access to religious speech might well create greater entanglement problems in the form of invasive monitoring to prevent religious speech at meetings at which such speech might occur.

Source: *Board of Education v. Mergens;* 496 U.S. 226 (1990). http://supreme.justia.com/cases/federal/us/496/226/case.html. Accessed on February 23, 2013.

Jamie S. Nabozny v. Mary Podlesny, William Davis, Thomas Blauert; 92 F.3d 446 (1996)

Although no federal law exists to protect LGBT students against harassment in schools, individuals who have experienced discrimination, bullying, physical and psychological attacks, and other forms of intimidation have sometimes found other mechanisms for suing their harassers. An example is the case cited here, in which the gay and lesbian legal advocacy group Lambda Legal Defense brought suit on behalf of a student, James S. Nabozny, who had experienced many years of harassment at his schools without receiving even the most modest support from school administrators. The defendants in the case are the school principal (Davis), the assistant principal (Blauert), and the principal in charge of discipline (Podlesny) (notes and references are omitted at points indicated by triple asterisks, ***).

(The court notes the bases for the suit brought by Lambda, namely that the defendants violated Nabozny's rights under the Fourteenth Amendment of the U.S. Constitution, an amendment that includes the Equal Rights Clause, guaranteeing equal protection under the law for all American citizens. Nabozny alleged, according to the court, that:)

... defendants: 1) violated his Fourteenth Amendment right to equal protection by discriminating against him based on his gender; 2) violated his Fourteenth Amendment right to equal protection by discriminating against him based on his sexual orientation; 3) violated his Fourteenth Amendment right to due process by exacerbating the risk that he would be harmed by fellow students; and, 4) violated his Fourteenth Amendment right to due process by encouraging an environment in which he would be harmed.

(The court begins by noting that the state of Wisconsin has a law prohibiting harassment based on, among other things, sexual orientation, and that the school had adopted a policy in accord with that laws.)

Wisconsin statute section 118.13(1), regulating general school operations, provides that:

No person may be denied . . . participation in, be denied the benefits of or be discriminated against in any curricular, extracurricular, pupil services, recreational or other program or activity because of the person's sex, race, religion, national origin, ancestry, creed, pregnancy, marital or parental status, sexual orientation or physical, mental, emotional or learning disability.

Since at least 1988, in compliance with the state statute, the Ashland Public School District has had a policy of prohibiting discrimination against students on the basis of gender or sexual orientation. The District's policy and practice includes protecting students from student-on-student sexual harassment and battery. Nabozny maintains that the defendants denied him the equal protection of the law by denying him the protection extended to other students, based on his gender and sexual orientation

. . .

The record viewed in the light most favorable to Nabozny, combined with the defendants' own admissions, suggests that Nabozny was treated differently from other students. The defendants stipulate that they had a commendable record of enforcing their anti-harassment policies. Yet Nabozny has presented evidence that his classmates harassed and battered him for years and that school administrators failed to enforce their anti-harassment policies, despite his repeated pleas for them to do so. If the defendants otherwise enforced their anti-harassment policies, as they contend, then Nabozny's evidence strongly suggests that they made an exception to their normal practice in Nabozny's case.

. . .

. . . the defendants ask us to affirm the grant of qualified immunity because "there was no clear duty under the equal protection clause for the individual defendants to enforce every student complaint of harassment by other students the same way." The defendants are correct in that the Equal Protection Clause does not require the government to give everyone identical treatment. Nothing we say today suggests anything to the contrary. The Equal Protection Clause does, however, require the state to treat each person with equal regard, as having equal worth, regardless of his or her status. The defendants' argument fails because they frame their inquiry too narrowly. The question is not whether they are required to treat every harassment complaint the same way; as we have noted, they are not. The question is whether they are required to give male and female students equivalent levels of protection; they are, absent an important governmental objective, and the law clearly said so prior to Nabozny's years in middle school.***

. . .

Our discussion of equal protection analysis thus far has revealed a well established principle: the Constitution prohibits intentional invidious discrimination between otherwise similarly situated persons based on one's membership in a definable minority, absent at least a rational basis for the discrimination. There can be little doubt that homosexuals are an identifiable minority*** subjected to discrimination in our society. Given the legislation across the country both positing and prohibiting homosexual rights, that proposition was as self-evident in 1988 as it is today. In addition, the Wisconsin statute expressly prohibits discrimination on the basis of sexual orientation. Obviously that language was included because the Wisconsin legislature both recognized that homosexuals are discriminated against, and sought to prohibit such discrimination in Wisconsin schools. The defendants stipulate that they knew about the Wisconsin law, and enforced it to protect homosexuals. Therefore, it appears that the defendants concede that they knew that homosexuals are a definable minority and treated them as such.***

. . .

We conclude that, based on the record as a whole, a reasonable fact-finder could find that the District and defendants Podlesny, Davis, and Blauert violated Nabozny's Fourteenth Amendment right to equal protection by discriminating against

person's presence affects in a significant way the group's ability to advocate public or private viewpoints. *** However, the freedom of expressive association is not absolute; it can be overridden by regulations adopted to serve compelling state interests, unrelated to the suppression of ideas, that cannot be achieved through means significantly less restrictive of associational freedoms. *** To determine whether a group is protected, this Court must determine whether the group engages in "expressive association." The record clearly reveals that the Boy Scouts does so when its adult leaders inculcate its youth members with its value system. *** Thus, the Court must determine whether the forced inclusion of Dale would significantly affect the Boy Scouts' ability to advocate public or private viewpoints. The Court first must inquire, to a limited extent, into the nature of the Boy Scouts' viewpoints. The Boy Scouts asserts that homosexual conduct is inconsistent with the values embodied in the Scout Oath and Law, particularly those represented by the terms "morally straight" and "clean," and that the organization does not want to promote homosexual conduct as a legitimate form of behavior. The Court gives deference to the Boy Scouts' assertions regarding the nature of its expression, *** The Court then inquires whether Dale's presence as an assistant scoutmaster would significantly burden the expression of those viewpoints. Dale, by his own admission, is one of a group of gay Scouts who have become community leaders and are open and honest about their sexual orientation. His presence as an assistant scoutmaster would interfere with the Scouts' choice not to propound a point of view contrary to its beliefs. *** This Court disagrees with the New Jersey Supreme Court's determination that the Boy Scouts' ability to disseminate its message would not be significantly affected by the forced inclusion of Dale. First, contrary to the state court's view, an association need not associate for the purpose of disseminating a certain message in order to be protected, but must merely engage in expressive activity that could be impaired. Second, even if the Boy Scouts discourages Scout leaders from disseminating views on sexual issues, its method of expression is protected. Third, the First Amendment does not require that every member of a group agree on every issue in order for the group's policy to be "expressive association." Given that the Boy Scouts' expression would be burdened, the Court must inquire whether the application of New Jersey's public accommodations law here runs afoul of the Scouts' freedom of expressive association, and concludes that it does. Such a law is within a State's power to enact when the legislature has reason to believe that a given group is the target of discrimination and the law does not violate the First Amendment. *** This Court rejects Dale's contention that the intermediate standard of review enunciated in United States v. O'Brien, 391 U. S. 367, should be applied here to evaluate the competing interests of the Boy Scouts and the State. Rather, the Court applies an analysis similar to the traditional First Amendment analysis it applied in Hurley. A state requirement that the Boy Scouts retain Dale would significantly burden the organization's right to oppose or disfavor homosexual conduct. The state interests embodied in New Jersey's public accommodations law do not justify such a severe intrusion on the freedom of expressive association. In so ruling, the Court is not guided by its view of whether the Boy Scouts' teachings with respect to homosexual conduct are right or wrong; public or judicial disapproval of an organization's expression does not justify the State's effort to compel the organization to accept members in derogation of the organization's expressive message. While the law may promote all sorts of conduct in place of harmful behavior, it may not interfere with speech for no better reason than promoting an approved message or discouraging a disfavored one, however enlightened either purpose may seem. ***

[Note; On May 23, 2013, the BSA's National Council approved a resolution removing the organization's policy denying membership to boys on the basis of sexual orientation alone effective January 1, 2014. The prohibition against gay men's serving as scoutmasters was retained.]

Source: *Boy Scouts of America et al. v. Dale.* 530 U.S. 640 (2000). http://supreme.justia.com/cases/federal/us/530/640/. Accessed on March 28, 2013.

Revised Sexual Harassment Guidance: Harassment of Students by School Employees, Other Students, or Third Parties (2001)

The mission of the Office for Civil Rights of the U.S. Department of Education is to "ensure equal access to education and to promote educational excellence throughout the nation through vigorous enforcement of civil rights." From time to time, it issues bulletins and other publications explaining the basis for its actions and the procedures by which complaints can be filled for redress against unwanted actions. The following passage provides the most recent statement of the office's position on the rights of LGBT students. (Notes and references are omitted at points indicated by triple asterisks, ***; Title IX is the section of the Education Amendments of 1972, which first provided protection for school students against sexual harassment.)

Although Title IX does not prohibit discrimination on the basis of sexual orientation, *** sexual harassment directed at gay or lesbian students that is sufficiently serious to limit or deny a student's ability to participate in or benefit from the school's program constitutes sexual harassment prohibited by Title IX under the circumstances described in this guidance.*** For example, if a male student or a group of male students target a gay student for physical sexual advances, serious enough to deny or limit the victim's ability to participate in or benefit from the school's program, the school would need to respond promptly and effectively, as described in this guidance, just as it would if the victim were heterosexual. On the other hand, if students heckle another student with comments based on the student's sexual orientation (e.g., "gay students are not welcome at this table in the cafeteria"), but their actions do not involve conduct of a sexual nature, their actions would not be sexual harassment covered by Title IX.***

Source: *Revised Sexual Harassment Guidance: Harassment of Students by School Employees, Other Students, or Third Parties.* January 2001. http://www2.ed.gov/offices/OCR/archives/pdf/ shguide.pdf. Accessed on February 22, 2013.

Henkle v. Gregory, 150 F.Supp.2d 1067 (2001)

In the fall of 1995, Derek R. Henkle, a sophomore at Galena High School in Washoe County, Nevada, appeared on a local television program in which students discussed issues of being out at their schools. From that point on, Henkle was subjected to continuous and intense harassment at his school, including one occasion on which his peers fashioned a lasso that they placed around his neck and pretended to hang him. Rather than attempting to protect Henkle, the school principal, Ross Gregory, acted as if Henkle was the problem, asking that he be transferred to another school twice and telling the student to "stop acting like a fag." In 2000, Henkle sued Gregory and other school officials, claiming the school had violated his First Amendment rights to free speech. Judge Robert A. McQuaid Jr. ruled in favor of Henkle (the plaintiff) on the First Amendment issue. The main points of his decision in this regard are as follows (omitted notes and references are indicated by a triple asterisk, ***).

"Students in public schools do not shed their constitutional rights to freedom of speech or expression at the schoolhouse gate." *** "[S]chool officials cannot suppress expressions of feelings with which they do not wish to contend." *** Thus, "[i]n the absence of a specific showing of constitutionally valid reasons to regulate their speech, students are entitled to expression of their views." *** Students' speech may be regulated where defendants show that engaging in forbidden conduct would "materially and substantially interfere with the requirements of appropriate discipline in the operation of the school." ***

Defendants argue that they did not violate Plaintiff's First Amendment rights because his speech was disruptive and as such was subject to being suppressed and regulated by Defendants.

. . .

In examining a First Amendment retaliation claim, courts engage in yet another three part inquiry. For the first two prongs of the inquiry, plaintiff must demonstrate: (1) the speech at issue was constitutionally protected; and (2) the speech was a substantial or motivating factor in the adverse action. *** If plaintiff satisfies this burden, the burden shifts to the defendants to demonstrate they would have taken the same actions against plaintiff, even in the absence of his protected conduct. ***

In light of the previous discussion, Plaintiff satisfied element one by alleging that his speech was constitutionally protected. *** Thus, we will turn our attention to element two.

[Plaintiff at this point provides examples of instances in which he was retaliated against for speaking out on gay issues.] . . .

Thus, at this stage of the proceedings, Plaintiff has made sufficient allegations, that his constitutionally protected speech was a substantial motivating factor in adverse action directed at him. . . .

Defendants assert they are entitled to qualified immunity because there was no clearly established right for a gay student to speak about or express his sexual preference in a school setting. ***

Government officials enjoy qualified immunity from civil damages unless their conduct violates "clearly established statutory or constitutional rights of which a reasonable person would have known." *** "A public official is not entitled to qualified immunity when the contours of the allegedly violated right were sufficiently clear that a reasonable official would understand that what he [was] doing violate[d] that right." *** Determining whether a public official is entitled to qualified immunity "requires a two-part inquiry: (1) Was the law governing the state official's conduct clearly established? (2) Under that law could a reasonable state official have believed his conduct was lawful?" ***

Defendants contend that the established constitutional right must be narrowly particularized, rather than generalized. They assert that without a case which specifically concerns sexual orientation speech by students there can be no clearly established law prior to 1997. The court disagrees. . . .

In *Tinker, supra,* the Supreme Court clearly established that students in public schools have the right to freedom of speech and expression. *** This is a broad right that would encompass the right of a high school student to express his sexuality. In *Chandler, supra,* the Ninth Circuit discussed in detail categories of student's speech. The court set forth two specific categories and a third category of "speech that falls into neither of these categories." This category clearly encompasses various types of speech, including the type involved with the Plaintiff. To require Plaintiff to particularize and prove the clearly established right that Defendants suggest would circumvent the right established by the Supreme Court. *** If Defendants' argument were to be accepted it would allow future Defendants to abuse the "clearly established right" standard so that each time a new fact situation arose they would be entitled to qualified immunity. . . .

The Defendants are not entitled to qualified immunity as a matter of law.

Source: *Henkle v. Gregory,* 150 F.Supp.2d 1067 (2001). http:// scholar.google.com/scholar_case?case=4160447112081253169 &q=henkle+v.+gregory&hl=en&as_sdt=2,38&as_vis=1. Accessed on March 29, 2013.

Suicide Risk and Prevention for Lesbian, Gay, Bisexual, and Transgender Youth (2008)

In 2008, the Suicide Risk Prevention Center (SRPC) prepared a report for the U.S. Substance Abuse and Mental Health Services Administration (SAMHSA) on the higher risk of suicide faced by LGB (and probably T) youth in the United States. In addition to reviewing the available scientific research on the topic, the authors of the report prepared a list of recommendations for agencies dealing with at risk LGBT youth. Those recommendations are reprinted here.

- Implement training for all staff members to effectively serve LGBT youth by including recognition and response to warning signs for suicide and the risk and protective factors for suicidal behavior in LGBT youth
- Include information about higher rates of suicidal behavior in LGBT youth in health promotion materials
- Assess and ensure that youth services and providers are inclusive, responsive to, and affirming of the needs of LGBT youth, and refer youth to these services and providers
- Develop peer-based support programs
- Include the topic of coping with stress and discrimination and integrate specific activities for LGBT youth in life skills training and programs to prevent risk behaviors
- Support staff advocacy for LGBT youth
- Incorporate program activities to support youth and their family members throughout the development of sexual orientation and gender identity, including awareness, identity, and disclosure. These programs must address young children and adolescents.
- Promote organizations that support LGBT youth, such as Gay-Straight Alliances and Parents, Families, and Friends of Lesbians & Gays (PFLAG)
- Institute protocols and policies for appropriate response if a client or student is identified as at risk of self-harm, has made a suicide attempt, or has died by suicide
- Make accurate information about LGBT issues and resources easily available
- Use an LGBT cultural competence model that enables individuals and agencies to work effectively with LGBT youth cultures
- Include LGBT youth in program development and evaluation
- Institute, enforce, and keep up to date non-discrimination and non-harassment policies for all youth

- Implement confidentiality policies that are clear, comprehensive, and explicit
- Assume that clients or students could be any sexual orientation or gender identity and respond accordingly
- Address explicitly the needs of LGBT youth in school-based programs and policies to prevent violence and bullying

Researchers and program developers, as well as funders, also play a role in reducing suicidal behavior in LGBT youth. The authors recommend that they:

- Use evaluation results, surveillance data, and research conclusions to develop evidence-based programs to build protective factors and to prevent suicide among LGBT youth
- Undertake large-scale epidemiological studies that include complex measures of sexual orientation and gender identity and include research on discrimination and mental illness
- Include LGBT youth in research development and evaluation
- In developing programs, emphasize protective factors for LGBT youth
- Develop research projects and funding for research on risk and protective factors for suicidal behavior for youth generally and for LGBT youth specifically and work with program staff to encourage getting research results into program design

Source: Effie Malley, Marc Posner, and Lloyd Potter. *Suicide Risk and Prevention for Lesbian, Gay, Bisexual, and Transgender Youth.* Newton, MA: Suicide Prevention Resource Center, 2008. http://www.sprc.org/sites/sprc.org/files/library/SPRC_LGBT _Youth.pdf. Accessed on March 30, 2013. Quoted by permission of SPRC.

It Gets Better (Obama Post) (2010)

More than 5,000 individuals and organizations have posted videos for the It Gets Better project started by Dan Savage and his husband Terry Miller in 2010. One of the earliest of those videos was posted by President Barack Obama. The transcript of that video is as follows.

Like all of you, I was shocked and saddened by the deaths of several young people who were bullied and taunted for being gay, and who ultimately took their own lives. As a parent of two daughters, it breaks my heart. It's something that just shouldn't happen in this country.

We've got to dispel the myth that bullying is just a normal rite of passage—that it's some inevitable part of growing up. It's not. We have an obligation to ensure that our schools are safe for all of our kids. And to every young person out there you need to know that if you're in trouble, there are caring adults who can help.

I don't know what it's like to be picked on for being gay. But I do know what it's like to grow up feeling that sometimes you don't belong. It's tough. And for a lot of kids, the sense of being alone or apart—I know can just wear on you. And when you're teased or bullied, it can seem like somehow you brought it on yourself—for being different, or for not fitting in with everybody else.

But what I want to say is this. You are not alone. You didn't do anything wrong. You didn't do anything to deserve being bullied. And there is a whole world waiting for you, filled with possibilities. There are people out there who love you and care about you just the way you are. And so, if you ever feel like because of bullying, because of what people are saying, that you're getting down on yourself, you've got to make sure to reach out to people you trust. Whether it's your parents, teachers, folks that you know care about you just the way you are. You've got to reach out to them, don't feel like you're in this by yourself.

The other thing you need to know is, things will get better. And more than that, with time you're going to see that your differences are a source of pride and a source of strength. You'll look back on the struggles you've faced with compassion and wisdom. And that's not just going to serve you, but it will help you get involved and make this country a better place.

It will mean that you'll be more likely to help fight discrimination—not just against LGBT Americans, but discrimination in all its forms. It means you'll be more likely to understand personally and deeply why it's so important that as adults we set an example in our own lives and that we treat everybody with respect. That we are able to see the world through other people's eyes and stand in their shoes—that we never lose sight of what binds us together.

As a nation we're founded on the belief that all of us are equal and each of us deserves the freedom to pursue our own version of happiness; to make the most of our talents; to speak our minds; to not fit in; most of all, to be true to ourselves. That's the freedom that enriches all of us. That's what America is all about. And every day, it gets better.

Source: White House. "It Gets Better Video Transcript." http://www.whitehouse.gov/it-gets-better-transcript. Accessed on April 9, 2013.

Student Non-Discrimination Act; H.R. 998/S. 555 (2011)

In 2011, Representative Jared Polis (D-CO) introduced the Student Non-Discrimination Act of 2011, establishing a framework for assisting GLBT youth who face discrimination and harassment. The bill establishes federal policy and provides mechanisms of relief for such individuals. The bill had 171 co-sponsors in the House. A comparable bill was introduced in the U.S. Senate by Al Franken (D-MN). The House bill was referred to the House Committee on Education and the Workforce but was never acted upon. The bill consists of 11 sections, most of which deal with administrative issues, such as definition of terms, findings,

*enforcement, and severability. The core of the bill is Section 4, enti-
tled "Prohibitions against Discrimination." It reads as follows.*

SEC. 4. PROHIBITION AGAINST DISCRIMINATION;
EXCEPTIONS.

(a) In General- No student shall, on the basis of actual or
perceived sexual orientation or gender identity of such individual or of a person with whom the student associates or has associated, be excluded from participation in, or be denied the
benefits of, or be subjected to discrimination under any program or activity receiving Federal financial assistance.

(b) Harassment- For purposes of this Act, discrimination
includes, but is not limited to, harassment of a student on the
basis of actual or perceived sexual orientation or gender identity
of such student or of a person with whom the student associates
or has associated.

(c) Retaliation Prohibited-

(1) PROHIBITION- No person shall be excluded from participation in, be denied the benefits of, or be subjected to discrimination, retaliation, or reprisal under any program or
activity receiving Federal financial assistance based on his or
her opposition to conduct made unlawful by this Act.

(2) DEFINITION- For purposes of this subsection,
'opposition to conduct made unlawful by this Act' includes,
but is not limited to—

(A) opposition to conduct reasonably believed to be made
unlawful by this Act,

(B) any formal or informal report, whether oral or written, to
any governmental entity, including public schools and employees thereof, regarding conduct made unlawful by this Act or
reasonably believed to be made unlawful by this Act,

(C) participation in any investigation, proceeding, or hearing
related to conduct made unlawful by this Act or reasonably
believed to be made unlawful by this Act, and

(D) assistance or encouragement provided to any other person in the exercise or enjoyment of any right granted or protected by this Act,

if in the course of that expression, the person involved does not purposefully provide information known to be false to any public school or other governmental entity regarding a violation, or alleged violation, of this Act.

Source: H.R. 998 (112th): Student Non-Discrimination Act of 2011. GovTrack.us. http://www.govtrack.us/congress/bills/112/hr998/text. Accessed on February 17, 2013.

Recommendations of the Massachusetts Commission on Gay, Lesbian, Bisexual, and Transgender Youth (2011)

The Massachusetts Commission on GLBT Youth is a state-chartered commission that is required to present an annual report on the status of gay, lesbian, bisexual, and transgender youth in the state. The 2011 report made the following recommendations to a number of state agencies.

[to the Department of Children and Families:]

Recommendation 1: GLBT specific trainings for workers and providers.

Recommendation 2: Development of GLBT specific practice guidelines.

Recommendation 3: Provide continued support to the DCF GLBT liaisons group.

Recommendation 4: Encourage members of GLBT community to become foster parents.

[to the Department of Elementary and Secondary Education:]

Recommendation 1: Eliminate educational barriers based on race and ethnicity.

Recommendation 2: Address transgender and gender non-conforming student needs.

Recommendation 3: Expand surveillance data on GLBT Youth.

Recommendation 4: Expand the scope of programs beyond focus on suicide and violence.

Recommendation 5: Expand the scope of programs to include elementary and middle schools.

Recommendation 6: Support Safe Schools Program for GLBT Students.

Recommendation 7: Amend "access to equal opportunity" regulations.

Recommendation 8: Include sexual orientation in curriculum frameworks.

Recommendation 9: Include sexual orientation in teacher licensure standards.

[to the Department of Public Health:]

Recommendation 1: Continue and enhance data collection on GLBT youth.

Recommendation 2: Ensure that evidence-based, culturally tailored strategies are being designed, adapted, and implemented to reduce health disparities among GLB youth of color and all transgender youth.

Recommendation 3: Assess the prevalence and nature of GLBT youth homelessness and fund GLBT youth homelessness prevention research.

Recommendation 4: Ensure that DPH and provider staff is trained on GLBT youth cultural competency.

Recommendation 5: Include GLBT youth populations in the mission and purview of the Office of Health Equity.

Recommendation 6: Provide continued support to the Massachusetts Commission on GLBT Youth's Mandate.

[to the Department of Youth Services:]

Recommendation 1: Provide GLBT cultural competency resources for staff and encourage staff to create safe spaces for GLBT youth.

Recommendation 2: Ensure safety, privacy, and medical care for transgender and gender-nonconforming youth.

Recommendation 3: Provide access to GLBT resources for youth and families.

Recommendation 4: Expand anti-discrimination policy to include gender identity and expression.

Recommendation 6: Ensure that current policies and practices around romantic or affectionate behavior are gender neutral (i.e. staff response and consequences are the same for same-sex and heterosexual behavior).

Source: Arthur Lipkin and Edward Byrne. *Annual Recommendations to the Great and General Court and Executive Agencies, October 2011.* Commission on Gay, Lesbian, Bisexual, and Transgender Youth, Commonwealth of Massachusetts. http://www.mass.gov/cgly/Oct2011_MCGLBTY_Annual_Rec .pdf. Accessed on March 8, 2013.

Letter from Secretary of Education Arne Duncan (2011)

In 1984, the U.S. Congress passed and President Ronald Reagan signed the Equal Access Act, an act designed to guarantee equal access to all public school students for their extracurricular clubs. Beginning in the mid-1990s, a number of court cases were initiated using the act to guarantee that LGBT youth would be allowed to form gay-straight alliance clubs in their schools. In 2011, U.S. Secretary of Education Arne Duncan wrote to all public school systems in the nation outlining federal law on the matter of equal access for GSA clubs. The major thrust of that letter was as follows (footnotes have been deleted, as shown by triple asterisks, ***).

Gay-straight alliances (GSAs) and similar student-initiated groups addressing LGBT issues can play an important role in promoting safer schools and creating more welcoming learning environments. Nationwide, students are forming these groups in part to combat bullying and harassment of LGBT students and to promote understanding and respect in the school community. Although the efforts of these groups focus primarily on the needs of LGBT students, students who have LGBT family members and friends, and students who are perceived to be LGBT, messages of respect, tolerance, and inclusion benefit all our students. By encouraging dialogue and providing supportive resources, these groups can help make schools safe and affirming environments for everyone.

But in spite of the positive effect these groups can have in schools, some such groups have been unlawfully excluded from school grounds, prevented from forming, or denied access to school resources. These same barriers have sometimes been used to target religious and other student groups, leading Congress to pass the Equal Access Act.

In 1984, Congress passed and President Ronald Reagan signed into law the Equal Access Act, requiring public secondary schools to provide equal access for extracurricular clubs. Rooted in principles of equal treatment and freedom of expression, the Act protects student-initiated groups of all types. As one of my predecessors, Secretary Richard W. Riley, pointed out in guidance concerning the Equal Access Act and religious clubs more than a decade ago, we "protect our own freedoms by respecting the freedom of others who differ from us." *** By allowing students to discuss difficult issues openly and honestly, in a civil manner, our schools become forums for combating ignorance, bigotry, hatred, and discrimination.

The Act requires public secondary schools to treat all student-initiated groups equally, regardless of the religious, political, philosophical, or other subject matters discussed at their meetings. Its protections apply to groups that address issues relating to LGBT students and matters involving sexual orientation and gender identity, just as they apply to religious and other student groups.

Today, the U.S. Department of Education's General Counsel, Charles P. Rose, is issuing a set of legal guidelines affirming the principles that prevent unlawful discrimination against any student-initiated groups. We intend for these guidelines to provide schools with the information and resources they need to help ensure that all students, including LGBT and gender nonconforming students, have a safe place to learn, meet, share experiences, and discuss matters that are important to them.

Although specific implementation of the Equal Access Act depends upon contextual circumstances, these guidelines reflect basic obligations imposed on public school officials by the Act and the First Amendment to the U.S. Constitution. The general rule, approved by the U.S. Supreme Court, is that a public high school that allows at least one noncurricular student group to meet on school grounds during noninstructional time (e.g., lunch, recess, or before or after school) may not deny similar access to other noncurricular student groups, regardless of the religious, political, philosophical, or other subject matters that the groups address.

I encourage every school district to make sure that its administrators, faculty members, staff, students, and parents are familiar with these principles in order to protect the rights of all students—regardless of religion, political or philosophical views, sexual orientation, or gender identity. I also urge school districts to use the guidelines to develop or improve district policies.

Source: "Key Policy Letters from the Education Secretary and Deputy Secretary." U.S. Department of Education. http://www2.ed.gov/policy/elsec/guid/secletter/110607.html. Accessed on March 26, 2013.

SAMHSA on Suicide Risk for LGBT Youth (2011)

In October 2011, Representative Jerrold Nadler (D-NY) wrote a letter to Pamela S. Hyde, administrator for the Substance Abuse and Mental Health Services Administration (SAMHSA) of the U.S. Department of Health and Human Services, asking what the agency was doing to reduce the risk of suicide for LGBT youth. Administrator Hyde responded with a five-page letter outlining the activities conducted by SAMHSA and other federal agencies to respond to this problem. The main points made by Hyde in her letter are as follows. Triple asterisks (***) indicate the omission of detailed information at various points in the letter.

SAMHSA has a number of programs and initiatives that focus on LGBT youth and suicide prevention. We have detailed these below in response to your questions.

1. *How are SAMHSA's programs and those that it supports nationwide with respect to suicide prevention specifically designed to help LGBT Americans?*

SAMHSA's Suicide Prevention Initiative and the Children's Mental Health Initiative have developed activities and materials specifically focused on LGBT youth. Selected efforts are described below.

(a) The *Suicide Prevention Resource Center (SPRC)* includes LGBT youth as one of its priority populations. The SPRC has produced publications and trainings geared toward improving awareness and capacity for suicide prevention for LGBT youth. Selected works include:

*[The letter next describes three publications developed specifically for LGBT youth. ***]*

(b) *SAMHSA's National Suicide Prevention Lifeline* links a network of crisis centers across the country. The Lifeline routinely refers LGBT youth to The Trevor Project. The executive director of The Trevor Project is an active member of the Lifeline's Consumer Survivor Subcommittee.

(c) *The Garrett Lee Smith State and Tribal Youth Suicide Prevention Program* funds State and Tribal grantees to conduct suicide prevention activities. Currently, nearly half of the 32 State grantees report activities focused on LGBT youth. Examples include:

*[The letter next describes programs in Colorado and Massachusetts that fit this description. ***]*

(d) *The Garrett Lee Smith Campus Suicide Prevention Program* funds colleges to address suicide prevention. Nearly a third of the 68 grantees report at least one activity focused on LGBT youth including:

*[The letter next describes programs at the University of Wisconsin–Oshkosh and the University of Kentucky–Lexington as examples of this work. ***]*

(e) *The National Workgroup to Address the Behavioral Health needs of Youth Who are LGBTQI2-S and Their Families* has been convened over the past few years by the SAMHSA Child Adolescent and Family branch. Comprised of a diverse group of stakeholders, this National Workgroup provides input about programs, materials, products and policies to improve the lives of LGBTQ youth and their families, including promoting suicide prevention efforts and enhancing family acceptance in the provision of services and supports.

(f) The *Children's Mental Health Initiative (CMHI)* grant program has been collecting sexual orientation and gender identity data since 2009 for all children and youth receiving mental health services and supports through the CMHI grant program. This data will be critical in better understanding the needs of LGBT youth in systems of care, including suicidal ideation and attempts and how best to meet their clinical and behavioral needs.

(g) SAMHSA's Homelessness Resource Center convened an *Expert Panel on Youth Who Are LGBTQI2-S and Homeless.* This panel generated a report with recommendations for culturally and linguistically competent care in shelters that serve the needs of LGBT youth who are homeless and at risk for multiple negative outcome including suicide. This report will inform future program efforts aimed at ameliorating the toxic effects of homelessness on LGBT youth.

[The letter concludes with the administrator's responses to four other questions from Nadler dealing with current and future programs for reducing suicide ideation among LGBT youth. ***]

Source: Letter to the Honorable Jerrold Nadler. http://www .keennewsservice.com/wp-content/uploads/2010/11/Response -from-SAMHSA-Nov-5-2010.pdf. Accessed on March 12, 2013.

A large number of books, pamphlets, articles, reports, and websites have been written on the topic of LGBT issues over the past half-century. The following annotated bibliography can do no more than provide a hint of those resources. The items listed have been categorized under four major heading: books, articles, reports, and Internet sources. Some overlap may occur, in which case both print and electronic references are provided for any specific item available in both formats.

Books

Aizumi, Marsha, with Aiden Takeo Aizumi. *Two Spirits, One Heart: A Son's Journey and a Mother's Love.* New York: Magnus, 2012.

> The author describes the experience in her young daughter's coming out as a lesbian and then transitioning as a man. The two major parts of the book are devoted to the daughter, Ashley, and the son, Aiden.

Belge, Kathy, and Marke Bieschke. *Queer: The Ultimate LGBT Guide for Teens.* San Francisco: Zest, 2011.

High school student Isaiah Baiseri holds a t-shirt that he designed for his school's gay-straight alliance in 2010. Gay-straight alliances promote respect and equality in schools. (AP Photo/Damian Dovarganes)

This book purports to help GLBT teens to know how to confirm their same-sex feelings; come out to family, friends, and others; develop their social life based on their same-sex feelings; and deal with homophobia they encounter in their lives. The book is based on helping teens to develop their own sense of "queerness."

Bernstein, Robert. *Straight Parents, Gay Children: Inspiring Families to Live Honestly and with Greater Understanding,* Revised edition. New York: Thunder's Mouth, 2003.

The primary purpose of this book is to help parents understand and deal with issues raised when they learn a child is gay, lesbian, bisexual, transgendered, or questioning. The author discusses a number of issues that may be associated with the coming out process, such as dealing with myths and misunderstandings about gays and lesbians, dealing with health and medical questions, helping to understand the religious and cultural bases of homophobia, and aiding children in adjusting to the social milieu in which they find themselves.

Bertram, Corrine C., M. Sue Crowley, and Sean G. Massey, eds. *Beyond Progress and Marginalization: LGBTQ Youth in Educational Contexts.* New York: Peter Lang, 2010.

The 11 essays in this book deal with a variety of issues related to the experiences of LGBTQ students, including topics such as the role of GSA clubs and advisors in schools, the process of becoming an ally of LGBTQ students, career aspirations and development of LGBTQ students, LGBTQ youth with disabilities, and how LGBTQ students can define themselves in positive ways and learn how to function effectively in largely negative school environments.

Biegel, Stuart. *The Right to Be Out: Sexual Orientation and Gender Identity in America's Public Schools.* Minneapolis: University of Minnesota Press, 2010.

The author reviews the problems faced by LGBT students in schools and the actions that school systems have and have not taken to protect them from harassment, bullying, physical harm, and other problems. He then reviews the history of legislation and case law dealing with these issues and summarizes the current legal status that LGBT students have.

Blackburn, Mollie V. *Interrupting Hate: Homophobia in Schools and What Literacy Can Do about It.* New York: Teachers College Press, 2012.

The author reviews the current status of heterosexism and homophobia in U.S. schools and suggests ways in which exercises that involve improved literacy by both students and teachers can reduce the effect of these mindsets on LGBT students.

Brill, Stephanie A., and Rachel Pepper. *The Transgender Child.* San Francisco: Cleiss, 2008.

The authors offer a host of suggestions for parents who know or suspect that their child may be gender-variant. They deal with all aspects of transgender issues, including medical, legal, developmental, educational, family, and social issues.

Cianciotto, Jason, and Sean Cahill. *LGBT Youth in America's Schools.* Ann Arbor: University of Michigan Press, 2012.

The authors provide a review of laws dealing with the treatment of LGBT youth in schools and other settings and of relevant social science research on the problems faced by LGBT youth during the process of growing up. They weave into each chapter a review of a specific individual whose life relates to the topic of that chapter.

Desai, Krishna. *It's Your Life: Opening Doors: Improving the Legal System's Approach to LGBTQ Youth in Foster Care.* Chicago: American Bar Association, Center on Children and the Law, 2010.

The author reviews the current legal status of LGBTQ youth in foster care and recommends improvements that can be made.

DeWitt, Peter. *Dignity for All: Safeguarding LGBT Students.* Thousand Oaks, CA: Corwin, 2012.

The author reviews the issues that LGBT youth face in schools, with special emphasis on harassment and bullying. He then points out a variety of steps that schools can take to help build a more supportive environment for such students, including the introduction of gay-straight alliances, the development of helpful school policies, and changes in curriculum that can raise consciousness of students and teachers about LGBT issues.

Dupper, David R. *School Bullying: New Perspectives on a Growing Problem.* New York: Oxford University Press, 2012.

This book deals with the general topic of school bullying but has an especially good chapter on the special problems faced by gay, lesbian, bisexual, and transgendered teens in schools today. Some useful suggestions for dealing with bullying are included.

Ehrensaft, Diane. *Gender Born, Gender Made: Raising Healthy Gender-Nonconforming Children.* New York: Experiment, 2011.

This book is intended for the parents of children who are questioning their gender status and for therapists who work with such adults and children. The author offers case studies that provide guidance for ways of dealing with both adults and children who are struggling with issues of gender identity.

Fisher, Sylvia K., Jeffrey M. Poirier, and Gary M. Blau, eds. *Improving Emotional and Behavioral Outcomes for LGBT Youth: A Guide for Professionals.* Baltimore: Paul H. Brookes, 2012.

The 17 chapters in this book deal with a variety of topics relating to social and psychological issues faced by LGBT youth in and out of the school environment. They cover topics such as public health issues, special problems faced by non-English speaking youth and of Native American youth, problems experienced by gender nonconforming children and transgender youth, and suicidal ideation and self-injury.

Giordano, Simona. *Children with Gender Identity Disorder: A Clinical, Ethical, and Legal Analysis.* New York: Routledge, 2013.

The title of this book suggests that the author adopts the existing psychiatric position that children who display cross-gender behaviors are mentally ill, but such is not the case. She discusses in considerable detail the history of cross-gender children and suggests ways in which their behavior and prognosis can be understood and they can be assisted in their development.

Gray, Mary L. *Out in the Country: Youth, Media, and Queer Visibility in Rural America.* New York: New York University Press, 2009.

The author describes her experiences in talking with LGBT youth in rural Kentucky and discusses the special problems these young men and women face in being out in the region and how they deal with social responses to their sexual orientation.

Haskell, Rebecca, and Brian E. Vurtch. *Get That Freak: Homophobia and Transphobia in High Schools.* Halifax, NS: Fernwood, 2010.

Although the topic of bullying of LGBT students in U.S. schools has received a fair amount of attention in the past decade, the same cannot be said for the situation in Canadian schools. This book summarizes interviews with a number of LGBT students in British Columbia who tell about their harassment and bullying while high school students, along with a review of the techniques they developed to survive and sometimes thrive in such an environment.

Horvitz, Lori. *Queer Girls in Class: Lesbian Teachers and Students Tell Their Classroom Stories*. New York: Peter Lang, 2011.

This book is a collection of essays by lesbian students and teachers describing their personal experiences in classrooms.

Huegel, Kelly. *GLBTQ: The Survival Guide for Queer & Questioning Teens*, 2nd revised and updated version. Minneapolis: Free Spirit, 2011.

The 11 chapters in this book deal with topics such as terminology, homophobia, coming out, life at school, friendships among GLBTQ youth, dating and relationships, sex and sexuality, staying healthy, religion and culture, transgender teens, and work, college, and beyond. The book is recommended both for GLBTQ youth and for adults who work with such individuals.

Jennings, Kevin. *Always My Child: The Concerned Parent's Guide to Understanding and Supporting Your Gay, Lesbian, Bisexual, Transgendered, or Questioning Son or Daughter*. New York: Fireside, 2002.

The author offers suggestions for parents dealing with the information that their child is gay or lesbian. He also discusses some of the signs that a parent can look for that a child may be gay or lesbian.

Krieger, Irwin. *Helping Your Transgender Teen: A Guide for Parents*. New Haven, CT: Genderwise, 2011.

This book provides information about the process of gender development during adolescence, focusing on the special issue of children whose gender identity is not consistent with their sexual identity. The author describes some of the problems that adolescents and parents may encounter in such cases and provides suggestions as to how adults and children can deal with these problems.

Lanse, Hal W. *The Rainbow Curriculum: Teaching Teens About LGBT Issues.* Indianapolis: CreateSpace Independent Publishing Platform, 2012.

> The author argues that schools provide instruction for all types of special groups or events, so why not a special curriculum for LGBT youth, which he provides in this book. The curriculum focuses on a history of gay and lesbian culture along with a special discussion of issues faced by LGBT youth in today's schools and culture in general.

LaSala, Michael C. *Coming Out, Coming Home: Helping Families Adjust to a Gay or Lesbian Child.* New York: Columbia University Press, 2010.

> This book discusses the elements involved in a child's coming out to her or his family as being lesbian, gay, bisexual, or transgendered, with the types of reactions that parents may give to such news and the "recovery" that may occur as they adjust to the news. The author also comments on the very positive aspects for a family of having a gay or lesbian child (the "gift" of having such a child) and the special problems posed by varying race and ethnic backgrounds.

Lowrey, Sassafras, ed. *Kicked Out.* Ypsilanti, MI: Homofactus, 2010.

> This book brings together stories from gay men and lesbians who are or were homeless during their teen years. The stories describe the problems faced by homeless LGBT youth, the long-term effects of homelessness, and the strategies developed to deal with the problems of homelessness.

Marcus, Eric. *Is It a Choice? Answers to the Most Frequently Asked Questions about Gay and Lesbian People*, 3rd ed. San Francisco: HarperSanFrancisco, 2005.

This book is in the format of questions and answers about many questions people have about homosexuality. Various chapters deal with topics such as coming out, dating and relationships, same-sex marriage, work and the military, the social life of gays and lesbians, religion, discrimination on the basis of sexual orientation, the media, sports, politics, and aging.

Marine, Susan B. *Stonewall's Legacy: Bisexual, Gay, Lesbian, and Transgender Students in Higher Education.* San Francisco: Jossey-Bass, 2011.

The author traces the evolving status of LGBT students in higher education, noting the increasing willingness of such students to be out or come out on campus and the mechanisms that institutions of higher learning have taken to acknowledge and accommodate the greater visibility of LGBT students on campus. The author also takes note of and comments on the special issues related to transgender students on campuses and the comparable accommodations that have been and are being made for the needs and expectations of those students.

McDougall, Bryce, ed. *My Child Is Gay: How Parents React when They Hear the News*, 2nd ed., St. Leonards, NSW: Allen & Unwin, 2006.

This book consists of letters from 50 sets of parents from Australia and New Zealand relating their own experiences upon learning that their child is gay or lesbian. The letters are written in the hope of helping other parents who have made similar discoveries to understand how they can deal with this news and how they can be supportive of their own children.

Ranney, Carol A. *So Someone You Know Is Gay? A Book for Christians Who Want to Love Like Jesus.* Indianapolis: CreateSpace Independent Publishing Platform, 2012.

The author writes from the perspective of a Christian parent who hopes to encourage fellow Christians deal with gays and lesbians in general, and LGBT youth in particular, in more compassionate ways. She refers extensively to Biblical references in her discussions of LGBT issues in general, as well as the specific problems associated with all forms of physical and psychological bullying.

Rivers, Ian. *Homophobic Bullying: Research and Theoretical Perspectives*. New York: Oxford University Press, 2011.

The author reviews available research on bullying of LGBT youth, giving special attention to issues such as short- and long-term effects of bullying, school situations that promote or tend to deter bullying, practical issues for parents and teachers, and the roles played by active confederates, passive bystanders, and indifferent onlookers.

Ryan, Caitlin. *Supportive Families, Healthy Children*. San Francisco: San Francisco State University, 2009.

This booklet was written by the director of the SFSU Family Acceptance Project. It explains why family support is so crucial for LGBT youth in dealing with the issues in their everyday lives and makes recommendations as to how parents can help support their children in this effort.

Sadowski, Michael. *In a Queer Voice: Journeys of Resilience from Adolescence to Adulthood*. Philadelphia: Temple University Press, 2013.

The author takes an unusual and effective approach in his a discussion of LGBT issues by interviewing boys and girls six years apart, during their high school years and again in early adulthood. The interviews reflect the mechanisms that individuals develop for dealing with homophobia and abuse during their teen years, and they also reflects some of the interviewees' early adulthood successes.

Schwartz, John. *Oddly Normal: One Family's Struggle to Help Their Teenage Son Come to Terms with His Sexuality.* New York: Gotham, 2012.

> Schwartz, a national correspondent for the *New York Times*, describes his experience of learning that his teenage son is gay when he was called to a local hospital after his son's failed suicide attempt. The author discusses a host of issues raised by this event, including the kinds of problems faced by LGBT students, resources that are and are not available for teenagers and their parents, and ways in which parents can help their LGBT children (and vice versa).

Suicide Prevention Resource Center. *Suicide Risk and Prevention for Lesbian, Gay, Bisexual, and Transgender Youth.* Newton, MA: Education Development Center, Inc., 2008.

> This report is a compilation and summary of research studies on suicide attempts and suicidal ideation among LGBT youth published between 1996 and 2007. In addition to summarizing the data from these studies, the report reviews services available for LGBT youth who are considering suicide, and it offers recommendations for improving the range of these services.

Vaccaro, Annemarie, Gerri August, and Megan S. Kennedy. *Safe Spaces: Making Schools and Communities Welcoming to LGBT Youth.* Santa Barbara, CA: Praeger, 2012.

> The authors review the problems faced by LGBT youth; the psychological literature that relates to growing up gay, lesbian, bisexual, or transgender; and the resources available to young people as they deal with these issues. The authors focus on the way that families, friends, and schools can aid LGBT youth in dealing with harassment, bullying, and other common problems.

Vitagliano, Paul. *Born this Way: Real Stories of Growing up Gay.* Philadelphia: Quirk, 2012.

> This anthology provides more than 100 snippets from the lives of boys and girls who knew that they were gay or lesbian at very young ages or at the very least understood that they were somehow different from their peers. It contains some wonderful photographs from these early lives.

Williams, Sally D. *"OMG, My Child Is Gay!" What You Should Do when You Learn Your Child's True Sexual Orientation.* Indianapolis: CreateSpace Independent Publishing Platform, 2012.

> The author describes many aspects of her discovery that her child is gay. She then discusses the many aspects of LGBT issues, including the role of the black church and other social institutions in understanding and dealing with such issues.

Articles

Some journals on general or specific issues of special interest to and about LGBT youth are the following:

Journal of Homosexuality. ISSN: 0091-8369 (print), 1540-3602 (online).

Journal of LGBT Issues in Counseling. ISSN: 1553-8605 (print), 1553-8338 (online).

Journal of LGBT Youth (formerly *Journal of Gay and Lesbian Issues in Education*). ISSN: 1936-1661 (print), 1936-1661 (online).

Almeida, Joanna et al. 2009. "Emotional Distress among LGBT Youth: The Influence of Perceived Discrimination Based on Sexual Orientation." *Journal of Youth and Adolescence.* 38(7): 1001–1014.

The authors report on a study of 1,032 students in Boston, of whom 10 percent were LGBT. They found that the LGBT students scored significantly higher on a number of measures of depressive symptomology, including suicidal ideation (30 percent compared to 8 percent among non-LGBT students) and thoughts of self-harm (21 percent versus 6 percent).

Aviv, Rachel. 2012, December 10. "Netherland." *New Yorker*, 60–69.

The author provides a vivid description of life for homeless LGBT youth on the streets of New York City.

Beachy, Robert. 2010. "The German Invention of Homosexuality." *Journal of Modern History*. 82(4): 801–838.

The author provides a lucid and informing review of the earliest steps in the development of a gay liberation movement in pre-Nazi Germany.

Birkett, Michelle, Dorothy L. Espelage, and Brian Koenig. 2009. "LGB and Questioning Students in Schools: The Moderating Effects of Homophobic Bullying and School Climate on Negative Outcomes." *Journal of Youth and Adolescence*. 38(7): 989–1000.

The authors report on a study of 7,376 seventh and eighth graders in a large Midwest county that explores the effects of school climate on student attitudes and behaviors. They found that reduced levels of bullying and homophobic comments and behaviors, as well as a generally more positive school climate with regard to nonconforming sexual orientation resulted in reduced levels of negative student attitudes and behaviors such as drug use, depression, suicidal thoughts, and truancy among lesbian, gay, bisexual, and questioning students.

Bittner, Robert. 2012. "Queering Sex Education: Young Adult Literature with LGBT Content as Complementary Sources of

Sex and Sexuality Education." *Journal of LGBT Youth.* 9(4): 357–372.

> The author recommends the use of young adult literature as a resource in teaching precollege students about LGBT issues.

Black, Whitney W., Alicia L. Fedewa, and Kirsten A. Gonzalez. 2012. "Effects of 'Safe School' Programs and Policies on the Social Climate for Sexual-Minority Youth: A Review of the Literature." *Journal of LGBT Youth.* 9(4): 321–339.

> The authors point out that little research evidence is available on the effects of so-called safe-school programs designed to protect LGBT students from physical and psychological bullying. This study summarizes some intervention strategies that have been suggested and examines the strengths and limitations of existing knowledge in the field.

Bouris, Alida et al. 2010. "A Systematic Review of Parental Influences on the Health and Well-Being of Lesbian, Gay, and Bisexual Youth: Time for a New Public Health Research and Practice Agenda." *Journal of Primary Prevention.* 31(5–6): 273–309.

> Researchers reviewed 31 studies on the effect of parental attitudes and actions on their LGBT children. They found that most studies focused on negative effects and noted that further research should study positive effects of parental actions. They also noted a dearth of studies on minority LGBT youth and on the perspectives of parents with regard to their children's sexual orientation.

Bozard, Lewis R., Jr., and C. J. Sanders. 2011. "Helping Christian Lesbian, Gay, and Bisexual Clients Recover Religion as a Source of Strength: Developing a Model for Assessment and Integration of Religious Identity in Counseling." *Journal of LGBT Issues in Counseling.* 5(1): 47–74.

Since religious beliefs are often at the core of negative actions related to homosexuality, LGBT youth who are also Christians face special problems in reconciling the problems in their everyday lives with their religious beliefs. The authors suggest an approach by which religious faith can actually be used to help LGBT youth deal with their problems.

Cloud, John. 2005, October 2. "The Battle over Gay Teens." *Time.* 42–48, 51.

The author reviews the changing status of LGBT youth in the United States and explores the implications that they are coming out more assertively and at ever younger ages.

Cohen-Kettenis, Peggy T., and Stephanie H. M. Van Goozen. 1997. "Sex Reassignment of Adolescent Transsexuals: A Follow-Up Study." *Journal of the American Academy of Child & Adolescent Psychiatry.* 36(2): 263–271.

The authors report on the status of 22 adolescents between the ages of 16 and 18 who underwent sex reassignment surgery at the Rudolph Magnus Institute of Neurosciences in Utrecht, the Netherlands. They report that "Starting the sex reassignment procedure before adulthood results in favorable postoperative functioning, provided that careful diagnosis takes place in a specialized gender team and that the criteria for starting the procedure early are stringent."

Coker, Tumaini R., Bryn Austin, and Mark A. Schuster. 2010. "The Health and Health Care of Lesbian, Gay, and Bisexual Adolescents."*Annual Review of Public Health.* 31: 457–477.

The authors review data on the health and health care of LGB adolescents, including health indicators and health risks such as substance use, eating disorders, suicidal thoughts and actions, risky sexual behaviors, exposure to violence and victimization, and homelessness. They also review health care options available to LGB youth and outline some ways in which researchers and clinicians can improve LGB adolescent health and health care.

Cooper, Robyn M., and Warren J. Blumenfeld. 2012. "Responses to Cyberbullying: A Descriptive Analysis of the Frequency of and Impact on LGBT and Allied Youth." *Journal of LGBT Youth*. 9(2): 153–177.

The authors conducted a survey of LGBT youth in 40 of the 50 U.S. states to determine how subjects (self-identified as gay, lesbian, or bisexual between the ages of 11 and 18) were subjected to online bullying and how they responded to such bullying.

Dessel, Adrienne, Michael Woodford, and Naomi Warren. 2011. "Intergroup Dialogue Courses on Sexual Orientation: Lesbian, Gay and Bisexual Student Experiences and Outcomes." *Journal of Homosexuality*. 58(8): 1132–1150.

The authors describe an interactive counseling technique that has been used to help students with issues related to racism and gender issues but has not widely been used for dealing with problems faced by LGBT youth. They report on a study in which intergroup dialogue was used to discuss and analyze LGBT issues and the effect of the technique on members of the group.

Eisenberg, Marla E., and Michael D. Resnick. 2006. "Suicidality among Gay, Lesbian and Bisexual Youth: The Role of Protective Factors." *Journal of Adolescent Health*. 39(5): 662–668.

The authors explore the effect of so-called protective factors in reducing the occurrence of suicidal thoughts and/or actions among 21,927 sexually active adolescents from the Minnesota Student Survey of ninth and twelfth graders. They found that family connectedness, teacher caring, other adult caring, and school safety contribute to a decrease in the level of suicidality among the population studied.

Espelage, Dorothy L. et al. 2008. "Homophobic Teasing, Psychological Outcomes, and Sexual Orientation among High School Students: What Influence Do Parents and Schools Have?" *School Psychology Review*. 37(2): 202–216. Available online at http://pdf.countyofdane.com/humanservices/youth/assessment_surveys/2009/homophobic_teasing_psych_outcomes_parent_influence.pdf. Accessed on March 8, 2013.

The authors review studies on the psychological effects of harassment of LGBTQ students.

Fitzgibbons, Richard P., Philip M. Sutton, and Dale O'Leary. 2009. "The Psychopathology of 'Sex Reassignment' Surgery: Assessing Its Medical, Psychological, and Ethical Appropriateness." *National Catholic Bioethics Quarterly*. 9(1): 97–125.

The authors present medical, psychological, and ethical reasons to oppose sex reassignment surgery, which they describe as "collaborating with madness."

Gastic, Billie. 2012. "Urban Students' Attitudes about Sexual Minorities across Intersections of Sex and Race/Ethnicity: Data from a Longitudinal Study." *Journal of LGBT Youth*. 9(1): 42–58.

The author explores differences in attitudes toward LGBT youth among peers of differing race, gender, and ethnicity.

Grossman, Arnold, and Anthony D'Augelli. 2006. "Transgender Youth: Invisible and Vulnerable." *Journal of Homosexuality*. 51(1): 111–128.

The authors report on a study of 24 young men and women who identify as transgender. They discuss three major issues: gender identity and gender presentation, sexual orientation, and vulnerability and health issues. The results of the research may be somewhat skewed because 95 percent of respondents were individuals of color, but the observations made by the researchers are insightful and useful.

Harper, Gary W., Asya Brodsky, and Douglas Bruce. 2012. "What's Good about Being Gay? Perspectives from Youth." *Journal of LGBT Youth.* 9(1): 22–41.

> The authors interviewed 63 gay and bisexual males from Chicago and Miami to determine how they viewed the positive aspects of their sexual orientation, as well as the coping mechanisms they had developed to deal with negative social messages provided by their peers.

Hillier, Lynne, Kimberly J. Mitchell, and Michele L. Ybarra. 2012. "The Internet as a Safety Net: Findings from a Series of Online Focus Groups with LGB and Non-LGB Young People in the United States." *Journal of LGBT Youth.* 9(3): 225–246.

> In a survey of LGBT and non-LGBT youth, the authors found that the former make greater and more imaginative use of the Internet to deal with some of the issues associated with coming out and being out in the gay and lesbian world than do their non-LGBT peers.

Jacob, Susan. 2013. "Creating Safe and Welcoming Schools for LGBT Students: Ethical and Legal Issues." *Journal of School Violence.* 12(1): 98–115.

> The author outlines a set of ethical principles and standards that she believes should guide the behavior of educators in helping LGBT students in elementary and secondary schools. She then reviews current laws related to the harassment of LGBT students.

Jennings, Todd, and Ian K. Macgillivray. 2011. "A Content Analysis of Lesbian, Gay, Bisexual, and Transgender Topics in Multicultural Education Textbooks." *Teaching Education.* 22(1): 39–62.

> The authors describe the results of their survey of 12 popular multicultural textbooks to discover the attention paid to LGBT youth issues. They suggest that their study

can serve as a baseline against which future studies of a similar type can be compared.

Kachgal, Tara M. 2011. "The 'Gay Comfort Level': Examining a Media Advocacy Group's Efforts to Combat Youth Homophobia." *Journal of LGBT Youth*. 8(1): 53–65.

> The author reviews a recommendation by the gay and lesbian media group GLAAD as to how schools can provide greater support for LGBT youth and finds it to be too accommodating. She suggests another approach to achieving the same results more in keeping with the objectives of the gay rights movement.

Knotts, Greg, and Dominic Gregorio. 2011. "Confronting Homophobia at School: High School Students and the Gay Men's Chorus of Los Angeles." *Journal of LGBT Youth*. 8(1): 66–83.

> The Gay Men's Chorus of Los Angeles's A-LIVE Music Project brings live music and a discussion of gay and lesbian topics to high school youth with the purpose of teaching about innovative ways of thinking critically about such topics. This article reviews a study conducted to determine the effects of the program on students' attitudes toward classism, homophobia, misogyny, and racism.

Kosciw, Joseph G. et al. 2013. "The Effect of Negative School Climate on Academic Outcomes for LGBT Youth and the Role of In-School Supports." *Journal of School Violence*. 12(1): 45–63.

> The authors report on a survey of 5,730 LGBT youth who attended secondary schools in the United States. They summarize the effects on such youth of negative and hostile school environments on academic achievement and social development, as well as the effects of positive forces provided by schools for LGBT youth.

Luecke, Julie C. 2011. "Working with Transgender Children and Their Classmates in Pre-Adolescence: Just Be Supportive." *Journal of LGBT Youth.* 8(2): 116–156.

> The author reports on the efforts of an elementary school to help the student population and the individual child involved in the transition from a gender variant boy to a gender expressed girl.

Madsen, P. W. B., and R.-J. Green. 2012. "Gay Adolescent Males' Effective Coping with Discrimination: A Qualitative Study." *Journal of LGBT Issues in Counseling.* 6(2): 139–155.

> This article summarizes the result of interviews with eight self-identified gay male teenagers who report on methods they have developed for dealing with the stress of coming out to parents, peers, and others.

Marshal, Michael P. et al. 2011. "Suicidality and Depression Disparities between Sexual Minority and Heterosexual Youth: A Meta-Analytic Review." *Journal of Adolescent Health.* 49(2): 115–123.

> The authors report on an exhaustive review of studies that have been conducted on the disparity between sexual minority youth and heterosexual youth on two measures: symptoms of depression and suicidal ideation. They find that the former group reports significantly higher rates of depression and suicidality, with the rate of such issues increasing with the seriousness of the subject's views on the topic.

Matthews, Cynthia H., and Carmen F. Salazar. 2012. "An Integrative, Empowerment Model for Helping Lesbian, Gay, and Bisexual Youth Negotiate the Coming-Out Process." *Journal of LGBT Issues in Counseling.* 6(2): 96–117.

> The authors note that the coming out process for LGBT youth can be particularly difficult when they experience

rejection from parents, friends, relatives, neighbors, and others. They recommend some techniques by which school counselors can make the coming out process easier and less stressful for LGBT youth.

McEntarfer, Heather Killelea. 2011. " 'Not Going Away': Approaches Used by Students, Faculty, and Staff Members to Create Gay-Straight Alliances at Three Religiously Affiliated Universities." *Journal of LGBT Youth*. 8(4): 309–331.

The author describes the methods used by students and faculty attempting to form gay-straight alliances at three religiously oriented universities, and she concludes with some suggestions as to how these methodologies can be used in similar and dissimilar situations in the future.

Nadal, Kevin L. et al. 2011. "Sexual Orientation Micro-aggressions: Processes and Coping Mechanisms for Lesbian, Gay, and Bisexual Individuals." *Journal of LGBT Issues in Counseling*. 5(1): 21–46.

The authors note that LGBT youth are faced not only with outright bullying and harassment, but also with more subtle forms of discrimination known as microaggressions. They report on a study of 26 LGBT youth to learn more about the nature of these microaggressions and the techniques that youth have developed to deal with them.

Paceley, Megan S., and Karen Flynn. 2012. "Media Representations of Bullying toward Queer Youth: Gender, Race, and Age Discrepancies." *Journal of LGBT Youth*. 9(4): 340–356.

The authors report on a study of the way in which LGBT bullying is reported in the mainstream media and found both racial and sexual biases, with whites and males receiving a disproportionate share of the coverage.

Padawer, Ruth. "Boygirl." 2012, August 8. *New York Times Magazine*. 19–23.

The author discusses, with specific examples, issues raised when young boys or girls prefer to assume gender roles of the opposite sex and the problems these decisions can cause for even the most progressive of parents.

Payne, Elizabethe C., and Melissa Smith. 2011. "The Reduction of Stigma in Schools: A New Professional Development Model for Empowering Educators to Support LGBTQ Students." *Journal of LGBT Youth*. 8(2): 174–200.

The authors describe a new program, the Reduction of Stigma in Schools, aimed at creating more supportive environments in schools for LGBT youth. They report on the results of implementing the program in an actual school setting with recommendations for expanding the use of the program in other schools.

Robinson, Joseph P., and Dorothy L. Espelage. 2012. "Bullying Explains Only Part of LGBTQ–Heterosexual Risk Disparities: Implications for Policy and Practice." *Educational Researcher*. 41(8): 309–319.

The researchers studied 11,337 adolescents in Dane County, Wisconsin, and found that harassment and bullying accounted for only a portion of the risk disparities between this group and their heterosexual peers. They discuss the meaning of this finding for the development of more supportive programs for LGBT youth in schools.

Robinson, Joseph P., and Dorothy L. Espelage. 2011. "Inequities in Educational and Psychological Outcomes Between LGBTQ and Straight Students in Middle and High School." *Educational Researcher*. 40(7): 315–330.

The authors report on their study that finds LGBT adolescents are at greater risk for suicidal thoughts, suicide attempts, victimization by peers, and elevated levels of unexcused absences than are their heterosexually identified peers, with the greatest risk occurring among bisexual and middle school students.

Russell, Stephen T., Caitlin Ryan, and Russell B. Toomey. 2011. "Lesbian, Gay, Bisexual, and Transgender Adolescent School Victimization: Implications for Young Adult Health and Adjustment." *Journal of School Health*. 81(5): 223–230.

The authors attempt to identify long-term effects on LGBT men and women arising out of harassment, bullying, and other negative actions in their youth. They find a strong link to future mental health issues and STI and HIV/AIDS, a moderate link to depression and suicidal ideation, but no link to future substance abuse.

Smolkin, Laura B., and Craig A. Young. 2011. "Missing Mirrors, Missing Windows: Children's Literature Textbooks and LGBT Topics." *Language Arts*. 88(3): 217–225.

The authors point out the importance of including LGBT topics in literature designed for school-age children. They report on a study of six major books in this field and find that all but one provide at least some discussion of LGBT-related topics and issues.

Spiggle, Thomas J. 2001. "Applying the Equal Access Act to Gay/Straight Alliances." *School Law Bulletin*. 32(2): 11–20.

The author reviews the general provisions of the Equal Access Act of 1984, originally passed to guarantee the right of religious groups to form clubs for secondary school students outside of regular school hours. He explores the relevance of the act to the creation of groups for LGBT students, such as gay and straight alliances, and finds that the arguments that permit the establishment of religious groups also apply to LGBT groups.

Talbot, Margaret. 2013. "About a Boy." *New Yorker*. March 18, 2013: 56–63.

This article describes the experiences of a young man who was born as a female but underwent sex reassignment surgery at the age of 14. It describes the forces that prompted this decision, the issues surrounding the decision, and the way those issues were resolved.

Toomeya, Russell B., Jenifer K. McGuireb, and Stephen T. Russella. 2012. "Heteronormativity, School Climates, and Perceived Safety for Gender Nonconforming Peers." *Journal of Adolescence*. 35(1): 187–196.

Gender nonconforming teenagers are likely to face a variety of physical and psychological threats in the school environment. The authors attempted to discover factors that increase or decrease such risks. They found that certain classes of students, such as older students and Latino teenagers, perceived gender nonconforming students as facing greater risks at their schools. They also found that schools that incorporated gay and lesbian themes in the regular curriculum had lower perceived risks for gender nonconforming students.

Reports

Committee on Lesbian, Gay, Bisexual, and Transgender Health Issues and Research Gaps and Opportunities. Board on the Health of Special Populations. Institute of Medicine. *The Health of Lesbian, Gay, Bisexual, and Transgender People.* Washington, DC: National Academies Press, 2011.

This book is a report on the special health issues faced by LGBT people in the United States. It focuses on questions such as what is currently known about the health status of LGBT populations, where gaps in the research exist, and what the priorities for a research agenda to address these gaps are. Chapter 4 of the book (pages 141–184) focuses especially on problems of LGBT children and adolescents.

Durso, Laura E., and Gary J. Gates. *Serving Our Youth: Findings from a National Survey of Service Providers Working with Lesbian, Gay, Bisexual, and Transgender Youth Who Are Homeless or At Risk of Becoming Homeless.* Los Angeles: Williams Institute with True Colors Fund and The Palette Fund, 2012.

This report summarizes the results of a web-based survey of 381 agencies nationwide that work with LGBT youth who are homeless. The report describes the types of agencies that work with homeless LGBT youth, the services they offer, and the characteristics of their clientele.

Growing Up LGBT in America. Washington, DC: Human Rights Campaign, [2012].

This report is a summary of responses to a series of 97 questions about LGBT issues by more than 10,000 participants nationwide. Issues queried included personal characteristics, state of coming out to families and friends, support from family and from school, and most common problems faced by LGBT youth.

Kann, Laura et al. 2011. "Sexual Identity, Sex of Sexual Contacts, and Health-Risk Behaviors Among Students in Grades 9–12: Youth Risk Behavior Surveillance; Selected Sites, United States, 2001–2009." *Mortality and Morbidity Weekly Report (MMWR).* 60(SS07): 1–133. http://www.cdc.gov/mmwr/preview/mmwrhtml/ss6007a1.htm#Tab3. Accessed on February 21, 2013.

Researchers from the Centers for Disease Control and Prevention (CDC) analyzed data collected for the Youth Risk Behavior Surveillance System to determine the risks perceived and faced by lesbian, gay, bisexual, and questioning youth in seven states and six large urban areas. They found that on average, LGBT youth faced an elevated risk of between 60 and 70 percent on all measurements in the survey compared to their heterosexual peers.

Kosciw, Joseph G. et al. "The 2011 National School Climate Survey: The Experiences of Lesbian, Gay, Bisexual and Transgender Youth in Our Nation's Schools." New York: Gay, Lesbian & Straight Education Network, 2012.

> Since 1999, the Gay, Lesbian & Straight Education Network (GLSEN) has been conducting a biennial national survey of the school experiences of LGBT youth across the nation. The survey is arguably the most complete and detailed record of the day-to-day experiences of gay and lesbian youth in America's schools. The 160-page 2011 report provides data and information on topics such as the use of homophobic, racist, and sexist remarks; overall school safety for LGBT youth; evidence of verbal and physical harassment in schools; effects of homophobic behavior on LGBT attendance and performance; availability and effectiveness of school clubs; and demographics of LGBT youth.

Lipkin, Arthur, and Edward Byrne. *Annual Recommendations to the Great and General Court and Executive Agencies, October 2011.* Commission on Gay, Lesbian, Bisexual, and Transgender Youth, Commonwealth of Massachusetts. Available online at http://www.mass.gov/cgly/Oct2011_MCGLBTY _Annual_Rec.pdf. Accessed on March 8, 2013.

> The Commission on LGBT Youth is established by state law and is required to provide annual reports on the status of this population annually. The report discusses strategic issues related to LGBT youth and outlines actions that can be taken by various state agencies, such as the Department of Children and Families, the Department of Public Health, the Department of Elementary and Secondary Education, and the Department of Youth Services.

Quintana, Nico Sifra, Josh Rosenthal, and Jeff Krehely. *On the Street: The Federal Response to Gay and Transgender Homeless Youth.* Washington, DC: Center for American Progress,

June 2010. http://www.americanprogress.org/wp-content/uploads/issues/2010/06/pdf/lgbtyouthhomelessness.pdf. Accessed on April 12, 2013.

> This report provides an extensive amount of data and statistics on the extent of homelessness among LGBT youth and the actions being taken (or not taken) by the federal government and other agencies to deal with this problem.

Ray, Nicholas, ed. *Lesbian, Gay, Bisexual, and Transgender Youth: An Epidemic of Homelessness*. Washington, DC: National Gay and Lesbian Task Force Policy Institute and National Coalition for the Homeless, 2006.

> This report focuses on the special problems faced by LGBT youth who are homeless. By some estimates, those individuals make up anywhere from 20 to 40 percent of all homeless youth. In addition to an analysis of problems such as health issues, substance abuse, victimization, mental health issues, and risky sexual behavior, the report offers five chapters on model programs that have been developed to deliver service to homeless LGBT youth.

Shields, J. P. et al. 2012. "Estimating Population Size and Demographic Characteristics of Lesbian, Gay, Bisexual, and Transgender Youth in Middle School." *Adolescent Health*. 52(2): 248–250.

> This research team attempted to estimate the percentage of middle school students who self-identified as gay, lesbian or transgendered in San Francisco public schools, as well as the characteristics of such students. They estimated that 3.8 percent of middle school students identified as gay, lesbian, or bisexual, and 1.3 percent as transgender.

Internet Sources

Baim, Tracy. "LGBT Youth Suicide Reports Show Need for More Studies." *Windy City Times*. http://www.windycitymedia

group.com/gay/lesbian/news/ARTICLE.php?AID=31546. Accessed on March 11, 2013.

This article summarizes a meeting held in San Francisco to review the information available about suicides among LGBT youth, the way in which that information can be used for prevention programs, and the type of additional research that still needs to be done.

"Bullying Prevention & Response Base Training Module." StopBullying.gov. http://www.stopbullying.gov/prevention/ in-the-community/community-action-planning/training-module -speaker-notes.pdf. Accessed on April 26, 2013.

This PowerPoint presentation provides a superb general introduction to the issue of bullying, with important statistical and factual information about the extent, causes, and prevention of bullying in American schools.

"Coming Out." LGBT Youth Scotland Green Light Project. https://www.lgbtyouth.org.uk/files/documents/guides/Coming _out_guide_-_LGB.pdf. Accessed on April 22, 2013.

This excellent brochure contains an extensive amount of information about and suggestions for coming out by LGBT youth to family and friends at home, at school, and at work with additional information on related topics such as homophobia and bullying, hate crimes, rights and legislation, and relationships.

Elias, Marilyn. "Gay Teens Coming Out Earlier to Peers and Family." *USA Today.* http://usatoday30.usatoday.com/ news/nation/2007-02-07-gay-teens-cover_x.htm. Accessed on April 15, 2013.

This article reviews the reasons LGBT youth come out earlier to their parents and friends and the effect this decision often has on youth who choose to do so.

Gamache, Peter, and Katherine J. Lazear. "Asset-Based Approaches for Lesbian, Gay, Bisexual, Transgender, Questioning,

Intersex, Two-Spirit (LGBTQI2-S) Youth and Families in Systems of Care." (FMHI pub. no. 252). Tampa: University of South Florida, College of Behavioral and Community Sciences, Louis de la Parte Florida Mental Health Institute, Research and Training Center for Children's Mental Health. http://rtckids.fmhi.usf.edu/rtcpubs/FamExp/lgbt-mono.pdf. Accessed on April 15, 2013.

This monograph provides an excellent overview of research on youth and families of sexual and/or gender minorities as a background for recommending future research, policy, and practice by experts in the field.

"A Gender Variance Who's Who." http://zagria.blogspot.com/. Accessed on March 26, 2013.

This extensive website has useful references on the general topic of transsexuality, including many biographical sketches of important individuals in history who were transsexuals.

"Give a Damn Campaign." http://www.wegiveadamn.org/. Accessed on April 12, 2013.

The Give a Damn campaign was created to provide information about and encourage action on a variety of issues, most of which focus on LGBTQ youth. Those issues include workplace discrimination, hate crimes, marriage, faith, youth in schools, youth and suicide, youth and homelessness, family acceptance, parenting, international issues, health care, and immigration.

"GLBTQ Issues." Advocates for Youth. http://www.advocates foryouth.org/glbtq-issues-home. Accessed on March 30, 2013.

This website provides a general introduction to issues of special interest and concern to LGBT youth and their allies, with some suggestions for possible means of resolving some of these issues.

GLBTNearMe.org. http://www.glbtnearme.org/GLBTNearMe Results.php?national=Yes. Accessed on March 7, 2013.

This website is one of the most complete and best lists of resources for LGBT youth, including separate sections on issues such as HIV/AIDS, bisexuality, crisis, culture, fundraising, workplace issues, health, the law, lesbians, media, and politics.

"GSA Federal Court Victories." American Civil Liberties Union Foundation. https://www.aclu.org/files/pdfs/gsa_cases _handout_2012_final.pdf. Accessed on March 26, 2013.

This page contains an annotated list of some major court decisions dealing with the rights of LGBT students wishing to form gay-straight alliance clubs in their schools.

"Homeless Lgbt Youth." *Huffington Post.* http://www.huffington post.com/news/homeless-lgbt-youth. Accessed on March 30, 2013.

This website brings together articles dealing with the issue of homelessness among LGBT youth in the United States.

"Homeless LGBT Youth and LGBT Youth in Foster Care." Safe Schools Coalition. http://www.safeschoolscoalition.org/ rg-homeless.html. Accessed on March 11, 2013.

This website brings together in one place a great deal of information and statistics on the special problems of homeless and fostered LGBT youth.

Hyatt, Shahera. *Struggling to Survive: Lesbian, Gay, Bisexual, Transgender, and Queer/Questioning Homeless Youth on the Streets of California.* Sacramento: California Youth Homeless Project, n.d. http://cahomelessyouth.library.ca.gov/docs/ pdf/StrugglingToSurviveFinal.pdf. Accessed on October 27, 2013.

This publication briefly presents a collection of personal stories of LGBTQ youth who have ended up homeless on the streets of California, explaining the factors that may lead to such events. It also provides policy recommendations for dealing with this issue.

"Key Policy Letters from the Education Secretary and Deputy Secretary." U.S. Department of Education. http://www2 .ed.gov/policy/elsec/guid/secletter/110607.html. Accessed on March 26, 2013.

> This website contains a letter from Secretary of Education Arne Duncan dealing with the legal rights of LGBT youth in American schools. It outlines protection offered by the Equal Access Act of 1984 and other relevant federal laws.

"Lesbian, Gay, Bisexual, & Transgender (LGBT)." U.S. Substance Abuse and Mental Health Services Administration. http://www.samhsa.gov/obhe/lgbt.aspx. Accessed on March 30, 2013.

> SAMSHA outlines its program for LGBT youth on this website and includes sections on data and educational resources as well as a directory of federal programs and services available to LGBT youth.

"Lesbian, Gay, Bisexual and Transgender Health." Centers for Disease Control and Prevention. http://www.cdc.gov/lgbt health/youth.htm. Accessed on February 17, 2013.

> This CDC page focuses on health issues of special significance to LGBT youth, with suggestions for ways in which schools, parents, and other adults can help young people who have come out or are coming out and are facing discrimination, bullying, harassment, and other issues in their communities.

"LGBT Homeless." National Coalition for the Homeless. http://www.nationalhomeless.org/factsheets/lgbtq.html. Accessed on March 11, 2013.

> This page contains basic information about homelessness among LGBT youth, as well as a variety of resources on the topic.

"LGBT Youth and Schools." American Civil Liberties Union. http://www.aclu.org/. Accessed on February 17, 2013.

This website provides information on the American Civil Liberties Union's program on LGBT Youth and Schools. It provides access to documents designed to assist LGBT youth with issues they may face in their everyday lives, such as their rights under the law, sources for assistance in dealing with problems in their lives, knowing how to recognize discrimination and what to do about it, and information on the Student Non-Discrimination Act (Senate bill 555).

"LGBT Youth & Suicide: Understanding & Reducing Risk." TeenScreen. National Center for Mental Health Checkups. http://www.teenscreen.org/resources/events-webinars/lgbt-youth -suicide-understanding-reducing-risk/. Accessed on March 30, 2013.

This website provides access to a webinar produced by the Image project at Northwestern University dealing with issues related to suicide and suicidal ideation by LGBT youth and methods that are available for working with individuals at risk.

"Library: LGBT Youth & Schools Resources and Links." American Civil Liberties Union. http://www.aclu.org/lgbt -rights_hiv-aids/library. Accessed on March 11, 2013.

This website provides an exhaustive list of resources of interest and value to LGBT youth.

"Live Out Loud!" http://www.liveoutloud.info/wp/. Accessed on March 30, 2013.

Live Out Loud is a program that matches young lesbians, gay men, bisexuals, and trangenders with adult role models for discussion, guidance, and planning for the future.

"New Alternatives for LGBT Homeless Youth." http://www .newalternativesnyc.org/. Accessed on March 30, 2013.

This New York City–based organization focuses on the needs of homeless LGBT youth in the city and describes options that have been developed to provide for these boys and girls, with suggestions for generalizing the program for other parts of the country.

Pickett, Brent. "Homosexuality." Stanford Encyclopedia of Philosophy. http://plato.stanford.edu/entries/homosexuality/. Accessed on March 7, 2013.

An excellent and extensive review of the history of same-sex relationships up to and including the development of current queer theory about same-sex relationships.

Ramsay, Richard F. "Gay, Lesbian, Bisexual & Transgender 'Attempted Suicide' Incidences/Risks Suicidality Studies From 1970 to 2013." http://people.ucalgary.ca/~ramsay/attempted-suicide-gay-lesbian-all-studies.htm. Accessed on March 11, 2013.

This website provides an enormous amount of data and statistics on suicide rates among LGBT youth in many cultures around the world. It is probably the most complete collection of such data currently available.

Redman, Daniel. " 'I Was Scared to Sleep': LGBT Youth Face Violence behind Bars." *Nation.* http://www.thenation.com/article/36488/i-was-scared-sleep-lgbt-youth-face-violence-behind-bars#. Accessed on March 30, 2013.

The author discusses the special problems faced by LGBT youth in prison, jails, and other correctional facilities.

Setoodeh, Ramin. "Young, Gay, and Murdered." U.S. News/Daily Beast. http://www.thedailybeast.com/newsweek/2008/07/18/young-gay-and-murdered.html. Accessed on April 15, 2013.

This article reports on the murder of 15-year-old Lawrence King by a fellow middle school student, Brandon McInerney, as an entre to a discussion of the issues schools face with so many boys and girls coming out at an earlier age.

StopBullying.gov. U.S. Department of Health and Human Services. http://www.stopbullying.gov/index.html. Accessed on February 14, 2013.

> This website is sponsored and operated by the U.S. Department of Health and Human Services to provide basic information about bullying and resources available for dealing with the practice. It includes sections such as "What Is Bullying," "Cyber Bullying," "Who Is at Risk," "Prevent Bullying," and "Respond to Bullying." The site also provides extensive resources on the topic of bullying, as well as a blog for those who wish to participate in discussions on the topic.

"Suicidal Behavior among Lesbian, Gay, Bisexual, and Transgender Youth Fact Sheet." American Association of Suicidology. http://www.suicidology.org/c/document_library/get_file?folderId =232&name=DLFE-334.pdf. Accessed on March 30, 2013.

> The fact sheet summarizes important studies on the risk of suicide and suicidal ideation faced by LGBT youth, with some suggestions for dealing with the problem based on this research.

Thilman, James. "Homeless LGBT Youth Describe Rejection by Their Christian Families." NewNowNext. http://www .newnownext.com/ali-forney-center-homeless-youth-christian -rejection/03/2013/. Accessed on March 30, 2013.

> A group of homeless LGBT youth talk about their personal experiences related to having been rejected and in some cases thrown out of their homes by their self-acknowledged Christian-identified families.

"Tips for Professionals Who Work with LGBT Youth." PFLAG New York. http://www.pflagnyc.org/safeschools/tips. Accessed on February 17, 2013.

> The state chapter of PFLAG (Parents and Friends of Lesbians and Gays) offers a list of a dozen important ideas for adults who work with LGBT youth.

"Title IX Protections from Bullying and Harassment in Schools: FAQs for LGBT or Gender Nonconforming Students and Their Families." National Women's Law Center. http://www.nwlc.org/sites/default/files/pdfs/lgbt_bullying_title_ix_fact_sheet.pdf. Accessed February 7, 2013.

> This fact sheet provides basic information on federal protection provided to LGBT and gender nonconforming students under Title IX of the Education Amendments of 1972.

"We Are the Youth." http://www.dailydot.com/society/top-10-lgbt-activists-2012/. Accessed on March 30, 2013.

> This website describes a traveling photojournalism program that brings a visual display and oral histories from gay, lesbian, bisexual, and transgender youth from across the United States. The program is sponsored by the Brooklyn Arts Council and, as of late 2013, was featuring more than 75 young women and men in its program.

"Youth OUTreach." LAMBDA. http://www.lambda.org/youth.htm. Accessed on February 17, 2013.

> This web page describes LAMBDA's outreach program to LGBT youth. It provides information on topics such as bullying, protecting oneself on the Internet, general facts about gay and lesbian youth, and special activities for lesbians and gay men under the age of 21. Access is also provided to resources on specialized topics such as famous gay people, how homophobia hurts teenagers, risks faced by transgendered youth, and information for parents of gay and lesbian children.

"Youth Resource." http://amplifyyourvoice.org/youthresource. Accessed on March 30, 2013.

> Youth Resource is a website sponsored and maintained by Advocates for Youth. It is designed to provide information for LGBT youth about sexual and reproductive health, with links to peer and professional health educators to answer specific personalized questions.

This chapter on chronology features important events in the history of lesbians, gay men, bisexuals, and transgenders. Of course, many events of significance have occurred over the past 2,000 or more years, but these items are among the most interesting and most important.

378 BCE Theban general Gorgidas organizes a special unit of warriors in the Theban army called the Sacred Band of Thebes. The unit consists of 150 pairs of male lovers who are said to have fought more valiantly than any other Greek unit because they fought for their lovers as much as they fought for their nation. The unit was annihilated by Philip II of Macedon in the Battle of Chaeronea in 338 BCE.

130 CE The young Bithynian man Antinous drowns in the Nile while on a voyage with his lover the Roman emperor Hadrian. Hadrian is so distraught that he founds cities in the youth's name, erects statutes to him in a number of locations, has medals struck in his remembrance, and elevates the youth to the Roman pantheon of gods.

Activists from a group called Young People against Homophobia protest with their mouths taped up, in front of the Education Ministry in Warsaw, Poland, in 2007. The protest was initiated after Poland's deputy education minister commented that teachers promoting homosexual behavior would be fired. (AP Photo/Czarek Sokolowski)

222   Emperor Elagabalus (Marcus Aurelius Antoninus Augustus, also known as Heliogabalus) dies in Rome at the age of 22. He is best known to have lived a bisexual life in which he was married to women five times and had extensive and intensive sexual relationships with countless numbers of males. He was assassinated at the age of 18, apparently in a plot masterminded by his grandmother.

Middle Ages   Extensive evidence suggests that same-sex relationships were not uncommon among knights in training, monks, and clerics in other religions, including Islam. Although such relationships were generally frowned upon among adult males, they were apparently not unusual between younger men and, occasionally, between younger males and older members of the clergy.

Thirteenth Century   Islamic scholar Imam An-Nawawi writes of the difference between individuals who would be classified today as transsexuals and transvestites. He says that there are two types of men who present themselves as women, "the first is the one in whom these characteristics are innate, he did not put them on by himself, and therein is no guilt, no blame and no shame, as long as he does not perform any illicit act or exploit it for money. The second type acts like a woman out of immoral purposes and he is the sinner and blameworthy."

1867   Lawyer, writer, and political activist Karl Heinrich Ulrichs speaks out for the repeal of antihomosexual laws in Germany. He is reputed to have been the first prominent individual in modern history to come out as a self-acknowledged gay man.

1869   Austro-Hungarian author Karl-Maria Kertbeny first uses the terms *homosexual* and *heterosexual* in print in a pamphlet opposing German antihomosexual laws.

1897   Sex researcher and political activist Magnus Hirschfeld founds the Scientific Humanitarian Committee to work for the repeal of Paragraph 175, the German law prohibiting homosexual activity.

1913   Reputedly the first use of the word *faggot* to describe gay men appears in a Portland, Oregon, newspaper that reported about a gay party that "All the fagots [sic] (sissies) will be dressed in drag at the ball tonight."

1919   German sexologist Magnus Hirschfeld founds the Institut für Sexualwissenschaft (Institute for Sexual Research) in Berlin.

1921   Herschfeld founds the Weltliga für Sexualreform (World League for Sexual Reform).

1922   A German man born as Rudolph Richter is medically castrated by Dr. Erwin Gohrbandt at the Charité Universitätsmedizin in Berlin, an act he had attempted himself at the age of six. She is later known as Dora and spends the rest of her life as a waiter and cook in upscale Berlin hotels. She is thought to have died in 1933 in the Nazi attack on Magnus Hirschfeld's Institut fuer Sexualwissenschaft, where she was working at the time.

1924   The first homosexual rights organization in the United States is founded in Chicago by a handful of married and single men, the Society for Human Rights. The group disbands after only a few months when the wife of one member reports the existence of the group to the police.

1930   Danish artist Lili Elbe undergoes the first male-to-female sex reassignment surgery in Germany. Born as Einar Mogens Wegener, Elbe had been married but may have been intersexed and first realized her desire to become a woman in the early 1910s. Elbe dies during the fifth of the surgeries required for the sex reassignment procedure.

1945   British physician Laura Maud Dillon undergoes the first female-to-male sex reassignment surgery and becomes known as Michael Dillon.

1946   An organization known as the COC (Cultuur en Ontspanningscentrum, or Center for Culture and Leisure) is founded in the Netherlands. The name is intended to be a "cover" for the organization's real purpose, a social club for lesbians and gay men. COC is now the oldest LGBT organization in the world.

1950   The Mattachine Society is formed in Los Angeles. It is the first even moderately successful organization of gay men to be established. The organization survived in one form or another until the end of the 1960s.

1955   The Daughters of Bilitis, a national organization for lesbians, is founded in San Francisco by Del Martin and Phyllis Lyon.

1961   Illinois becomes the first state in the United States to decriminalize sodomy between same-sex partners.

1966   A riot at a Compton's Cafeteria in the Tenderloin District of San Francisco presages the Stonewall riots of three years later. The Compton's Cafeteria riot occurs when management calls the local police to evict a group of rowdy transgendered individuals, who end up fighting back against the police. Within days, a united group of gay men, lesbians, and transgendered individuals picket the cafeteria and create the first unified LGBT efforts in history. Historians mark the riot as the beginning of transgender-focused groups and activities in the United States.

1966   Stephen Donaldson (born Robert Anthony Martin Jr.) founds the Student Homophile League at Columbia University, in New York City, the first gay student group to receive official recognition by an educational institution.

1969   Rioting occurs at the Stonewall Inn, a bar frequented by gay men in the Greenwich area of New York City. The event is considered by some historians as the beginning of the modern gay and lesbian movement in the United States.

1969   In an effort to begin organizing against actions typified by the attack on the Stonewall Inn, a group of gay men and lesbians form the Gay Liberation Front (GLF) in New York City.

1970   The first gay pride parade, under the name of the Christopher Street Liberation Day March, is held in midtown Manhattan. An estimate 2,000 people march in the parade. (Attendance at the 2012 parade was estimated at 1.5 million.)

1970   The first organization in the United States intended exclusively for LGBT youth, New York City's Gay Youth, is formed as an offspring of the Gay Liberation Front (GLF).

1972   Jeanne Manford marches with her son Morty in the Christopher Street Liberation Day March (the predecessor of today's modern gay pride parades). Jeanne later becomes a major force in the formation of Parents and Friends of Gays and Lesbians (PFLAG), one of the most supportive groups for LGBT youth in the United States.

1972   Paramus (New Jersey) High School teacher John Gish is fired for accepting the presidency of the local gay activist alliance. Gish appeals the decision, and the case continues for eight years. Gish's firing is finally upheld by New Jersey State Education commissioner Fred G. Burke, who calls the teacher's actions "conduct unbecoming to a teacher."

1972   East Lansing (Michigan) becomes the first city in the United States to adopt a policy prohibiting discrimination against lesbians and gay men in city hiring based on sexual orientation.

1972   Bisexual activist Don Fass founds the National Bisexual Liberation group, possibly the first national group of its kind in the United States. Fass also publishes the first newsletter for bisexuals, the *Bisexual Expression*.

1973   The American Psychiatric Association removes homosexuality as a mental disorder from its *Diagnostic and Statistical Manual of Mental Disorders* (DSM-II). Two years later, the American Psychological Association takes a similar action.

1974   The Charles Street Meetinghouse, in Boston, receives a $52,371 grant from the city's Youth Advocacy Commission of Treatment Alternatives to Street Crime for the establishment of the Gay Youth Advocacy program, the first such government program in the United States directed at LBGTQ youth. The program is later renamed Project Lambda. The program ends in 1976 when it loses funding from the city.

1977 The Oklahoma state legislature unanimously passes a law requiring the dismissal of gay and lesbian schoolteachers and prohibiting the favorable mention of same-sex behavior in schools. In 1985, the U.S. Supreme Court invalidates the part of the law that prohibits advocacy of same-sex issues in *Board of Education v. National Gay Task Force* (470 U.S. 903).

1977 Christian activist, former Miss America candidate, and popular singer Anita Bryant forms the Save Our Children campaign in Dade County, Florida, in an attempt to overturn the county board's decision to adopt an antidiscrimination ordinance on behalf of gay men and lesbians. The SOS campaign is eventually successful in having the ordinance overturned.

1978 Proposition 6 (the so-called Briggs Initiative), banning lesbian and gay schoolteachers and forbidding the positive mention of homosexuality in classrooms in California, is defeated in the November election.

1978 In response to a raid conducted by Boston police on a private home where illegal sexual activity was thought to be occurring, a group of gay men form the North American Man/Boy Love Association (NAMBLA). The organization is still in existence today.

1979 The first national same-sex march for civil rights, the National March on Washington for Lesbian and Gay Rights, is held in Washington, DC. An estimated 75,000–150,000 men and women attend.

1980 Cumberland (Rhode Island) High School senior Aaron Fricke invites a male friend to be his date at the high school prom. The school forbids the couple from attending the event. A U.S. district court rules that the high school may not prohibit Fricke and his friend from attending the prom.

1980   Georgetown University, run by the Jesuit Order of the Roman Catholic Church, expels its gay student group from campus, forbidding it to use any university facilities. The student group sues to overturn the university action and in 1987 wins approval from the District of Columbia Court of Appeals to use university facilities, although the university is not required to officially recognize the group (*Gay Rights Coalition v. Georgetown University*, 536 A.2d 1).

1980   The Human Rights Campaign (HRC) is founded to work for the civil rights of lesbians and gay men.

1983   The Boston Bisexual Women's Network is formed, one of the first and longest-lived bisexual organizations in the United States.

1983   Kindergarten teacher Linda Conway is fired from her teaching job in Hampshire County, West Virginia, because she "looks like a lesbian." She denies the accusation, sues the school board for reinstatement, but loses her case in a jury trial and again in the state court of appeals (*Conway v. Hampshire County Board of Education*, 352 S.E.2d 739).

1984   The U.S. Congress passes and President Ronald Reagan signs the Equal Access Act, requiring all public school systems to provide equal access to all extracurricular clubs. The act is initially intended to protect religious clubs but is later interpreted to protect a much wider variety of student organizations, including gay-straight alliances.

1988   Teacher Kevin Jennings founds the first gay-straight alliance in the United States at the Concord Academy, a private school in Concord, Massachusetts.

1990   The World Health Organization (WHO) removes homosexuality from its list of mental disorders.

1990   Jennings and his domestic partner at the time, Robert Parlin, found Gay and Lesbian Independent School Teachers Network (GLISTN), a group of individuals concerned about the special problems faced by LGBT youth in private schools.

Shortly thereafter, the organization changes its name to the Gay and Lesbian School Teachers Network (GLSTN).

1991 Parlin founds the first gay-straight alliance at a public school in the United States at South Newton High School, in Newton, Massachusetts.

1993 Transgender teenager Teena Brandon is raped and murdered in Humboldt, Nebraska, by a group of his friends when they discover he was born female. After his death, Brandon became better known as Brandon Teena in respect to his preferred gender identification. Teena's story is later told in the Golden Globe–winning film *Boy's Don't Cry* (1999), starring Oscar award–winner Hillary Swank.

1994 GLSTN becomes a national organization and changes its name to Gay, Lesbian and Straight Teachers Network (GLSTN).

1994 The first gay prom sponsored by a local school district is held at Diamond Bar High School in Walnut Valley, California. The event is called the Live to Tell prom.

1996 The U.S. Court of Appeals for the Seventh Circuit rules in the case of *Nabozny v. Podlesny, Davis, Blauert* that a student could sue a school district under the Fourteenth Amendment of the U.S. Constitution on the basis of not receiving equal protection provided other students in the school, based on his or her sexual orientation.

1997 GLSTN changes its name to Gay, Lesbian and Straight Educators Network (GLSEN).

1998 A group of gay-straight alliances in the San Francisco Bay area join to form a regional organization, GSA Network, which later (in 2004) becomes a national organization of gay-straight clubs.

1999 A court rules in *East High Gay/Straight Alliance v. Board of Education of Salt Lake City School District* that the school district cannot prohibit a gay-straight alliance from organizing and meeting in a manner as do other noncurricular clubs in the system.

2000   In *Boy Scouts of America et al. v. Dale* (530 U.S. 640), the U.S. Supreme Court rules that the Boy Scouts of America may legally refuse to accept homosexual boys as members and to ban adult homosexuals as scout leaders since to do otherwise would be to violate the principles on which the organization stands.

2000   In *Colin ex rel. Colin v. Orange Unified School District*, a court rules that the school district cannot prohibit a gay-straight alliance from using the word *gay* in its name.

2002   Seventeen-year-old Gwen Araujo (born Edward Araujo, Jr.) is beaten and strangled to death by four men who discover that she is a preoperative transsexual. The four men base their not guilty plea on a so-called *trans panic* defense, claiming that their acts were caused by panic attacks when they found out that Araujo was actually a male and not the female with whom they had or were planning to have sexual relations.

2003   A court rules in *Boyd County High School Gay Straight Alliance v. Board of Education of Boyd County, Kentucky* that the school board violated the federal Equal Access Act by allowing religious and other noncurricular clubs to meet on school property while forbidding the gay-straight alliance to do the same.

2004   The British Parliament passes the Gender Recognition Act, which allows transsexuals to legally change their gender.

2005   Sixteen-year-old Mahmoud Asgari and 18-year-old Ayaz Marhoni are hanged in Iran for allegedly raping a 13-year-old boy. Independent observers claim that the two boys were killed for consensual homosexual acts.

2006   After adopting a policy to ban all noncurricular clubs in an effort to prevent a gay-straight alliance from organizing and meeting, the White County, Georgia, school district accedes to a court order to reinstate all clubs, including the GSA, and to institute a program of sensitivity training dealing with LGBT issues. The action is ordered in *White County High School Peers in Diverse Education v. White County School District*.

2006 The California legislature passes and Governor Arnold Schwarzenegger signs the Gwen Arajuo Justice for Victims Act, the first state law prohibiting the so-called gay panic or trans panic defense in criminal trials. (See also 2002, Gwen Araujo.)

2008 The Osseo Area School District is ordered to pay attorney's fees of more than $450,000 after losing *Straights & Gays for Equality v. Osseo Area School District No. 279*, in which the court found that the school district attempted to mask its policy toward noncurricular school clubs to avoid allowing a GSA club to meet on school grounds.

2008 A decision by the school board in Okeechobee, Florida, to deny a request by students to form a GSA is overturned by a local court, and the board is ordered to pay $326,000 in attorney's fees. The board had claimed that permitting the club to meet would violate its abstinence-only policy, an assertion that the court rejected.

2010 Dan Savage and his partner Terry Miller upload their first video in the It Gets Better program to YouTube.

2010 Rutgers University freshman Tyler Clementi commits suicide after learning that his roommate has videotaped a sexual encounter between Clementi and a friend.

2011 Senator Al Franken (D-MN) and 39 co-sponsors introduce Senate bill 555, the Student Non-Discrimination Act of 2011, ensuring that "all students have access to public education in a safe environment free from discrimination, including harassment, bullying, intimidation, and violence, on the basis of sexual orientation or gender identity." The bill dies in committee.

2012 The American Civil Liberties Union of Florida files suit against superintendent of schools Jim Yancey and the local school board because the principal at Vanguard High School in Ocala, Florida, is "uncomfortable with having a club based on sexual orientation at the high school level." The school board then votes to permit a GSA to form at the school.

2013   The National Council of the Boy Scouts of America approves a resolution removing restrictions against membership for boys solely on the basis of their sexual orientation, effective January 1, 2014. It retains its ban on gay men as scoutmasters.

2013   The U.S. Supreme Court, in two separate rulings, invalidates major portions of the Defense of Marriage Act of 1996 and invalidates bans against same-sex marriage in California.

Introduction

This chapter lists some of the most common terms used in discussions about LGBT youth and related topics. Not everyone agrees with every definition for every term, but the definitions given here have been used relatively widely in the literature in the form given or one close to it.

affirmed gender   The gender that a person has established for himself or herself that may or may not be the same as that assigned at birth by parents and the general society.

ally   A nongay, nonlesbian, nonbisexual, nontransgendered person who supports the interests and concerns of these groups and often works with them to obtain equality for all LGBT persons.

androgyne   A person with (usually) physical and (sometimes) psychological characteristics (or both) that are generally ascribed to both male and female genders.

asexual   The condition of lacking in sexual interest in either male or female gender.

berdache.   *See* **two-spirit people**.

bisexual   A person who is sexually interested in someone of the same gender and someone of the opposite gender in roughly equal proportions.

bullying   Physically, mentally, emotionally, and/or otherwise intimidating and/or harming another individual, often because she or he is a member of a specific group, such as being LGBT or of another religious belief, race, or ethnic group.

cisgender   A person whose gender identity is the same as her or his biological gender at birth, such as a biological female who identifies in her lifestyle as a female. The term is often used in contrast to people who are transgendered. The prefix *cis-* means "on the same side of."

[to] come out   A term that may refer to any one of a series of events ranging from acknowledging one's sexual orientation to oneself to making that acknowledgment to the general public.

crossdresser   A person who enjoys dressing in the clothing of a person of the opposite gender. Now preferred to the older term *transvestite.*

drag queen   A (usually) homosexual male who enjoys dressing in women's clothing and (often) performing in public as a female.

dysphoria   A state of unease, anxiety, depression, or dissatisfaction with some condition. Gender dysphoria, for example, refers to a condition in which a person is uneasy with her or his biological sex.

feminine   Having the appearance and behavior usually associated with members of the female gender, whether or not one is of that biological sex.

FTM (F2M)   A female who has undergone a gender transformation to become a male.

gay   A common term for a male homosexual.

gay-straight alliance   A club, usually at the precollege level, consisting of LGBT and their non-LGBT allies.

gender   The full set of characteristics by which society recognizes an individual as a man or a women. Gender may or may not correspond to the biological sex with which one is born.

gender expression   The gender one chooses to present in public, which may or may not be the same as one's biological sex. Also known as **gender presentation**.

gender fluid The tendency of a person to present to the general public a masculine gender on some occasions and a female gender on other occasions.

gender nonconforming The tendency of an individual to dress and act in a manner more commonly associated with the opposite gender, as when a young girl prefers to dress and act as a boy.

hermaphrodite. *See* **intersex**.

heterosexism The belief that all people either are or should be heterosexual.

heterosexual A term sometimes used to describe a person whose sexual attraction is primarily to someone of the opposite sex, although probably better reserved for use as an adjective to refer to certain types of sexual acts or feelings with someone of the opposite sex.

heterophobia The irrational hatred and/or fear of heterosexuals.

heterosexuality The tendency of a person to feel strong sexual attraction primarily to someone of the opposite sex.

homophobia The irrational hatred and/or fear of homosexuals.

homosexual A term sometimes used to describe a person whose sexual attraction is primarily to someone of the same sex, although probably better reserved for use as an adjective to refer to certain types of sexual acts or feelings with someone of the same sex.

homosexuality The tendency of a person to feel strong sexual attraction primarily to someone of the same sex.

intersex person An individual who has sexual anatomy characteristic of both males and females. Also known as a **hermaphrodite**.

(being) in the closet The intentional concealment of an individual's own gender identity or sexual orientation.

lesbian A female who is sexually attracted primarily to other females.

masculine   Having the appearance and behavior usually associated with members of the male gender, whether or not one is of that biological sex.

MTF (M2F)   A male to female transsexual.

pansexual   An individual who is sexually attracted to all types of individuals of both sexes and both genders.

pederasty   A sexual relationship between an adult male and a younger boy.

pedophilia   A sexual attraction for young boys and young girls. The attraction may be primarily for boys or for girls but is most commonly for either sex.

queer   A somewhat ambiguous term that was originally adopted by some gay men and lesbian to self-identify themselves as same-sex-loving individuals but which has grown to have a host of other meanings that may include bisexuals, transsexuals, LGBT allies, intersex people, fetishists, and other others with nontraditional sexual orientation.

questioning   A term used to describe individuals who are uncertain of their own gender identity or sexual orientation.

sex   The biological and physiological characteristics that define males and females.

sexual orientation   A person's emotional, romantic, and/or sexual attraction toward males, females, or both.

suicidal behavior   All those thoughts and activities related to the possibility of taking one's own life, including suicidal ideation, suicide attempts, and successful suicides.

suicidal ideation   The process of thinking about committing suicide, which may range from undifferentiated fantasies to carefully worked out plans for the action.

trans man   A female-to-male transsexual.

trans woman   A male-to-female transsexual.

transitioning   The process through which a person goes in living with one gender or one sex to the opposite gender or opposite sex.

transphobia   The irrational fear and hatred of transsexuals.

two-spirit people   Individuals in Native American and Canadian First Nation tribes who display mixed gender roles, intermediate between those of males and females. Two-spirit people were previously known as *berdaches*.

About the Author

David E. Newton holds an associate's degree in science from Grand Rapids (Michigan) Junior College, a BA in chemistry (with high distinction) and an MA in education from the University of Michigan, and an EdD in science education from Harvard University. He is the author of more than 400 textbooks, encyclopedias, resource books, research manuals, laboratory manuals, trade books, and other educational materials. He taught mathematics, chemistry, and physical science in Grand Rapids, Michigan, for 13 years; was professor of chemistry and physics at Salem State College in Massachusetts for 15 years; and was adjunct professor in the College of Professional Studies at the University of San Francisco for 10 years.

Previous books for ABC-CLIO include *Global Warming* (1993), *Gay and Lesbian Rights: A Resource Handbook* (1994, 2009), *The Ozone Dilemma* (1995), *Violence and the Mass Media* (1996), *Environmental Justice* (1996, 2009), *Encyclopedia of Cryptology* (1997), *Social Issues in Science and Technology: An Encyclopedia* (1999), *DNA Technology* (2009), *Sexual Health* (2010), *Same-Sex Marriage: A Reference Handbook* (2010), *Substance Abuse: A Reference Handbook* (2010), *World Energy Crisis: A Reference Handbook* (2012), *Marijuana: A Reference Handbook* (2013), *The Animal Experimentation Debate: A Reference Handbook* (2013), *Vaccination Controversies: A Reference Handbook* (2013), and *Steroids and Doping in Sports: A Reference Handbook* (2013).

Other books include *Physics: Oryx Frontiers of Science Series* (2000), *Sick!* (4 volumes; 2000), *Science, Technology, and Society: The Impact of Science in the 19th Century* (2 volumes; 2001), *Encyclopedia of Fire* (2002), *Molecular Nanotechnology: Oryx Frontiers of Science Series* (2002), *Encyclopedia of Water* (2003), *Encyclopedia of Air* (2004), *The New Chemistry* (6 volumes; 2007), *Nuclear Power* (2005), *Stem Cell Research* (2006), *Latinos in the Sciences, Math, and Professions* (2007), and *DNA Evidence and Forensic Science* (2008).

He has also been an updating and consulting editor on books and reference works, including *Chemical Compounds* (2005), *Chemical Elements* (2006), *Encyclopedia of Endangered Species* (2006), *World of Mathematics* (2006), *World of Chemistry* (2006), *World of Health* (2006), *UXL Encyclopedia of Science* (2007), *Alternative Medicine* (2008), *Grzimek's Animal Life Encyclopedia* (2009), *Community Health* (2009), *Genetic Medicine* (2009), *Gale Encyclopedia of Medicine* (2010), *Gale Science in Context* (2011, 2013), *Cities of the United States* (2011), *Gale Encyclopedia of Fitness* (2012), and *Gale Encyclopedia of Alternative Medicine* (2013).